# Francis Bacon:
# Painting, Philosophy, Psychoanalysis

FRANCIS BACON
STUDIES II

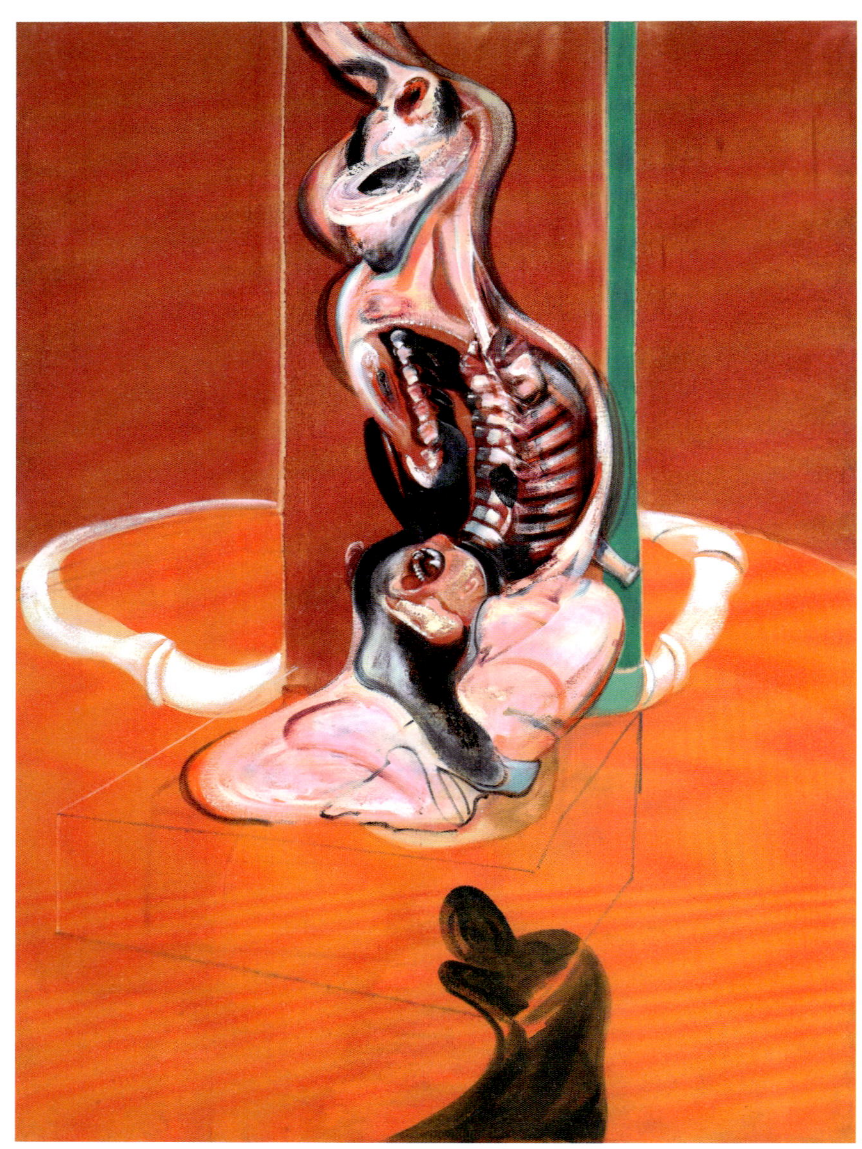

1. *Three Studies for a Crucifixion*, 1962 (right panel)

# Francis Bacon:
# Painting, Philosophy, Psychoanalysis

Edited by Ben Ware

Howard Caygill

Gregg M Horowitz

Darian Leader

Catherine Malabou

Dany Nobus

Renata Salecl

Ben Ware

Alenka Zupančič

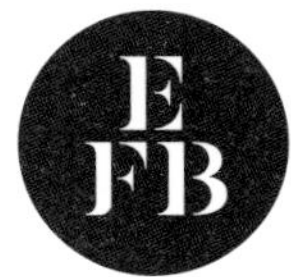

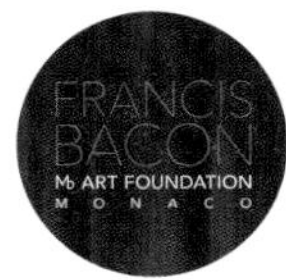

The Estate of Francis Bacon Publishing,
supported by Francis Bacon MB Art Foundation Monaco,
in association with Thames & Hudson

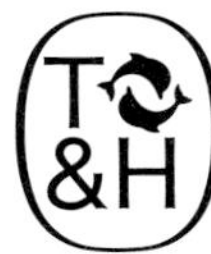

# Contents

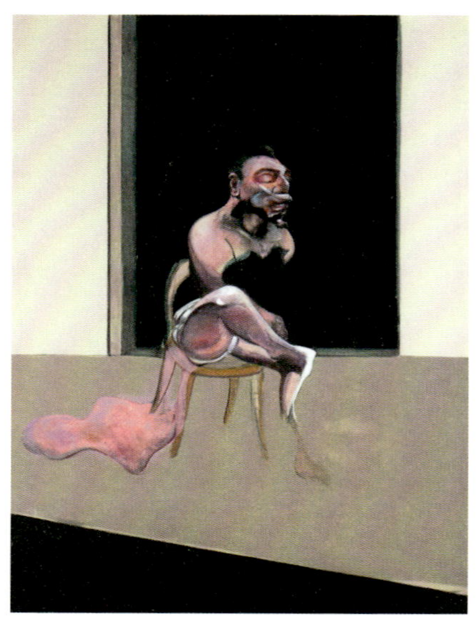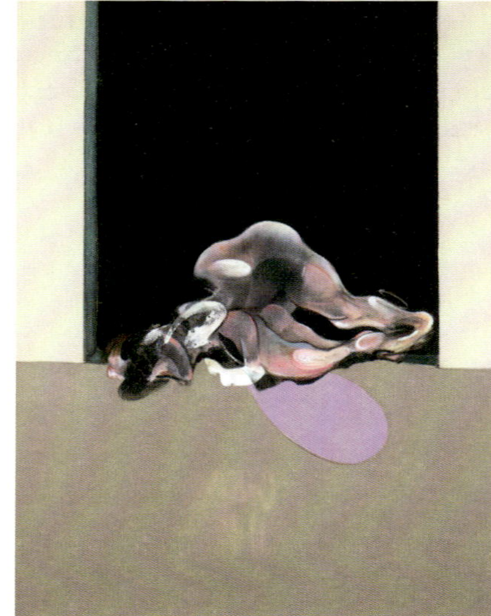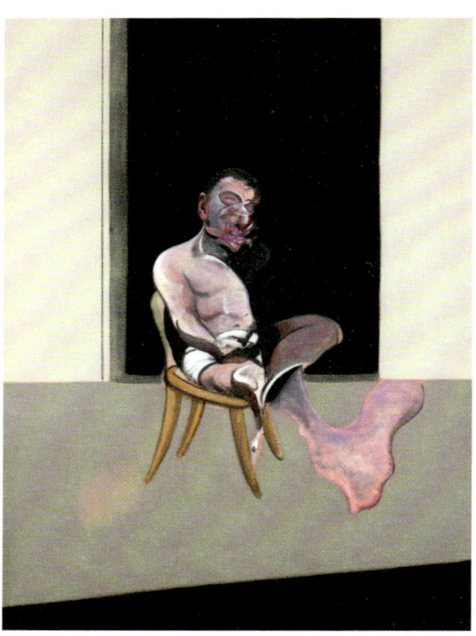

**2.** *Triptych August 1972*

# Preface

This, the second volume in the series Francis Bacon Studies, represents a departure from its predecessor (published in May 2019), in that the eight essays have been produced under an 'external' editor, Ben Ware. Dr Ware was responsible not only for his own essay, and the introduction to this book, but also for suggesting and inviting the other seven distinguished authors who have contributed to it. Their insightful and original texts form a concrete demonstration of the ways in which our understanding of Bacon's art is being enlarged through the application of a widening scope of disciplines and methodologies.

Martin Harrison

Editor: Francis Bacon Studies

# Contributors

**Howard Caygill** is Professor of Modern European Philosophy in the Centre for Research in Modern European Philosophy, Kingston University. He is the author of *Walter Benjamin: The Color of Experience*, *The Kant Dictionary* and *Levinas and the Political*. His most recent publications are *On Resistance: A Philosophy of Defiance* (2014) and *Kafka: In Light of the Accident* (2017).

**Gregg M Horowitz** is Emeritus Professor of Philosophy at Pratt Institute in Brooklyn, New York. He writes on aesthetics and the philosophy of art, psychoanalysis and political theory. His publications include the books *Sustaining Loss: Art and Mournful Life* (2001) and *The Wake of Art: Philosophy, Criticism and the Ends of Taste* (1998), with Arthur C. Danto and Tom Huhn.

**Darian Leader** is a psychoanalyst working in London and a member of the Centre for Freudian Analysis and Research and of the College of Psychoanalysts–UK. His essay 'Bacon and the Body' was published in Francis Bacon Studies I (2019), and he is the author of numerous books, including: *Why Do Women Write More Letters Than They Post?* (1997); *Freud's Footnotes* (2000); *Stealing the Mona Lisa: What Art Stops Us from Seeing* (2002); *The New Black: Mourning, Melancholia and Depression* (2009), and *What is Madness?* (2012).

**Catherine Malabou** is Professor of Philosophy at the Centre for Research in Modern European Philosophy at Kingston University, and Distinguished Professor of Comparative Literature and European Languages at the University of California at Irvine. Her books include *The Future of Hegel: Plasticity, Temporality and Dialectic* (2004); *What Should We Do with Our Brain?* (2009); *Ontology of the Accident* (2010); *The New Wounded: From Neurosis to Brain Damage* (2012) and, most recently, *Morphing Intelligence, From IQ Measurement to Artificial Brains* (2019).

**Dany Nobus** is Professor of Psychoanalytic Psychology at Brunel University London, and former Chair of the Freud Museum London. He is the author of *Jacques Lacan and the Freudian Practice of Psychoanalysis* (2000); *Knowing Nothing, Staying Stupid: Elements for a Psychoanalytic Epistemology* (with Malcolm Quinn) (2005) and, most recently, *The Law of Desire: On Lacan's 'Kant with Sade'* (2017), along with numerous papers on the history, theory and practice of psychoanalysis.

**Renata Salecl** is a Slovene philosopher, sociologist and legal theorist. She is a senior researcher at the Institute of Criminology, Faculty of Law at the University of Ljubljana, and is Professor of Psychology, Psychoanalysis and Law at Birkbeck College, University of London. Among her many books are *The Spoils of Freedom* (1994); *(Per)Versions of Love and Hate* (1998) and *The Tyranny of Choice* (2010).

**Ben Ware** is a research fellow in Philosophy at King's College London. His work explores the intersections between philosophy, modernist aesthetics, politics and psychoanalysis. He is the author of *Dialectic of the Ladder: Wittgenstein, the 'Tractatus' and Modernism* (2015) and *Living Wrong Life Rightly: Modernism, Ethics and the Political Imagination* (2017). His next book, and the final work in his trilogy on modernism and philosophy, will be entitled *Negative Passions*.

**Alenka Zupančič** is a Slovene philosopher and social theorist. She works as research advisor at the Institute of Philosophy, Scientific Research Center of the Slovene Academy of Sciences. She is also a professor at the European Graduate School in Switzerland. She is the author of numerous articles and books, including *Ethics of the Real: Kant and Lacan* (1997); *The Shortest Shadow: Nietzsche's Philosophy of the Two* (2003); *Why Psychoanalysis: Three Interventions* (2008); *The Odd One In: On Comedy* 2008) and, most recently, *What is Sex?* (2017).

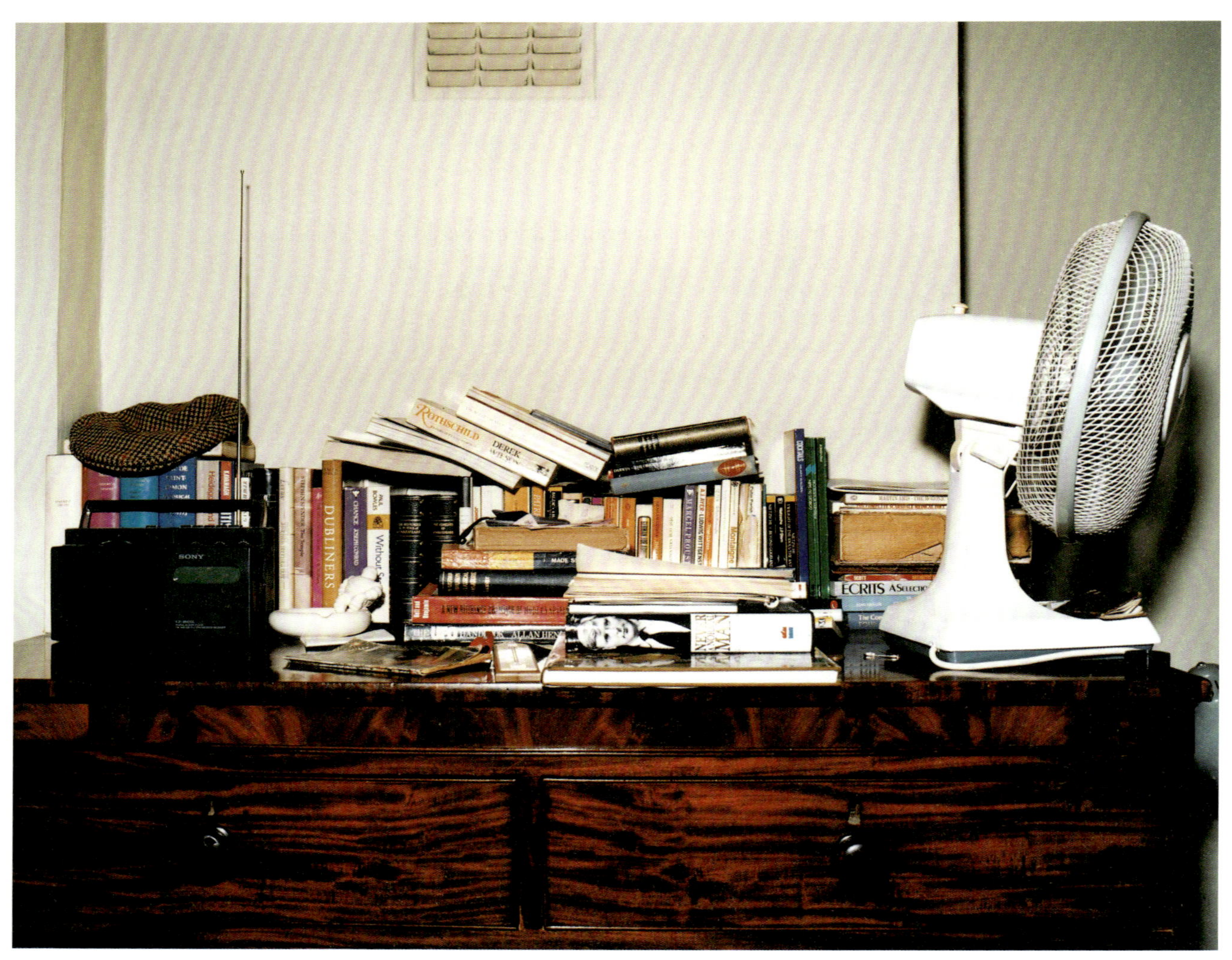

3. Perry Ogden, 1998. Books on chest of drawers in Bacon's bedroom, 7 Reece Mews

# Introduction

Ben Ware

In Perry Ogden's collection of photographs of Francis Bacon's studio, *7 Reece Mews*, there are several images devoted exclusively to the artist's books.[1] In one image, copies of Nietzsche's *Beyond Good and Evil* and *Twilight of the Idols/The Antichrist* sit alongside A. J. Ayer's primer on Wittgenstein, Michael Murray's collection *Heidegger and Modern Philosophy* (containing contributions from Arendt, Gadamer and Ricoeur) and a copy of Lacan's *Écrits*; in another, Freud's *Moses and Monotheism* is stacked beneath copies of George Steiner's *In Bluebeard's Castle*, John Passmore's *A Hundred Years of Philosophy* and the George Braziller 1971 edition of Gilles Deleuze's *Masochism*. Bacon, as has been noted, read widely and voraciously; but it is interesting to see here, alongside key works of literary modernists (Joyce, Eliot, Pound, Proust, Genet) and books on art, photography and music (Picasso, Brassaï, Stravinsky), an explicit interest in philosophy and psychoanalysis. In one of Ogden's pictures, standing proudly on top of one of the stacks (and much more easily accessible than the surrounding works on Velázquez and Seurat) is R. J. Hollingdale's edited volume *A Nietzsche Reader*[2] – a book whose section on 'Art and Aesthetics' begins with the following lines from the philosopher's *Human, All Too Human*:

> In regard to knowledge of truths, the artist possesses a weaker morality than the thinker; he does not wish to be deprived of the glittering, profound interpretations of life and guards against simple and sober methods and results … [The artist] refuses to give up the presuppositions which are *most efficacious* to his art, that is to say, the fantastic, mythical, uncertain, extreme, the sense of the symbolical, the overestimation of the person, the belief in something miraculous in genius.[3]

Given Bacon's clear interest in both philosophy and psychoanalysis, it is therefore surprising that relatively little work on Bacon's painting has been undertaken from either of these perspectives. On the rare occasions that contemporary work *has* moved in this direction it has tended, more often than not, to be haunted by two spectres — existentialism and Deleuze. On the existentialist account (perhaps the most clichéd of all philosophical approaches to Bacon), the artist's work is understood to deal primarily with the 'demonic forces in every man which try to take possession of him … the anxiety at the thought of living … feelings of emptiness, meaninglessness and despair'.[4] Works such as *Head VI*, 1949, [55] and *Study for Portrait*, 1949, [57] are taken to present 'extreme situations', evoking the claustrophobia, torment and absurdity encountered in existentialist texts such as Sartre's *Huis Clos*.[5] As one commentator puts it: 'the screams and cries that many of Bacon's figures emit can … be viewed as [arising from a] confrontation [with] the primal horror of existence'.[6] Moreover, Bacon is said to present the spectator with a Godless world; or, more specifically, his painting provides a 'visual representation of the death of God' – evidenced by the fact that traditional theological symbols such as the Pope and the crucified Christ become, in the artist's hands, subjects of 'ridicule and subversion'.[7] Such a reading is, to be sure, helped along by Bacon himself, who, in his famous interviews with David Sylvester often adopts a kind of reach-me-down existentialist register:

> I think that man now realizes that he is an accident, that he is a completely futile being, that he has to play out the game without reason. I think that, even when Velasquez was painting, even when Rembrandt was painting, in a peculiar way they were still, whatever their attitude to life, slightly conditioned by certain types of religious possibilities, which man now, you could say, has had completely cancelled out for him. Now, of course, man can only attempt to make something very, very positive by trying to beguile himself for a time by the way he behaves, by prolonging possibly his life by buying a kind of immortality through the doctors. You see, all art has now become completely a game by which man distracts himself.[8]

Bacon is, however, no existentialist painter (whatever that might mean). If existentialism turns absurdity and meaninglessness into a kind of universal doctrine, then Bacon's work simply takes it literally – often, we should say, to the point of *parody*. At the same time, Bacon's paintings are not 'about' alienation or despair; they are not attempts to say anything philosophical about the so-called *condition humaine*. Rather than articulating a 'message', Bacon's whole artistic enterprise – at least as *he* conceives of it – is concerned with unlocking 'sensation'; with bringing the image – usually a distorted reworking of a photograph or a film still – directly and violently onto the beholder's 'nervous system'.[9] As he famously puts it, paraphrasing Paul Valéry, 'I want ... to give the *sensation* without the boredom of its conveyance.'[10]

This brings us directly to Deleuze – the second philosophical ghost hovering over Bacon's work. The publication of Deleuze's 1981 study *Francis Bacon: Logique de la Sensation* [*Francis Bacon: The Logic of Sensation* (2003)] was, without a doubt, a landmark event: the first philosophical monograph on Bacon's painting and one which, given the author's stature, inflicted a kind of intellectual shock and awe on theoretically minded Bacon scholarship. Deleuze's central thesis is, in some respects, a relatively simple one; and its basic outline is given on the first page of the Preface to the English edition:

> Francis Bacon's painting is of a very special violence. Bacon, to be sure, often traffics in the violence of a depicted scene: spectacles of horror, crucifixions, prosthesis and mutilations, monsters. But these are overly facile detours, detours that the artist himself judges severely and condemns in his work. What directly interests him is a violence that is involved only with colour and line: the violence of a sensation (and not of a representation), a static or potential violence, a violence of reaction of expression.[11]

Deleuze here thus distinguishes between sensational violence (the spectacle of mutilations, monsters and screams) and the violence of a sensation (associated with colour and line), which, for him, is the real concern of Bacon's art. The paintings, he argues, reprising Bacon's own claims, bypass representation and act directly and violently upon the spectator's 'nervous system'.[12] Bacon's Figures, Deleuze continues, 'are not racked bodies', but rather 'ordinary bodies in ordinary situations': Figures which are 'made of flesh' and which are whipped and shaped by 'invisible forces'. 'If there is feeling in Bacon', then, 'it is not a taste for horror, it is pity, an intense pity: pity for the flesh';[13] a remark which once again presents itself as philosophical fact while simultaneously channelling the words of Bacon himself:

> I've always been very moved by pictures about slaughterhouses and meat, and to me they belong very much to the whole thing of the Crucifixion. … Of course, we are meat, we are potential carcasses. If I go into a butcher shop I always think it's surprising that I wasn't there instead of the animal.[14]

Deleuze's study thus applies his own ready-made philosophical system (invisible forces, the body without organs) to Bacon's painting at the same time as it reproduces many of Bacon's own claims about his art and aesthetic outlook. The effect can, at times, be disorienting. Who, exactly, is speaking at any given moment? Is it Bacon or is it Deleuze? Is philosophy leading art or is art leading philosophy? Perhaps most problematic is Deleuze's suggestion that all Bacon's works operate according to the same 'logic of sensation'. By focusing exclusively on the affective dimensions of the paintings, Deleuze fails to give an account of what it is that actually compels our interest in them: why, we might ask, do they continue to matter to us in the way that they do? Despite these limitations, Deleuze's treatment of Bacon continues to hold sway among many of the artist's philosophical exegetes. For them, Bacon is a kind of modernist Spinoza, affirming life and transmuting 'cerebral pessimism' into 'nervous optimism'.[15] Moreover, the point is not – or at least not primarily – to interpret his work, but rather to hold oneself open to the 'intense modes of sensation' which the works themselves convey through rhythm, colour and line.[16]

While not seeking to downplay the philosophical and aesthetic significance of Deleuze's intervention, the time is now right to open up a new dossier on Bacon: one which pays serious attention to the *diverse* philosophical and psychoanalytic dimensions of his painting, while departing (in the form of a dialectical shifting of the gears) from the Baconian theoretical narratives of the past. The essays in this collection constitute a significant step in this direction. Dealing with a wide variety of topics and ranging across a broad conceptual field, they bring us to see Bacon's works in radically new and unexpected ways. Howard Caygill reads a number of Bacon's paintings in the light of recent work on cynegetics or the philosophy of the hunt; Darian Leader argues that Bacon's art serves as an invitation to question and rethink the mirror phase theory of Jacques Lacan; Catherine Malabou discovers in Bacon a new, post-deconstructive approach to 'form' that strikingly anticipates contemporary definitions of cerebral plasticity; Dany Nobus understands Bacon's artistic practice as a kind of psychoanalytic 'painting cure' that captures the 'truth of the appearance' through a 'pasting of the paint'; Gregg M Horowitz argues that Bacon, who characteristically maintains a cool distance from his subjects, establishes an 'unusual intimacy' in his 1969 *Study of Henrietta Moraes Laughing* by painting what Horowitz calls 'impediment to her absence'; Renata Salecl looks at the distortion of faces in Bacon's portraits and self-portraits and asks what has changed in people's self-perception in times of selfies, neuroscience and new social media; Ben Ware opens Bacon up to philosophical exploration beyond an aesthetics of sensation, making the case for reading the artist (at least in certain works) as a painter of the *negative*; Alenka Zupančič picks up on the notion of 'objective humour' in Hegel's *Aesthetics*, and argues that this notion, which remains somewhat vague and obscure in Hegel, gains concrete consistency in Bacon's art, providing a new perspective on many key aspects of his work.

The essays in this collection do not claim that philosophy and psychoanalysis hold the 'key' to unlocking Bacon's art. Rather, their outlook (implicitly or explicitly) is much more dialectical: it is art that invites us to new levels of intellectual consideration, forcing us to rethink, clarify, modify and rearticulate our philosophical and psychoanalytic ideas. *At the same time*, it is philosophical and psychoanalytic criticism that constitute the consummation – that is to say, the completion – of the work of art, the means by which it is brought to self-knowledge. '[T]he [art]work is incomplete', writes Walter Benjamin;[17] but the same holds true for philosophy and psychoanalysis. Each sphere – art and criticism – thus requires the other in order to discover the truth about itself.

# Endnotes


1.  Perry Ogden & John Edwards, *7 Reece Mews: Francis Bacon's Studio* (London: Thames & Hudson, 2001). I'm indebted to Dany Nobus for drawing my attention to these photographs and to Philip Roe and Logan Sisley at Dublin City Gallery The Hugh Lane, for additional research and information on the philosophical books in Bacon's library. Nobus elegantly expands upon the significance of the appearance of Lacan's *Écrits* in Bacon's collection in the Epilogue of his essay in this volume.

2.  In addition to the books already listed (i.e. those photographed by Ogden in *7 Reece Mews*), the following works were also in Bacon's possession: Wittgenstein's *Philosophical Investigations*, Bertrand Russell's *History of Western Philosophy*, Voltaire's *Philosophical Dictionary*, Roland Barthes's *Mythologies*, Walter Kaufmann's *Nietzsche: Philosopher, Psychologist, Antichrist*, Ernest Jones, *The Life and Work of Sigmund Freud* and Freud's *On Metapsychology*. This is by no means an exhaustive list, but it gives further evidence of the diversity of Bacon's philosophical and psychoanalytical interests.

3.  Friedrich Nietzsche, *A Nietzsche Reader*, ed. & trans. R. J. Hollingdale (London: Penguin, 1981), p. 125.

4.  Paul Tillich, 'A Prefatory Note', in Peter Selz, *New Images of Man* (New York: Museum of Modern Art, 1959), p. 10. The publication accompanied an exhibition at MoMA, which featured several of Bacon's paintings. Tillich's essay and Selz's introduction are very much canonical examples of existentialist approaches to late modernist art. As Selz puts it: 'The revelations and complexities of mid-twentieth-century life have called forth a profound feeling of solitude and anxiety. The imagery of man which has evolved from this reveals sometimes a new dignity, sometimes despair, but always the uniqueness of man as he confronts his fate. Like Kierkegaard, Heidegger, Camus, these artists are aware of anguish and dread, of life in which man – precarious and vulnerable – confronts the precipice, is aware of dying as well as living' (ibid., p. 11).

5.  See, for example, John Russell, *Francis Bacon* (London: Thames & Hudson, 1993), p. 35.

6.  Rina Arya, 'The Existentialist Dimensions of Bacon's Art', in *Francis Bacon: Critical and Theoretical Perspectives*, ed. Rina Arya (Oxford: Peter Lang, 2012), p. 89.

7.  Ibid., pp. 100 & 92.

8.  David Sylvester, *Interviews with Francis Bacon* (London: Thames & Hudson, 2016), p. 34.

9.  Ibid., p. 12.

10.  Ibid., pp. 73, 75 (emphasis added).

11.  Gilles Deleuze, *Francis Bacon: The Logic of Sensation*, trans. Daniel W. Smith (London: Bloomsbury, 2013), p. xii.

12.  Ibid., p. 26 ff.

13.  Ibid., p. xii.

14.  Sylvester, op. cit., pp. 25 & 53.

15.  *Deleuze and the Non/Human*, ed. Jon Roffe & Hannah Stark (London: Palgrave, 2015), p. 35.

16.  See Darren Ambrose, 'Deleuze's Bacon: Automatism and the Pictorial Fact', in *Francis Bacon: Critical and Theoretical Perspectives*, op. cit., p. 173. For a defence of Deleuze's reading of Bacon from a psychoanalytic perspective, see Tomas Geyskens, 'Painting as Hysteria – Deleuze on Bacon', in *Sexuality and Psychoanalysis: Philosophical Criticisms*, ed. Jens De Vleminck & Eran Dorfman (Leuven: Leuven University Press, 2010), pp. 215–29.

17.  Walter Benjamin, 'The Concept of Criticism', in *Walter Benjamin: Selected Writings, Volume 1, 1913–1926* (Cambridge, MA: The Belknap Press of Harvard University Press, 2004), p. 154.

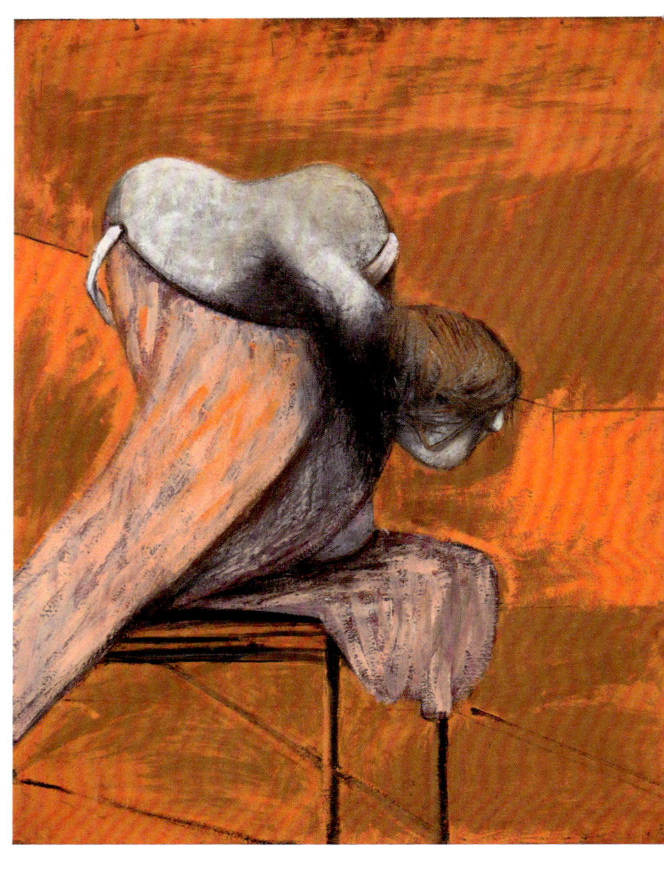

*4. Three Studies for Figures at the Base of a Crucifixion*, 1944

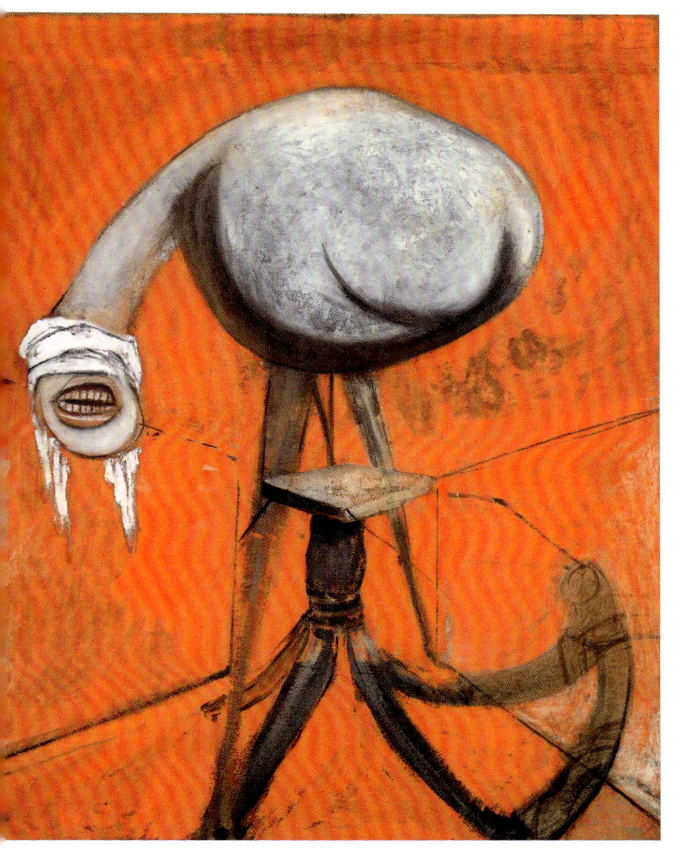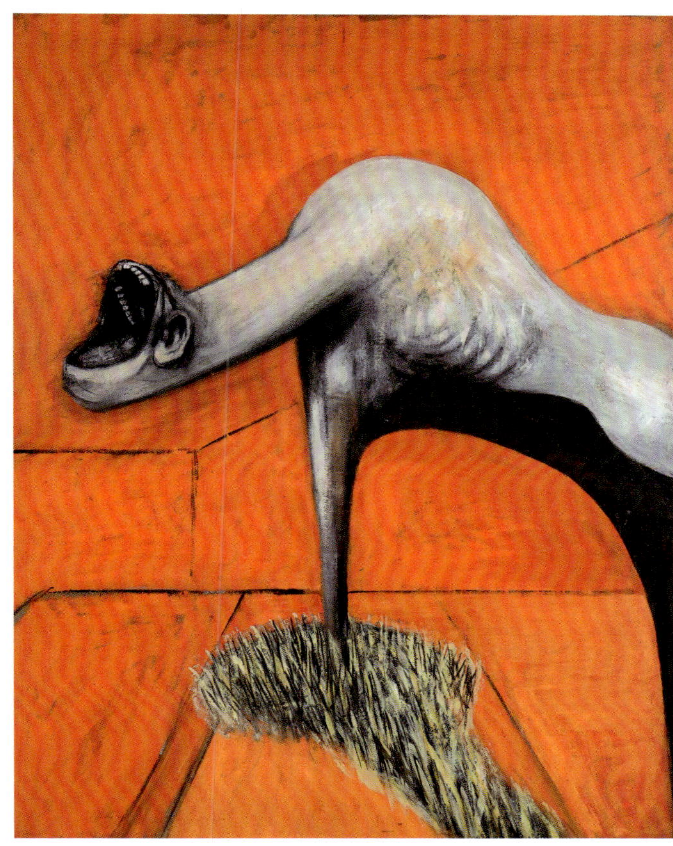

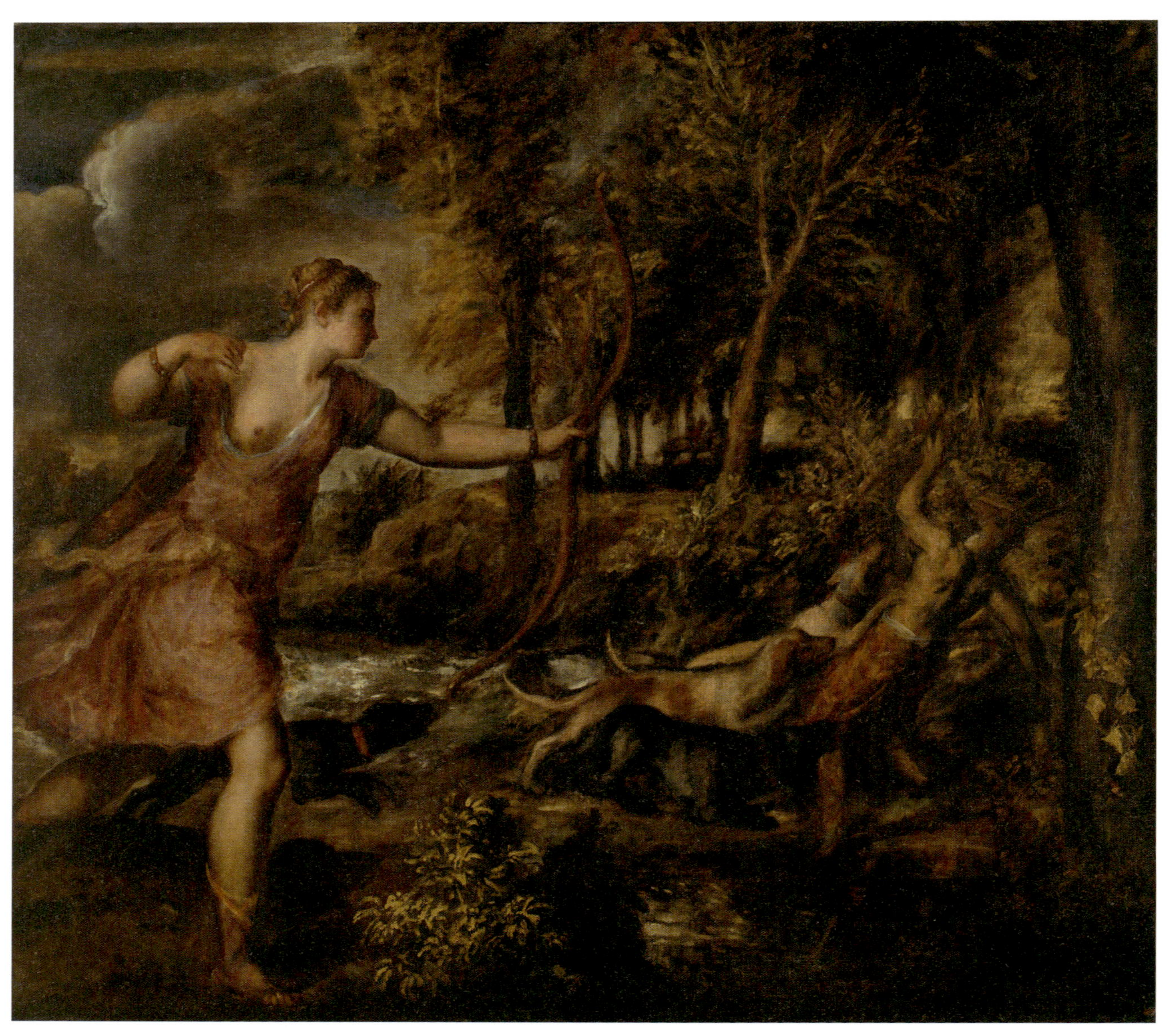

5. Titian, *The Death of Actaeon*, c. 1565–76

# Bacon's Cynegetic Vision

Howard Caygill

*When I look at Actaeon being torn to bits by the hounds, I think also of the Eumenides, and it makes me think of how perhaps they could be used.*
– Francis Bacon, 1972

### Cynegetics or The Theory of the Hunt

Deleuze opens the preface to the English translation of *Francis Bacon: The Logic of Sensation* with the claim that 'Francis Bacon's painting is of a very special violence.'[1] But by locating this violence in the tension between force and flesh Deleuze overlooks its specific, *cynegetic* character as a violence proper to the *hunt*. And despite the importance he lends to the theme of 'escape' in his readings of Bacon's paintings, it is never explicit who or what is escaping … or being escaped. Hunters and the hunted, the metamorphoses of predator and prey, the use and avoidance of bait, lures and traps along with pursuit, evasion, flight, camouflage and capture, consistently inform Bacon's practice and his reflections on it in interviews and conversations. Hugh Davies noted that 'The themes of pursuit and of the predatory observer became central to Bacon's work after 1960',[2] and his friend and biographer Michael Peppiatt observed that 'An awareness of life as a perpetual hunt – the stalker and his prey, the aggressor and his victim – was to be fundamental to Bacon.'[3] The hunt provides his terminology of reflection and the key to his apparent distortions of the lexicon of aesthetics. His sustained fascination with the hunt of the matricidal Orestes by the Furies/Eumenides (which he shared with T. S. Eliot), along with the figure of the hunted hunter Actaeon, point to an engagement with cynegetic 'logic' paralleled only in the writings of Kafka and Ernst Jünger. He pursued the hunt across the terrains of photography, medical imagery, zoology, sexual adventure and, of course, painting.

Until recently the specific violence of cynegetic thought and practice remained camouflaged in the margins of art history, philosophy, classical studies, strategy and politics. But increasingly writers including Vidal-Naquet, Roberto Calasso and Grégoire Chamayou have begun to recover its specificity as a pre-political, pre-logical mode of thought present at the origins of humanity and persisting with unobtrusive and quiet menace into modernity. In *The Black Hunter* Vidal-Naquet examines the relation of the hunt to the ancient Greek city and its spatial organisation and rites of passage, and the ways in which the polis and the invention of philosophy were directed against *cynegetics* or the theory and logic of the hunt. Roberto Calasso in *Il cacciatore celeste* [*The Celestial Hunter*] elaborates upon the intuitions of Bataille and Blanchot linking the hunt with anthropogenesis and the shared origins of human thought and art, finding that the 'most ancient thought' survives in '*aphorisms on the hunt*', while Chamayou in *The Manhunt: A Philosophical History*, *Drone Warfare* and *The Ungovernable Society* sees in the manhunt an emergent figure and organising principle of modern politics and warfare. The contemporary recovery and articulation of cynegetics in all these cases is inseparable from the twentieth-century experience of total domination and its conversion of politics into police actions and manhunts across a range of actions including the National Socialist Final Solution and contemporary drone warfare. Ernst Jünger's allegorical depiction of Hitler and National Socialism as a hunter with a hunter-band in *On the Marble Cliffs* proved a prescient intuition while Kafka's depictions of hunter-angels in *The Trial* and *The Castle*, along with their uncanny fusions of religion, justice, politics and logic, appear as extended commentaries on both the aphorisms of the hunt and the disquieting features of a cynegetic modernity.

The need to address cynegetics and figures of the hunter and the hunted was anticipated by Kafka and explicitly discussed by the painter Titorelli in a central episode of *The Trial*. While on a studio visit to the painter, Josef K., the protagonist hunter/prey of the novel, remarks on an allegorical figure of the Goddess of Justice in an incomplete portrait of a judge. It is unsafe for Titorelli explicitly to warn Josef K. of the gravity of his predicament – he would surely be overheard – so he instead shows his warning through some revisions to his work in progress. The Goddess of Justice is with a few strokes transformed first into the Goddess of War and then finally into the Goddess of the Hunt. Titorelli visually counsels Josef K., not to believe he is undergoing a legal process, nor that he is at war with the court but to understand he has become the prey of an implacable hunter and should act accordingly. He should not insist on imaginary rights nor believe that he has the power to fight the court, but should make himself scarce by disappearing from sight, adopting camouflage and leaving no traces behind him that would help the chase. Josef K. does not understand let alone heed the warning, allowing himself to be trapped and finally executed 'like a dog'. Yet at the same time as being a victim of the court, Josef K. is himself a sexual predator and, as a banker, a financial predator, and so exemplifies the figure of the hunter/prey that fascinated Kafka and would also fascinate Bacon in the figures of Orestes and Actaeon.

Bacon's use of cynegetic vocabulary and techniques when describing his practice is consistent and forceful. It quietly underlies his descriptions of the predicament of painting sketched in his interviews with David Sylvester. It emerges when he describes painting as 'trying to trap' an image or having to 'in a sense, set a trap by which you hope to trap this living fact alive. How well can you set the trap? Where and at what moment will it click?'[4] He describes the hunt for the image in terms of attempting 'to make the construction by which this thing will be caught raw and alive and left there and, you may say, finally fossilised ...'.[5] On a later occasion he described the subject of a painting as 'the bait' and the construction of an artificial structure as the way 'to trap the reality of the subject matter that one has started from'.[6] He describes his triptychs of heads such as *Three Studies of Isabel Rawsthorne on Light Ground*, 1965, as 'rather like police records' or the photographic recording of captured criminals. His practice is repeatedly described in terms of stalking an image-prey that is in the process of evading capture by fleeing, avoiding his traps or camouflaging itself. And just as with Pasteur's medical hunt for pathogens, for Bacon

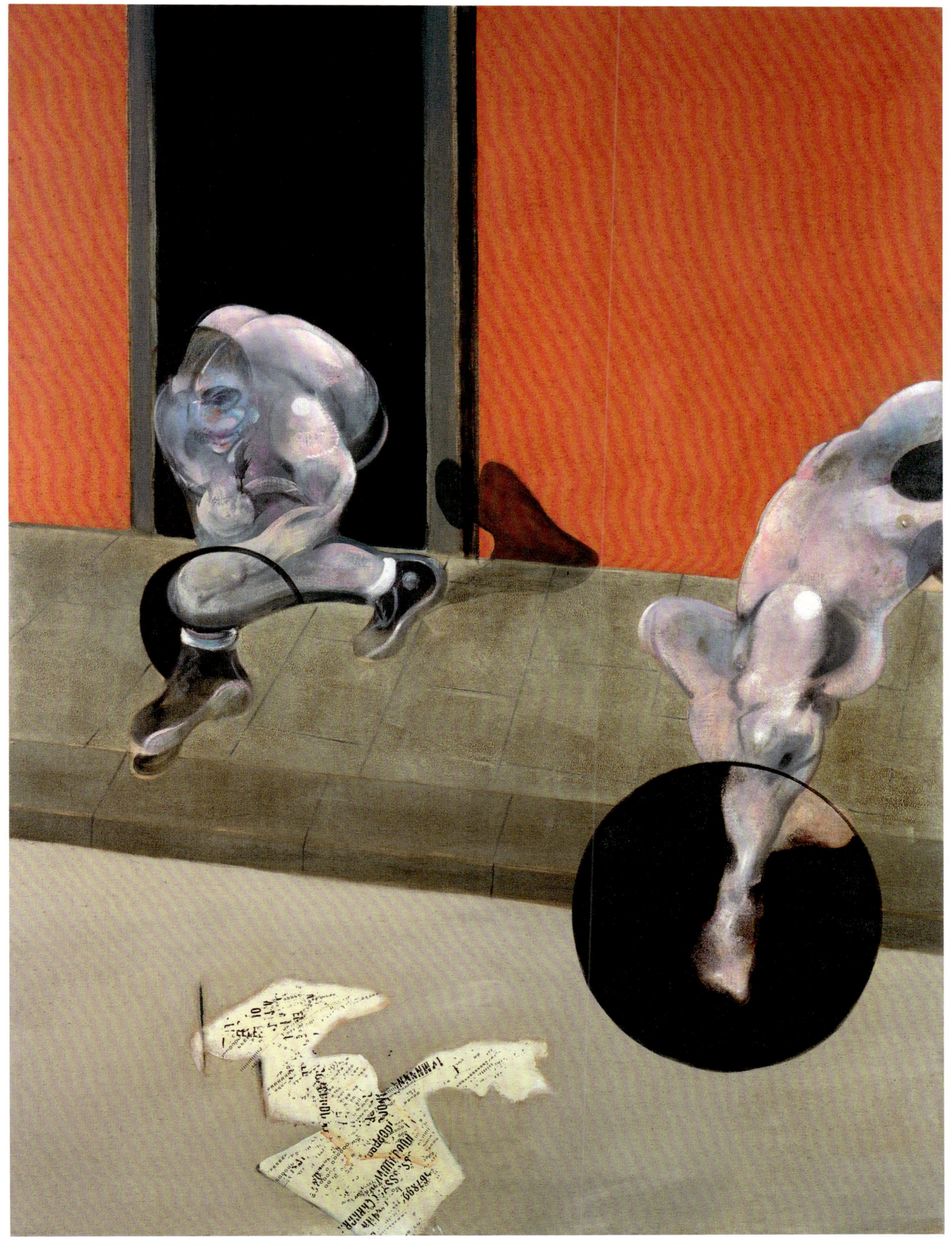

6. *Figures in Movement*, 1973

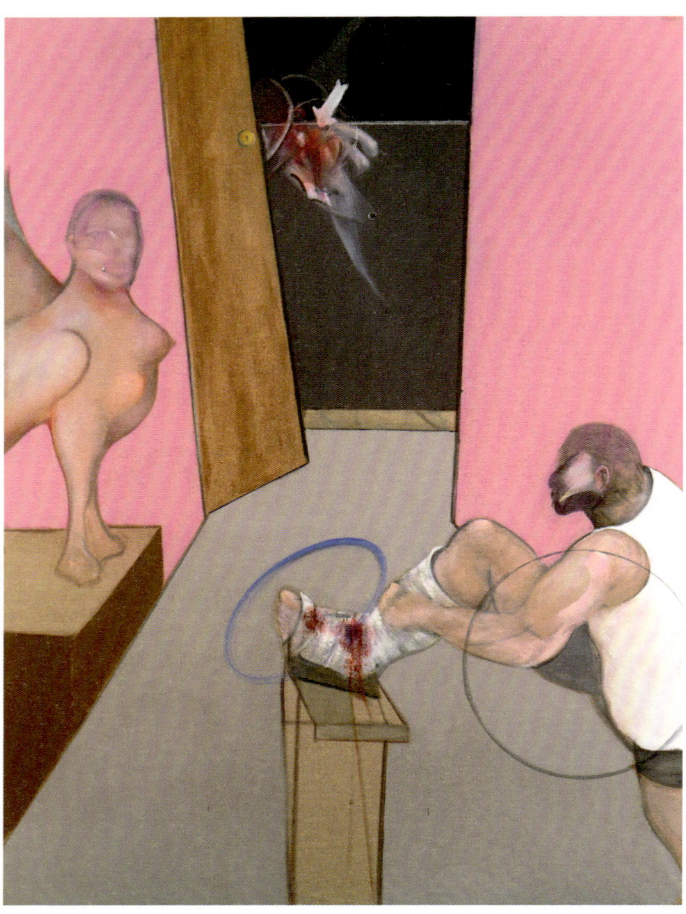

7. *Oedipus and the Sphinx after Ingres*, 1983

chance favours the prepared mind or rather the patient hunter. The successful hunts or the paintings that survive are those that hold the image in a trap, close off all means of escape and expose the prey on the canvas.

Bacon's fascination with the cynegetic paradigm informing medical imaging and photographic practice is all the more striking through its direct and indirect entries into his paintings. In medical pathology the hunt for aetiologies behind pathological appearances has informed pathological anatomy since Rudolf Virchow's *Cellular Pathology* (1858). Bacon's fascination with pathological texts is well known, not only diagnostic texts such as his much-prized hand-painted book of pathologies of the mouth but also instruction manuals in pathological image capture such as Kathleen Clara Clark's *Positioning in Radiography* (1939). Some of the pedagogical contrivances for teaching effective X-ray capture described and applied by Clark appear in Bacon's later work such as the *Figures in Movement*, 1973, [6] and the *Oedipus and the Sphinx after Ingres*, 1983. [7] The former image directly translates the circular X-ray target image from Clark into the constitution of the image – both setting and showing how the trap has been set – while the latter goes further in showing the contrivances through which the image has been pursued and captured: the arrow pointing outside the open door of what resembles a medical waiting

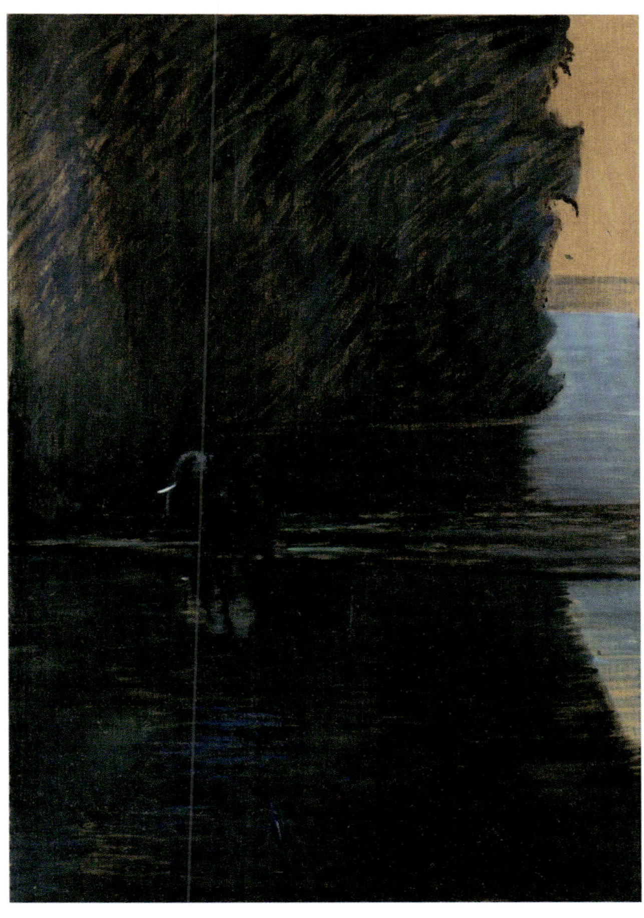

8. *Elephant Fording a River*, 1952

room indicates an approaching fury while the athletic Oedipus's presentation of his injured foot has been prepared and targeted by a blue circle for potential X-ray capture. Another circle brings Oedipus's muscular arm under examination, the arrow and the two circles providing the trap or 'construction' by which the 'thing has been caught raw and alive'.

The cynegetic model is also prominent in photographic practice, not only in art photography as a metaphorical hunt for the photograph with Cartier Bresson, but also literally in Marius Maxwell's *Stalking Big Game with a Camera in Equatorial Africa* (1924) that Bacon possessed and admired. Maxwell is highly attentive to the ways in which animals try to evade his photographic capture through camouflage or blending with the background, and his technique consists in stalking the moments in which the target is momentarily exposed against the background, being made visible by certain angles and effects of light or contrasts of tone. Bacon's consistent interest in landscape, already documented in his early work of the 1930s, is brought together with Maxwell's advice on how photographically to hunt an animal by making it stand out against its background, and is carried over into his work of the early 1950s and beyond. His *Elephant Fording a River*, 1952, [8] has been directly linked with Maxwell's text and shows an elephant almost invisible but betrayed by its reflection and the light shining off its tusk.[7] The similar capture of a figure exposed against a ground characterises *Study for Crouching Nude*, 1952, [9] where the presence of the body is betrayed by reflected light and the prominent shadow. The passing by of the body has been betrayed by the light and the shadow falling on it, allowing it to be literally captured and exhibited in a curved enclosure, surrounded by a high wall of unprimed canvas, a system of protective railings and a transparent rectangular cage. The painting fuses the moment of arrest when the body is exposed and trapped and then left fixed for display and petrification.

While Bacon's observations on his practice and his use of hunt manuals for organising his images point to a powerful cynegetic impulse informing the technical accomplishment and organisation of his paintings, there is also a further and perhaps more significant dimension to be pursued. It is not just that Bacon approaches his painting as a hunter of the image – setting traps, blocking escapes and exposing the camouflaged – and it is not just by some accident of the chase that he is sometimes lucky in capturing his prey. Rather the notion of the hunt profoundly informs his deeper and abiding fascination with Greek tragedy and the recurrent figure throughout his work of the pursuing Eumenides/Erinyes or Furies cast by Aeschylus as hunters, along with the hunted/hunter figures of Actaeon and Oedipus. *Oedipus and the Sphinx after Ingres*, 1983, is such a cynegetic vision with the figure of Oedipus captured by the painter at a moment just before his capture by the hunter Fury at the door, indicated by an arrow. Discussions of this dimension of Bacon's work are, however, rare – Jonathan Littell's *Triptyque: Trois études sur Francis Bacon* is an exception in which he is able to see things in Bacon through his own extended meditation on the Eumenides in his novel *The Kindly Ones*.[8] But the relationship between the hunt, tragedy, religion and the city is far more profound in itself and in the paintings of Bacon than is widely appreciated.

Bacon's esteem for Greek tragedy, especially Aeschylus and specifically the *Oresteia* is well documented, indeed so much so that it seems as if Bacon took unusual care to ensure it was recorded for posterity. His fascination with the Furies/Eumenides surfaced throughout his paintings, from *Three Studies for Figures at the Base of a Crucifixion*, 1944, [4] to *Triptych Inspired by the Oresteia of Aeschylus*, 1981. [10] He claimed to 're-read Aeschylus all the time, but unfortunately in translation. As I don't read Greek, which really is one of my great regrets'[9] and found the '*Oresteia* by Aeschylus … absolutely incredible'.[10] Peppiatt reports that Bacon came to the *Oresteia* through T. S. Eliot's *The Family Reunion* in which the Furies/Eumenides are central as 'the sleepless hunters/that will not let me sleep' and one of the most prominent of Eliot's many uses of the theme of the hunt. Eliot's play sent Bacon to the Irish classics scholar William Bedell Stanford's *Aeschylus in his Style* (1942) that remained an important book for him and for his painting. Stanford believed that the transformation of the Furies into the Eumenides at the close of the *Oresteia* merely brought out an aspect to the Furies that was always there, and that the Furies live on within the Eumenides. Bacon was clearly fascinated by this ambivalence and when he referred to the Eumenides clearly also meant the Furies. Peppiatt also perceptively links Bacon's phrase 'I feel myself very close to the world of Greek tragedy … often in my painting, I have this sensation of following a long call from Antiquity'[11] with his comment in a 1964 televised interview that he too was often visited by the Furies.

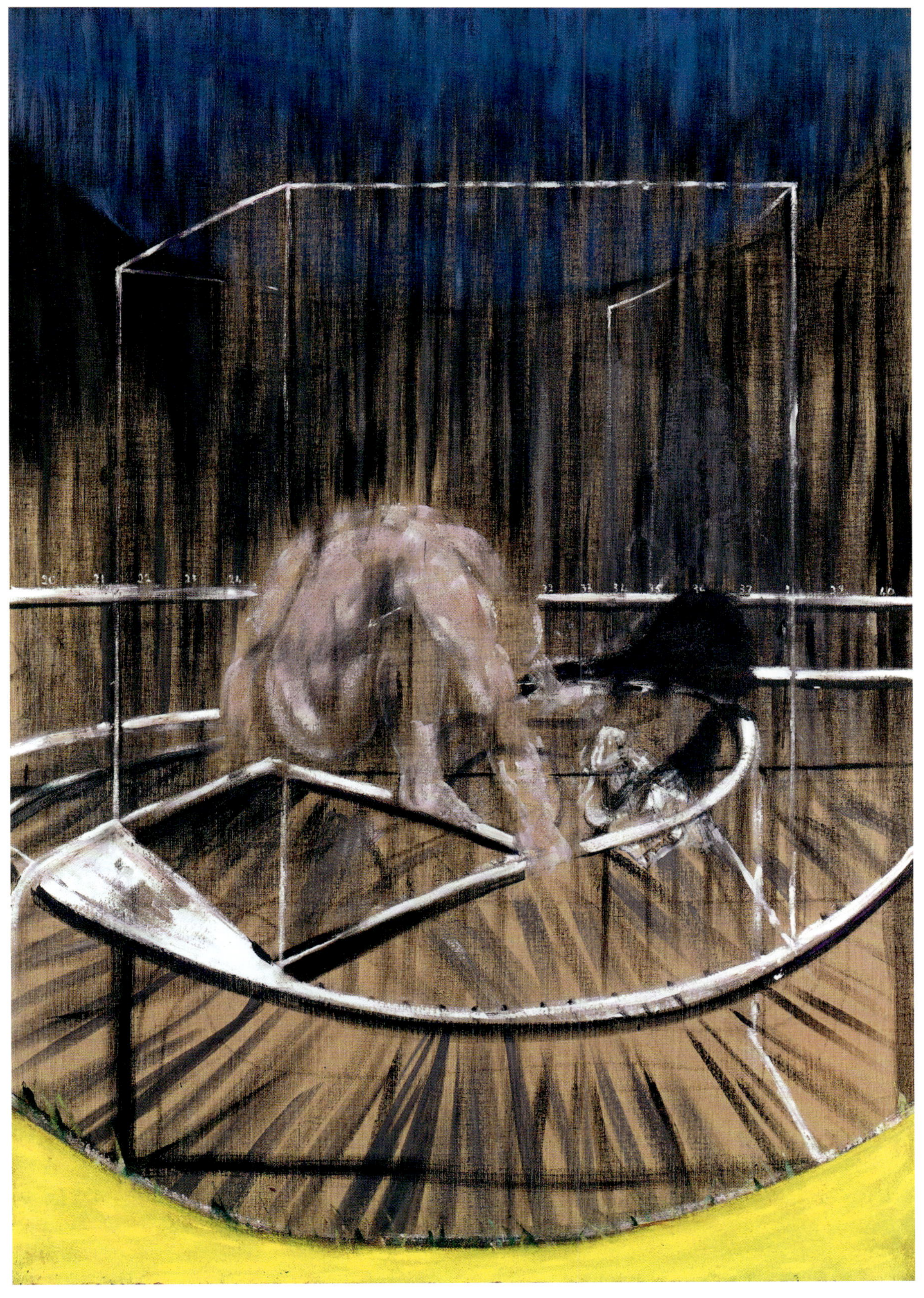

9. *Study for Crouching Nude*, 1952

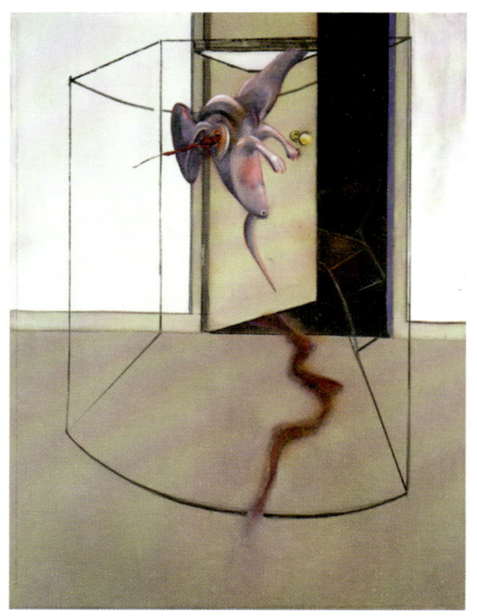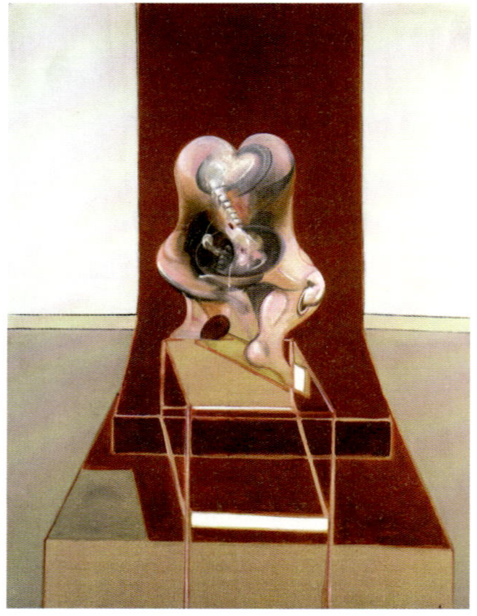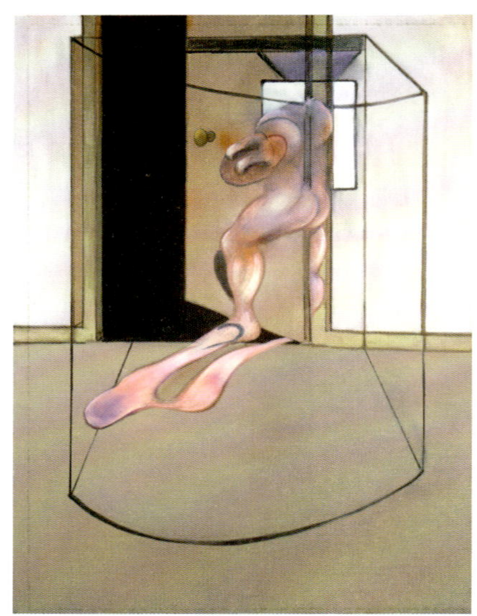

10. *Triptych Inspired by the Oresteia of Aeschylus*, 1981

However, the Furies have increasingly been recognised as but the most prominent of many cynegetic motifs in the *Oresteia* which is otherwise structured around the hunt and specifically the chase of humanity by vengeful Gods. Vidal-Naquet and Calasso's work has emphasised this feature of tragedy, pointing also to the complicated relationship between the terrain of the hunt in the forests and mountains and the space of the city and its immediate surroundings. In a 1969 essay 'Hunting and Sacrifice in Aeschylus's *Oresteia*' that preceded his more extensive studies of the Black Hunter, Vidal-Naquet points to the repeated appearances of the hunt motif in the *Oresteia* and its proximity and distance to the institution of sacrifice. He describes the *Eumenides* in terms of 'a man-hunt in which Orestes is the quarry and the Erinyes the hounds'[12] but also the peculiar metamorphosis of hunter into hunted that informs Aeschylus's cycle: 'it is the very same characters, Agamemnon and Orestes, who play the role first of hunters and then of hunted, first of the sacrificers and subsequently of the sacrificed (or those threatened with this fate).'[13] Vidal-Naquet understands the link between hunt and sacrifice in terms both complementary and opposed, noting 'that the hunt is the opposite to the classical Olympian sacrifice' because 'In general, hunting is linked with Gods who are hostile to the city, the Gods of nature in the wild like Artemis and Dionysus.'[14] The exception is offered by the case of human sacrifice and the man-hunt; yet the case of the sacrificial hunt works in two directions, the substitution of an animal for the hunted human, or a human for the hunted animal as in Euripides' *Bakkhai* and the Dionysian chase. There is, moreover, an indeterminacy or a movement between the two conditions: it is very easy for the hunter to suddenly find themselves prey.

Vidal-Naquet emphasises the movement between hunter and hunted through a contrast between the chase of the *Oresteia*, largely the work of Apollo and Artemis, and that of Dionysos, the third of the uncanny hunter-gods, in the *Bakkhai*. In the latter, Agave the mother chases and kills her son, who had hidden in a tree to spy on the Dionysian rites, imagining him to be prey. She carries his severed head back to the city, still imagining it to be variously Dionysos's ivy wreath, a lion cub and a calf: 'And so Agave praises Bacchus, the skillful hunter, the great huntsman ... Where

Dionysos has been so clever is in making Agave *hunt* her son, even though she subsequently treats him as a domestic animal ...'.[15] Indeed, Dionysos hunts the mother through her hunting the son who is following and hunting her and then mistaking him for prey; she is herself at many levels both huntress and prey. For Vidal-Naquet's reading of Euripides this equivocation is carried out unconsciously by the mother, with Dionysos hunting her by fostering the illusion that she is hunting prey and not her son. However, this is not the case with the *Oresteia:* 'What Agave does unconsciously is done in full consciousness by the hunter sacrificers of Agamemnon. The wild beast that they slaughter as if it were a domestic animal is actually their closest kin, their daughter, or their husband.'[16] The father who traps and kills his daughter is then trapped and killed by his wife who is then pursued and killed by her son, who is then pursued by the Furies ...

The chase of Orestes, in both senses of the double genitive, makes its way across the two tragedies that follow *Agamemnon* in the *Oresteia: The Libation Bearers* and *The Eumenides*. Orestes hunts his mother and then is hunted by the Furies: 'So Orestes, the hunter in *The Libation Bearers*, has now become the quarry. He is a fawn that escapes the net, a cowering fawn, a hare whose sacrifice will pay for the death of Clytemnestra. Once again Aeschylus uses the technical vocabulary of the hunt. The Erinyes are the huntresses but they are huntresses that are purely animal. The wildness that was one side of the personalities of Agamemnon, Clytemnestra, and of Orestes himself is unmitigated in their case'.[17] Vidal-Naquet, like Stanford and following him Bacon, believes 'The Nature of the Erinyes is not altered when they become the Eumenides.'[18] The transformation of the huntresses into protectors of fertility under the protection of the city of Athens coincides with the growing power of the city and its sacrifices to the Olympian Gods. In the case of the *Oresteia* the Goddess Athena undertakes the pursuit of justice previously conducted by the Furies in their hunt for vengeance and directs fury away from civil war towards war against the enemies of the polis. The cycle of hunted hunter seems to be broken and the hunt transformed into the law of the polis.

Many modern readers of the *Oresteia* did not necessarily accept the happy Athenian, Olympian sacrificial and *political* ending of the vengeful chase of the House of Atreides. For them the hunt did not end with the foundation of the polis and the epoch of law and philosophy but continued regardless. For T. S. Eliot in *The Family Reunion* it is clear that the Furies were still abroad and the hunt still on, and Bacon believed this too, especially following the experience of World War II. The resolution of cynegetics into law and philosophy promised by Athena remained incomplete and premised on a suppression but not an overcoming of the hunt.

Perhaps the most powerful philosophical argument for this position is represented by the work of Roberto Calasso in his remarkable studies of the tension between the hunt and the sacrifice conducted through readings of Kafka, Baudelaire, the Vedas and most synthetically in *The Celestial Hunter*. For Calasso, not only does the hunt continue with the foundation of the city, but it remains essential for it – the Eumenides never ceased to be Furies even after being welcomed into the polis. In a remarkable passage from *The Celestial Hunter* Calasso brings together the hunter-gods, the city and the human hunter/prey: 'While life in the city throbbed on, another life – in parallel – corresponded to it on the mountain. Indefatigable and solitary Apollo and Artemis and even Dionysos continued to hunt ... Nothing

of all that constitutes the life of the city could subsist without that chase, without
those ambushes in the mountains, without those arrows shot and that blood. It
could be said that society would never have felt sufficiently alive and perhaps even
real without that parallel superfluous and vagrant life of the hunter-gods lost in
the woods. Like the monk's prayer the silent chase of the hunters kept up the walls
that girded the city; indeed, it was that very chase that girded it like a perpetual
tornado.'[19] The movements of Vidal-Naquet's divine hunter enemies of the city for
Calasso generate the vortex in which the city can hold itself together and endure
through time but at the price of holding off the moment when the hunter becomes
the hunted. The hunt may resume at any moment, and it is this sense of the fragility
of the moment of cynegetic suspense that is captured by art and artists.

Bacon's paintings approach and capture precisely this moment, when the
deadly turbulence of the hunt reveals itself behind the fixed façades and masks of
civility. He understands this revelation in terms of the tragic, as the moment of
realisation of becoming prey, of the pursuit of the hunter, and of the attempts to
evade, escape or otherwise hide from pursuit. In many ways his view of the hunt was
more implacable than the model of Aeschylus which ends with a resolution of the
chase. The hunt of the Erinyes/Eumenides was driven by the guilt of the prey, driven
by the pursuit of justice against the matricidal hunter Orestes. But Bacon's pairing
of the Eumenides with the figure of Actaeon adds a darker dimension to the chase.
For Actaeon is not *guilty*, is not the heir of a family curse playing out on the tragic
stage. He accidentally transgressed through no major fault of his own, but though
innocent, he too is hunted down and torn apart by his own hounds. He is the victim
of chance and accident but is pursued by Artemis/Diana with the same if not more
implacable determination than which the Erinyes pursued Orestes.

**The Hunting of Actaeon**

On 4 March 1972 Bacon participated in a BBC radio broadcast with Andrew Forge and
Michael Levy as part of the public campaign to acquire Titian's late painting *The
Death of Actaeon* for the National Gallery. The painting had been on loan for ten years
to the National Gallery by the Trustees of the Seventh Earl of Harewood and recently
sold to the Getty Museum in Los Angeles for £1,763,000. The export licence was
delayed for a year to give the National Gallery the chance to raise matching funds.
The campaign was a success, partly due to a substantial donation by Bacon himself,
and the painting purchased on 6 July 1972.

In the broadcast Bacon made not only a powerful case for keeping the painting
in the National Gallery, but also a remarkable statement of his own aesthetic and
the intimate relationship he saw between the cynegetic and the tragic. Peppiatt
is entirely justified in observing that 'What he said about this masterpiece related
profoundly to his own view of life and his own painting'.[20] *The Death of Actaeon*
is one of the most devastating cynegetic visions ever painted and depicts the
metamorphosis of the hunter Actaeon into a stag savaged by his own hounds as
punishment for inadvertently witnessing the huntress Goddess Artemis/Diana
bathing naked. Actaeon is brutally punished for bad luck, suffering the necessity of
divine punishment for a chance transgression. This capture of the moment when
the luck of the hunter ran out and he became the hunted disrupted the controlled

process of painting evident in Titian's early version of a Dionysian hunt – *Bacchus and Ariadne* across the room in the National Gallery – and provoked Bacon's extreme fascination.

He begins the broadcast by pointing to the way *The Death of Actaeon* complements *Bacchus and Ariadne* hung on the opposite wall of the gallery. As a late work, it contrasts starkly with the light and relief of the earlier painting and enables Bacon to make a powerful contrast between the techniques of the early and late Titian. Asked by Andrew Forge about the nature of this contrast and the different processes of painting exposed in the early and late Titians, Bacon replied: 'I think the process is totally different in all his very late pictures, they are really painted in a very profound sense in the way that the earlier paintings are nearer to illustrational paintings.'[21] Bacon's celebrated aversion to narrative, illustrational painting and to the critical pursuit of such narratives in his own painting is joined here with an appreciation of the process of painting in the late Titian. Nevertheless, while he sees *The Death of Actaeon* as the unravelling of a 'tragic act', this is not accomplished as an illustration of a story or myth, but as its embodiment in painting and indeed, for Bacon, in a specific part of the painting. By using the term 'tragic' to describe the death of Actaeon he is placing it in the context of the hunt and the predicament of the hunter/hunted in the *Oresteia*, a link that is made explicit in his bringing together of Actaeon and the Eumenides later in the broadcast.

In many ways Bacon's reading of *The Death of Actaeon* offers a lesson in how to read his own work. He makes his first approach to the painting by pointing to the way that:

> the whole psyche has locked into the technique and especially in the corner where Actaeon has been turned into a stag and the hounds yelping and setting on him, one sees this extraordinary way Titian has been able to weave these forms as though he used the light to work into the paint, so that the images are never absolutely definite and yet they are the suggestion of a tremendously tragic act going on in this corner and one sees the more substantial form of Diana in the left-hand side that perhaps enhances the ambiguity of this tragic act.[22]

Bacon first points to the way 'the whole psyche has locked into the technique', showing how the moods of divine vengeance and the desperation of the hunter turned prey to his own dogs is not just a theme but is expressed in the frantic technique which, recalling Calasso's 'perpetual tornado', whirls around the prey. Indeed, Bacon's attention is fixed on the corner where Actaeon is caught in the moment of metamorphosis into a stag falling in panic under his own excited and 'yelping' hounds. Bacon admires 'the extraordinary way Titian has been able to weave these forms' of the hunter dogs and the man/stag unfolding the tragic act in this corner and makes an analogy between this weaving of attacking and succumbing forms with a use of 'the light to work into the paint'.[23] The light is not delineating outline but is holding the paint at a moment between rising into and out of visibility. This capture of a moment of metamorphosis is never definite – this is not an illustration of a story but a performance of the hunting-down of Actaeon and so the images are blurred as if the time of the hunt was moving just a little too fast to be captured hard and fast by the image. And yet this blur of a metamorphosis that cannot be captured visually suggests a 'tremendously tragic act' but one not represented in the painting as a whole, but just in the corner. The ambiguity of this tragic act – the hunter falling prey to his own hounds through no subjective fault or intent of his own, just the bad luck of coming across Artemis/Diana naked in the forest – is enhanced by the figure of the vengeful hunter/Goddess remorselessly pursuing him. She is solid, implacable, incapable of metamorphosis, and holds an invisible arrow to an invisible string that enters vision in the pell-mell of the hunter's own dogs, her chosen arrow or weapon of vengeance.

Bacon is insistent that the tragedy of this image does not consist in an illustration of the mythological story narrated by Ovid in the *Metamorphoses* – this is more the case with Titian's earlier treatment of the same theme in *Diana and Actaeon* – but with the capture and dismemberment of the image itself. He replies to a question about whether he gets involved in the narrative when looking at the painting with an emphatic 'yes' followed by a 'but' and then 'I'm less conscious in a sense of the subject than I am of the extraordinary quality, technical quality, by which he has been able to return this very tragic event back into me and unlock the valves of sensation about life in general which is the way that I always see painting'.[24] The tragic event of the hunter/hunted is returned by Titian to his viewer, in this case Bacon, in a way that 'unlocks the valves of sensation about life'. This painting does not give knowledge or information but it disables the defences raised by sensation and makes them vulnerable to the tragic predicament – the suffering and injustice – of life as a hunt.

Bacon reflects further on the 'unlocking of the valves of sensation' through some thoughts on the 'tragic impact' of the image. He justifies the differences in scale and technique between the vengeful Goddess on the left and the diminished falling Actaeon on the right by observing 'If the scale of Actaeon attacked by the hounds had been kept on the same scale as Diana it couldn't have had this tragic impact as though Actaeon is being demolished by the hounds that have been set on him and he has already diminished to a stag and also it is further removed, he's further from the foreground than the Goddess.'[25] The Goddess enters left, implacably pursuing Actaeon while revealing a breast to the viewers of the painting who thus perform the same voyeuristic 'crime' of Actaeon and contemplate the disproportionate punishment visited on him that is also equally their due. Actaeon's death is seen by Bacon as a diminishment, a reduction of the human to the animal but also to an ironic spectacle with the macabre humour of the hunter falling to his own hounds who fail to recognise him. While the diminishment of the figure of Actaeon and the relegation of his tragic end to a corner of the painting enhance the 'tragic impact', this is given further intensity by a contrast between the integral figure of Diana and the torn-up figure that is Actaeon. Bacon comments: 'Well, something torn to bits, that's what it's about, it's the tearing of an image of a human image to bits.'[26] The tearing-apart of human prey and image, this punishment by dismemberment, connects Artemis with Dionysos whose revels dismembered prey, occasionally human prey, as is shown across the room in the torn flesh accompanying the Dionysian procession of *Bacchus and Ariadne*.

Bacon concludes his broadcast by reflecting on the implications of *The Death of Actaeon* for 'the whole problem of painting today'. He makes a direct translation from this painting with its tragic figure of the hunter/hunted to his own painting, by reflecting first on the opposition of abstraction and figuration and then on the application of the cynegetic/tragic predicaments of Actaeon and the Eumenides to contemporary 'everyday subjects'. He begins with the contrast: 'If you think how abstract painting has taken over and how people find it almost impossible to be figurative, you will see, in this painting, not that this kind of painting could be done today, but there are all sorts of suggestions by which forms could be used and redeveloped in another way with everyday subjects.'[27] Bacon opposes to abstraction not so much a figurative or mimetic painting, but a painting in which forms such as pursuit by an implacable and irresistible power, mutilation, metamorphosis or reduction to the animal and being torn apart could be brought into the painting of modern life or 'everyday subjects'. Equally important, however, is the chance character of the transgression; there is a modernity in the violent death of Actaeon for no particular reason that distinguishes his fate from that of the guilty tragic hero.

Bacon proceeds by placing the fate of Actaeon alongside that of the hunter/hunted Orestes. He reflects 'When I look at Actaeon being torn to bits by the hounds, I think also of the Eumenides, and it makes me think of how perhaps they could be used.' He had of course consistently used them since his 1944 breakthrough painting *Three Studies for Figures at the Base of a Crucifixion* and would use them again, but differently. From now on the figure of the Erinyes/Eumenides hunting down the guilty will resolve into the single figure of the Goddess administering dreadful punishment for no reason other than bad luck. Bacon brings together Actaeon and the Eumenides by maintaining the fury of the chase but without the juridical context of vindicating a crime on the guilty. He justifies the use of these cynegetic figures because of the impact they have on the 'nervous system' or the 'valves of sensation about life in general'. The figure of the hunted hunter confuses action and passion, perpetration and suffering, and killing and being killed. Bacon believes that such images provoke automatic nervous responses – non-conscious memories – of the inextricable exhilaration of the chase and the panic of being chased. These affects are vested in the images with which we surround 'everyday life': 'Because we don't only live our life, as it were, only in the material and physical sense; we live it through our whole nervous system, which is, of course, only a physical thing, but it's a whole kind of long process of human images that have been passed down and yet nobody knows how to go on using them. This is very suggestive in this painting of how forms and images could be remade again to carry things as definite as the death of Actaeon.'[28] What Bacon sees in the Titian is a remaking of this death, the use of painting not to illustrate a nasty mythical story but to relive the killing of a victim of the bad luck of being in the wrong place at the wrong time.

A fascinating case of his own remaking of *The Death of Actaeon* is Bacon's painting *Seated Figure* completed two years after the broadcast. The direction of action has been reversed, with the single avenging figure approaching from the right, but the hunt is still on. Bacon described the 'phantasmal figure' entering stage right as a Eumenides[29] but in this cynegetic vision it pursues an Actaeon figure sprawled on a chair in black trunks convulsing in an attempt to escape the avenging Diana figure literally coming out of the blue. As in *The Death of Actaeon* it is the moment

when the light switch at the back of the room has been switched on and the prey
has not only been sighted but knows itself to have been seen and vainly squirms
to escape. The X-ray target is inscribed around his knees – Actaeon's lower legs
metamorphosed with his head in the Titian painting – and the blooded hunter-angel
is in suspended approach.

There is however an important difference between this death of Actaeon and
that of Titian, for Bacon draws out and makes explicit what is implicit in Titian,
namely the ability of painting to arrest the moment of the victim's death. Jean-Pierre
Vernant describes how the torn-up body of Actaeon was never buried, provoking
his *eidolon* or ghost to 'stir up all sorts of mischief against the population'.[30] The
injustice of his death provoked a further cycle of random vengeance on his part
which was only arrested when, on the advice of the oracle of Delphi, 'an effigy be
made of Actaeon and that it be bound with iron chains to the very stone where the
ghost appeared'.[31] In *Seated Figure* the painted image of the head is secured to a
blank canvas by a black line, collapsing together the moment of the prey's senseless
suffering and the image painted to atone for it. With this, the avenging Goddess is
thwarted of her victim and both are held arrested, as with Titian, in the medium of
painting, except that for Bacon the suffering and its placatory commemoration are
held by the device of the painting within the painting.

Hugh Davies and Sally Yard are perhaps mistaken when in their reading they
describe the approaching figure in *Seated Figure* as an Erinyes (or more properly for
Bacon, a Eumenides). Yet the figure of Diana hunting the unwitting transgressor
recalled directly to Bacon those of the Eumenides hunting the guilty from Aeschylus.
These hunter-avengers from Aeschylus's *Oresteia* played an important and consistent
role in all periods of Bacon's work and are his most consummate cynegetic visions.
They increasingly become fused with the figure of Artemis/Diana into a single figure
of pursuit. But now in an intensification of the hunt, and of tragedy, they not only
pursue the guilty matricide but also the innocent prey who suffered the misfortune
of stumbling across a naked Goddess in the forest. The intense and sustained
malevolence of the Atreides and their equally violent pursuit by the Furies is distinct
in antiquity from the pursuit of Actaeon but increasingly blurred in the work of
Bacon. Yet if the figures of the Erinyes and Diana are fused in this way, then the
vicious and uncontained pursuit of the innocent for unwitting wrong or no wrong at
all becomes conceivable and perhaps even 'everyday'.

**The Metamorphoses of the Eumenides**

We have seen that Bacon repeatedly returns to the figure of the Erinyes/Eumenides
from Aeschylus's *Oresteia* in his conversations and in his paintings. They provide
a fixed point of reference throughout his work, indicating the moment when the
hunter becomes the hunted, the perpetrator the victim. In spite of his admiration
for Greek tragedy and especially the *Oresteia* he did however retain some scepticism
concerning the apparently happy ending to the cycle, with the Furies accepting
Athena's hospitality in her city – 'I will embrace/one home with you, Athena' – and
her decision to absolve Orestes of the murder of his mother. This ends not only the
torment of Orestes who hunted down his mother spurred on by Apollo and was then
hunted down in turn by the Erinyes but closes the cycle in the laws of the polis,

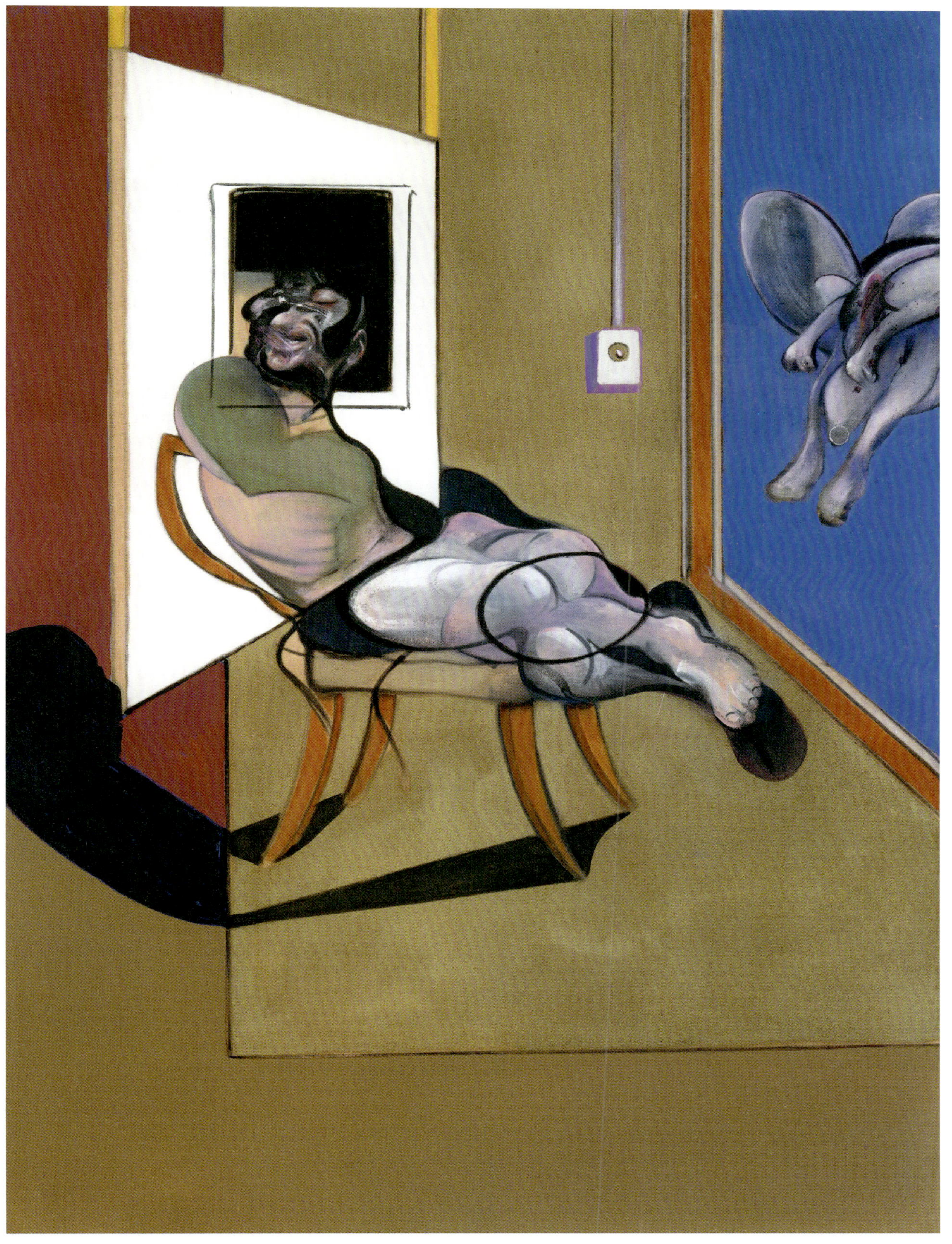

11. *Seated Figure*, 1974

opening the space for philosophy, politics and reason. The cycle of violent death that preceded Agamemnon but continued through the sacrifice of his daughter Iphigenia, his murder in revenge by his wife Clytemnestra and her murder by her son Orestes driven by Apollo, seems to be closed at the end of the cycle. The Erinyes pursued vengeance, hunting down those who hunted their own families before being received and exalted by Athena and Athens. Bacon though finds that they are still on the chase and that the Athenian resolution had not held, nor the analogous attempt to still the Furies and close the cycle of vengeance that they feed and fed on that is represented by the sacrifice of Christ and the Christianity Nietzsche described as a 'Platonism for the masses'.

They return in the painting – crucial for Bacon and acknowledged by him as the point of departure for his career as a painter – *Three Studies for Figures at the Base of a Crucifixion*, 1944. Their presence at the base of the crucifixion was acknowledged by Bacon on a number of occasions,[32] but the juxtaposition of Eumenides and a crucifixion raises a number of troubling questions. Are they there at the end of their pursuit of Jesus watching justice being done? If so, then the crucifixion would represent the capture of their prey but would also imply either that Jesus like Orestes had committed acts which caused them offence or, more likely, was an unwitting, even innocent, victim like Actaeon. The postures of the figures are ambivalent; they may indeed be read as baying at the end of a chase as the prey is captured and demolished, as with Actaeon at the hands of Diana and his hounds, but they are equally plausibly straining to be unleashed at the beginning of a hunt for vengeance. In the latter case, the scenario would be one of an innocent man suffering the mortal injustice of judicial murder, leaving the Erinyes/Eumenides – with the emphasis on the latter – straining to be released for the pursuit of the guilty perpetrators. But this is of course problematic since they are at the base of a crucifixion, the event that should mark the end of an era of vengeance and the beginning of one of love and forgiveness. In this case the hunters are being held back from pursuing vengeance, not this time by Athena but by the incarnation of a merciful and loving God. In this sense they should seem more Eumenides than Erinyes, except that in Bacon's image the submission seems less welcomed than in Aeschylus, with the figures straining to pursue vengeance for an event that understood itself as the end of vengeance.

The interpretation of the three figures is further complicated by Martin Hammer's research into the presence of Nazi propaganda imagery at a virtually concealed level of the paintings, whether in the architecture of Reich Chancellery in the backgrounds, or in the features of leading Nazis drawn from photographs in the faces of the figures.[33] According to this scenario the Eumenides/Erinyes are pictured within a context of Nazi Germany and its war and may be read as straining to pursue the Nazi murderers of the innocent victims of war and genocide. In this case the Nazi hunters become the guilty hunted in a manner entirely consistent with the pursuit of vengeance in the *Oresteia* but without the message of forgiveness of even the most heinous sins and offences promised by Athena and the crucifixion. Will the Nazis who implacably hunted down their victims now in turn be hunted down, or will there be a political settlement of their guilt as with Orestes or will they be forgiven? The vicious tension of the figures embodies these dilemmas. Already the fact that the mourners Mary, Mary Magdalen and John have been replaced by the vengeful Alecto, Megaera and Tisiphone suggests a fundamental change from a scene of mourning to one of revenge, but a vengeance that is contained and somehow held back or inhibited.

The questions surrounding the three figures are further intensified by the absence of the image of the crucifixion at whose base they are being held. Bacon's fascination with the image of the crucifixion is well attested, as is his work on crucifixions in the years prior to the *Three Studies*. If the accompanying crucifixion had survived, it might have served to clarify the role of the Erinyes/Eumenides and the reasons for their being introduced to the scene of the death of an innocent. Yet it might also have reduced the power of the *Three Studies* by situating them too unambiguously within a coherent and thus less charged pagan or Christian narrative. By remaining studies and not being situated within a completed work the images maintained the edge of being an unfinished and even unfinishable work, a feature evident in the frequent change of title from the first exhibition's *Three Studies for Figures at the Base of a Crucifixion* in 1945 to *Studies for Figures at the Base of a Crucifix* in 1946, *Study I, Study II* and *Study III* in 1949 to the neutral *Three Studies for a Larger Composition* in 1954.[34] There was to be no easy resolution of the question of the pursuit of guilt and vengeance by the three Erinyes/Eumenides unless their hunt for the guilty was generalised into a vision of the hunt for its own sake, regardless of guilt and innocence.

The resolution of the three Furies into a single Artemis/Diana figure of vengeance is carried over into the explicitly titled *Triptych Inspired by the Oresteia of Aeschylus*, 1981. [10] The inspiration in question is not an illustration of the themes and narrative of the tragic cycle but an analogous opening of the valves of sensation by the plays and the painting. Michael Peppiatt links the triptych to *Seated Figure*, 1974, [11] through the single 'unlovely grey fleshed apparition' that for him 'recalls Bacon's famous howling figures of 1944 and less directly, the animal bearing its fangs in *Fragment of a Crucifixion*, 1950 [37]; but nothing else in the long interim.'[35] But he moves too quickly to link the appearances through a narrative of 'the undisguised avowal of the guilt the artist still felt about Dyer's death'[36] with the single Fury figure representing 'a deeply uneasy conscience'.[37] Perhaps the compression of the three Eumenides into a single figure means quite the opposite, that this pursuit is no longer motivated by guilt and offence but by bad luck.

The three paintings of the triptych share the same internal skirting-board even though the floor colouring differs between the rooms. The room in the painting on the left has a door on the left jamb held open by a chair on the edge of a dark space, the centre room has a throne on a plinth with a burgundy backdrop while the painting of the room on the right is broadly symmetrical with that on the left but with the door hung on the right. Both left and right rooms have a symmetrical linear scaffolding that frames the action. The open door on the left seems inspired by the trap set by Clytemnestra in *Agamemnon* with the trail of dirty blood oozing like soiled bathwater out under the door from the scene of the kill. Agamemnon has been lured to his death, trapped in the bath in a web of robes and hacked to death by Clytemnestra's axe. The door itself seems to be divided by a white triangular space transposed from the angle of the open door through which a single Fury has entered with arms raised, it seems in exhilaration at the success of the trap. Like the analogous Fury in *Seated Figure*, and consistent with one of the descriptions of the Erinyes in the *Oresteia* as grey and haemorrhaging blood, this one is bloodied with a single malevolent eye. Its appearance at the moment of capture and kill of the prey, the moment of success in the hunt is shared by both images. The kinetic quality of this and the earlier Furies, hurling themselves towards their prey, distinguishes them from the static Furies of the *Three Studies* and brings them into proximity with the implacable figure of Diana in Titian's *The Death of Actaeon*.

The triptych loosely follows the three plays of the *Oresteia*, with the trapping and murder of Agamemnon in the first painting, and the episode of the libation bearers in which Clytemnestra, following a premonitory dream, offers libations to her victim in the centre. Here the figure is seated on a throne placed on a plinth covered with the red robe that inveigled Agamemnon to his death. There is indeed a bowl for the libation in the lap of the figure seated on a throne on a plinth, that on inspection resembles a womb containing a damaged embryo attacked by a Fury, with what appears like a fist striking the rim of the bowl on the left. The image presents literally Clytemnestra's terrifying dream of giving birth to a serpent, interpreted by Orestes her son in terms of the 'clots and stains' of a 'violent prodigy' with whom he identifies – 'I turn serpent, I kill her'.[38] In spite of its struggle, the serpent-embryo-Fury remains connected to the mother's body by an umbilical cord with the sharp articulations of a spine. The body is sectioned at the top in the form of a romantic heart and seems to be contorted around a complex amalgam of maternal love and loathing. The doubling of the womb and libation bowl certainly evokes a fear of vengeance at the hands of the still-loved son, but not guilt. The contents of the bowl will not assuage the spirit of the murdered dead but will serve to exacerbate his vengeance.

The suggestion in the central painting that the embryo was a developing Fury is unfolded in the third painting in which a heroic human figure with the arms of the Fury in *Seated Figure* is bisected by the door. The parallel with the demolished figure of Actaeon in metamorphosis is striking, except this Orestes figure is metamorphosing into a Fury with the outstretched arms of the Fury now fused with the torso and buttocks of Orestes and his deliquescing lower body. The hunt and possession of Orestes by the Fury is almost accomplished although the open door that in the *Oresteia* opens onto the sanctuaries of Apollo and Athena now offers only unmitigated darkness. The redemption through Athena and the hospitality offered by the city to the Furies is here replaced by a perverse metamorphosis in which the pursuer does not just obliterate the prey but entirely possesses it without alleviation.

Aeschylus's cynegetic drama of the hunt of Orestes is translated by Bacon into an implacable vision of a hunted hunter in the act of being possessed by the pursuit. As an intensification of the Actaeon motif, it frees the tragic hunt from any suggestion of guilt and atonement. Bacon's vision is of a world of hunters and hunted without the alleviations of law, philosophy and redemption. Perhaps this cynegetic vision that he shares with Kafka makes him the consummate modernist painter with a rare and disquieting understanding of a darker history of the twentieth century. His vision is entirely consistent with the insights of Calasso, Vidal-Naquet and Chamayou into the abiding and uncanny significance of the hunt motif and its continued operation beneath the appearances of law and justice.

**Endnotes**

1. Gilles Deleuze, *Francis Bacon: The Logic of Sensation*, trans. Daniel W. Smith (London & New York: Continuum Books, 2003), p. x.
2. Hugh Davies & Sally Yard, *Bacon* (New York: Abbeville Press, 1986), p. 8.
3. Michael Peppiatt, *Francis Bacon: Anatomy of an Enigma* (London: Constable, 2008), p. 18.
4. David Sylvester, *The Brutality of Fact: Interviews with Francis Bacon* (London: Thames & Hudson, 2016), pp. 17, 66.
5. Ibid., p. 76.
6. Ibid., p. 202.
7. Dennis Farr et al., *Francis Bacon: A Retrospective*, (New York: Harry N. Abrams Inc., 1999) pp. 72–73.
8. Jonathan Littell, *Triptyque: Trois études sur Francis Bacon* (Paris: Éditions Gallimard, 2011).
9. Michel Archimbaud, *Francis Bacon in conversation with Michel Archimbaud* (London: Phaidon Press, 1993), p. 112.
10. Ibid., p. 119.
11. Michael Peppiatt, *Francis Bacon in Your Blood: A Memoir* (London: Bloomsbury, 2015).
12. Jean-Pierre Vernant & Pierre Vidal-Naquet, *Myth and Tragedy in Ancient Greece*, trans. Janet Lloyd (Cambridge, MA: Zone Books, 1988), p. 142.
13. Ibid.
14. Ibid., p. 145.
15. Ibid., p. 152.
16. Ibid.
17. Ibid., p. 157.
18. Ibid., p. 158.
19. Roberto Calasso, *Il cacciatore celeste* (Milan: Adelphi Edizioni, 2016), p. 21.
20. Peppiatt, *Francis Bacon: Anatomy of an Enigma*, p. 302.
21. Francis Bacon, *'The Death of Actaeon'*, BBC Archive, 4 March 1972.
22. Ibid.
23. Ibid.
24. Ibid.
25. Ibid.
26. Ibid.
27. Ibid.
28. Ibid.
29. Sylvester, op. cit., p. 130.
30. Jean-Pierre Vernant, *Myth and Thought among the Greeks*, trans. Janet Lloyd with Jeff Fort (Cambridge, MA: MIT Press, 2006), p. 330.
31. Ibid., p. 304.
32. See Sylvester, op. cit., p. 130
33. Martin Hammer, *Francis Bacon and Nazi Propaganda* (London: Tate Publishing, 2012), p. 79.
34. Ibid., p. 71.
35. Peppiatt, *Francis Bacon: Anatomy of an Enigma*, op. cit., p. 334.
36. Ibid., p. 333.
37. Ibid., p. 334.
38. See *The Libation Bearers* in Aeschylus, *The Oresteia*, trans. Robert Fagles (Harmondsworth: Penguin Books, 1975), pp. 435–36.

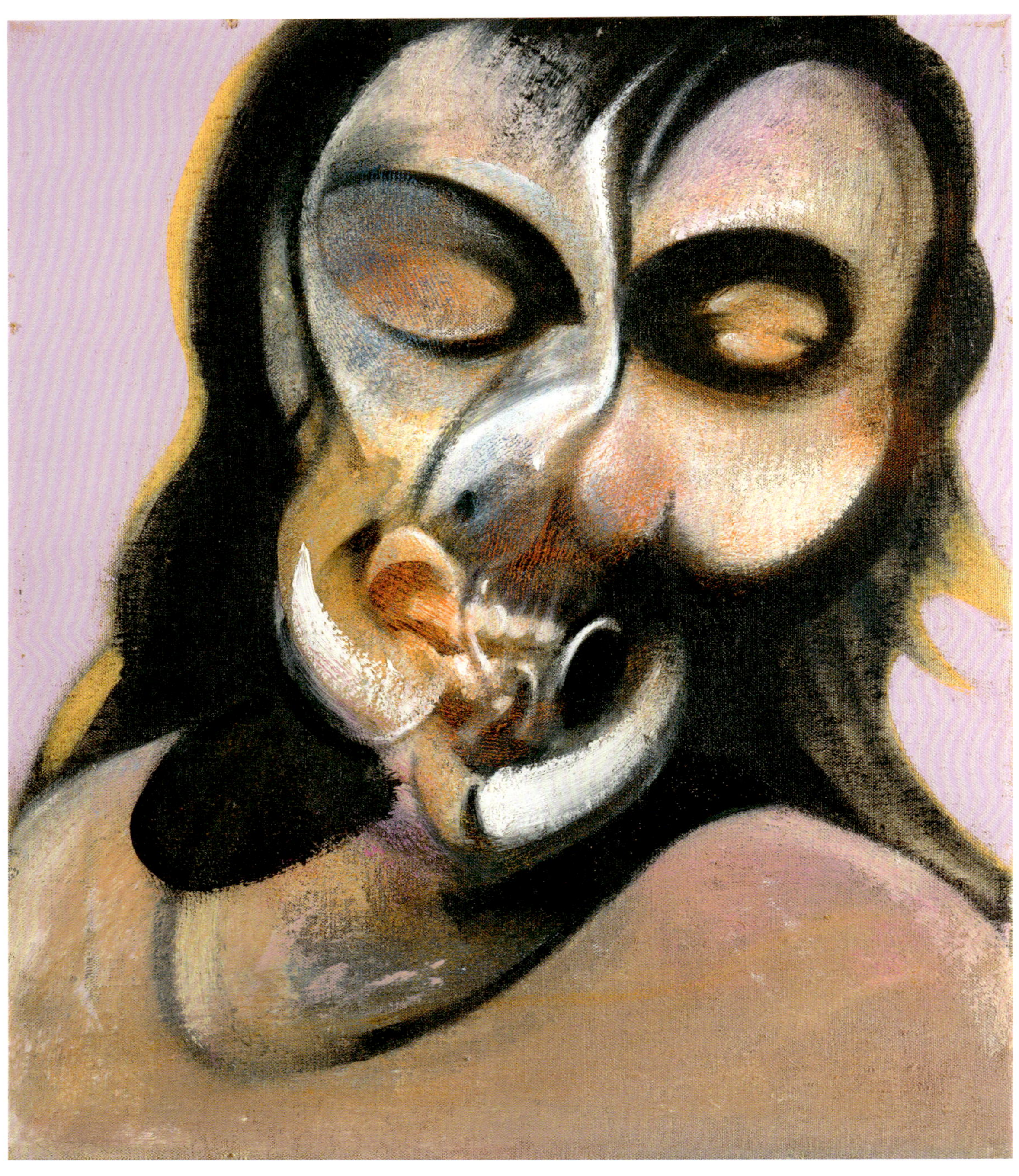

12. *Study of Henrietta Moraes Laughing,* 1969

# Scratching the Surface:
# Distance and Intimacy in *Study of Henrietta Moraes Laughing*

Gregg M Horowitz

### I  The Eyes, Then the Mouth

*I like, you may say, the glitter and colour that come from the mouth.*
– Francis Bacon[1]

Martin Harrison says of Francis Bacon's *Study of Henrietta Moraes Laughing*, 1969, [12] that 'our gaze is drawn to the eyes — perhaps in the transitional motion of blinking and moves ineluctably to the mouth — the site of the 'laugh'.'[2] It is natural for us to look first at the eyes in a portrait. Since what the sitter for a portrait is typically doing is also looking, if not directly at us, then at least at the world in which she is being painted, the eyes are where the action is. Why, though, in Bacon's painting, is our gaze then drawn, as Harrison puts it, ineluctably, irresistibly – as if against our will or hers – to Moraes's mouth? Do her eyes repel our gaze? Does the draw of her mouth overcome our first, natural gaze at her eyes? Does the drama of this painting play itself out in the overcoming of our natural attention to Moraes's eyes? And once our gaze has been drawn to her mouth, what then might we do to overcome that fascination and return it again to her eyes? Another way to ask this last question: is there anything we can do, once our eyes have been drawn ineluctably to Moraes's mouth, to once again treat Bacon's study of her as a portrait?

There is one straightforward reason why our gaze at the *Study* drifts down Moraes's face: her eyes look to be closed, while her mouth is wildly agape. Harrison aptly describes Moraes's eyes as 'perhaps in the transitional state of blinking', which is to say, her eyelids seem to be down, thereby withdrawing themselves as candidates for the centre of action in the painting. Perhaps not all the way down, but enough at least for us to be freed to look down at the real action in the *Study*, which is, as the title of the painting tells us, her laugh. There is, I believe, a more perspicacious way than 'closed' to describe Moraes's eyes, but, in any case, this explanation, which treats the component parts of the painting in a literal-minded way, tells us very little about the drama unfolding in the picture. As we know from several self-portraits by Rembrandt, a painter about whom Bacon thought a lot, a sitter's eyes need not be visible in a painting to grip us. In the *Study*, Moraes's eyes patently remain an eventful and compelling site, regardless of whether they are open, closed, or something else entirely. If we find nonetheless that we cannot resist looking down to Moraes's mouth, it cannot be because Bacon has withdrawn attention from her eyes. As for that mouth: to say that the mouth grabs hold of our attention simply by virtue of being the site of the eponymous laugh understates what is happening in the lower portion of the painting: the laugh is tearing Moraes's head apart. Harrison acknowledges this violence negatively, when he puts the word 'laugh' in shudder quotes. Something more savage than a simple displacement of the painting's action happens at Moraes's tripartite mouth.

Mouths often exert a centripetal force in Bacon's work. Famously, his figures are frequently screaming. But not, to my eyes, in agony. In one of his interviews with David Sylvester, Bacon says, 'You could say that a scream is a horrific image; in fact, I wanted to paint the scream more than the horror.'[3] This strange thought poses an interesting question: what is the interest of a scream without the horror? Bacon proffers a deeply painterly answer: a scream is what opens the mouth so that glitter and colour come shining out of the head. This is a surprising thought, as one might be forgiven for expecting that the gleaming opening in the head would be the eyes, the lamp of the body. Perhaps, though, the light in the eyes is for Bacon too much a cliché of soulfulness. This would be a plausible surmise, as Bacon's attraction to mouths does not rest on any interest in the emotions of his figures. Mouths, for Bacon, are where heads lose their formal integrity, their capacity for self-containment, and thereby show us, as Bacon puts it, another world of glitter and colour. In other words, they, and not eyes, are where painting comes to life.

In the same interview, Bacon also tells Sylvester that he has tried to paint smiles, but that he has never been able to. Smiles do not crack the head open enough for the gleam of the mouth to become the scene of painting. Sometimes, however, laughs, the alarming cousin of smiles, do the trick.

## II    Intimacy and Impediment

*The ego is first and foremost a bodily ego; it is not merely a surface entity, but is itself the projection of a surface.* – Sigmund Freud[4]

In order to make sense of the relation between Moraes's eyes and mouth, let us start over again, but this time in a more general register. It is a hallmark of adamant figuration in the twentieth century that convincing depictions of the human body require more than the illusion of the subject's presence. Mere depictions of the human body, however skilfully they deploy the massive powers accumulated in – accumulated as – the history of European figurative painting, amount to no more than echoes, *mere images*, of the body rather than authoritative encounters with the reality of embodiment. Something more emphatic is called for. Let Chaim Soutine, Käthe Kollwitz, Lucian Freud, Willem de Kooning, Alice Neel, and, more recently, Kara Walker, Cecily Brown and Mickalene Thomas, stand as examples of modern artists who, when they lash themselves to the mast of figuration, take up the traditions of figure painting at a moment when visual likeness and the reality of the body have been cleaved apart. What such painters know in their bones is that the problem of making the painted body a painting of a real body cannot be solved simply by adding something to its form, for down that path we find only the devastating judgment that the human form is incapable of establishing the significance of the human body. We find, in short, abstraction. What is called for to maintain the practice of figure painting is not a practice of addition but of stripping bare, of flaying the human body to render its material presence, which has slipped the bonds of familiar visual forms, urgent, raw, unavoidable. What is called for, in short, is not simply form (which in figurative painting remains the *sine qua non*) but anti-formal means of achieving intimacy with whatever that form can still bring to bear in on us.

Missing from my list of painters of the emphatic figure is, of course, Bacon. That should seem strange, since no artist is more commonly identified with 'deformed' bodies expressive of some sort of agony. Yet their rawness and intensity notwithstanding, Bacon's paintings rarely, I think, bring us into intimate contact with their subjects. I am even tempted to say that they never do, and that grasping Bacon's artistic achievement requires acknowledging that he is simply not a painter of intimacy with bodies. For reasons that will become clear when I return to the *Study*, foreclosing the question of intimacy in Bacon's painting is too peremptory. Still, I start by defending the generalisation. Bacon's figures are typically set back at a painted distance from the picture plane, penned inside sketchy enclosures (notional boxes, cages, rings, doorways) or splayed out on sketchy surfaces (notional platforms, stages, ledges, crosses). No matter how vividly we imagine hearing their screams (or laughs), we can hear at most echoes. Further, Bacon's figures appear to be in the grip of forces of uncertain origin that contort and rearrange their bodies and faces. The figures can be apprehended as bodies, but only if we experience them as inhabitants of another dimension. There is, in other words, something science fictiony about Bacon's pictures, as if they were depicting a world shaped by laws of physics different from ours. (In the 2014 remake of *RoboCop*, for instance, *Triptych Inspired by the Oresteia of Aeschylus*, 1981, [10] looms over the office of the evil mastermind as the emblem of a new and inhuman order of law-keeping.) As we gaze in at Bacon's figures across this abyss of non-recognition, we cannot help but sense that we do not share with them in what Maurice Merleau-Ponty called the flesh of the world. We do not see them as human like us, but as characters in the worlds of the paintings they inhabit.

All this being granted, one cannot deny that Bacon is nonetheless an emphatically figurative painter of some sort. How, then, should we describe the figures in Bacon's paintings given that they are neither classical in form nor presented to us with the material urgency found in Soutine or Freud? I will address this question by exploring how Moraes is made available to us in the *Study* not despite but precisely by means of the obstacles to intimacy Bacon places between her and us. Anticipating my focus on one painting, let me offer a more concrete version of the question I just now posed: how does Bacon use impediments to intimate encounter in the *Study of Henrietta Moraes Laughing* to bring us face-to-face with …? The natural way to complete that sentence is: with Henrietta Moraes. But that cannot be quite right, as anyone can see by looking at the *Study*, so to rush to that conclusion without tarrying with the impediments to encountering her would be just as overhasty as deciding high-handedly that there is no intimacy to be found in Bacon. I will say for now only that to make a case for intimacy in the *Study* requires that we come to see it as the outcome of a complex process of mediation that is negotiated at the surface of his paintings.

Let me try to be clearer about what exactly I am denying in denying that we typically experience Bacon's figures intimately. Elsewhere in his conversation with Bacon, Sylvester proposes the roughly existentialist thought that what Bacon paints is a primordial violence to which his models have been subjected. Although this is a familiar sort of response to Bacon as a painter of body-horror, Bacon himself rejects in short order the fervid pathos of Sylvester's line of reasoning.[5] But one finds in the world of Bacon interpretation similar albeit less overwrought versions of the idea that Bacon's paintings depict the plight of 'modern man' in the grip of the forces of an indifferent universe. Gilles Deleuze, for instance, argues that the affect at work in Bacon is pity.

> What fascinates Bacon is not movement, but its effect on an immobile body: heads whipped by the wind or deformed by an aspiration, but also all the interior forces that climb through the flesh. To make the spasm visible the entire body becomes plexus. If there is feeling in Bacon, it is not a taste for horror, it is pity, an intense pity: pity for the flesh, including the flesh of dead animals.[6]

The interpretation of Bacon as an artist whose paintings succeed when they solicit compassion from us, when they induce us to respond mimetically to the suffering of his subjects, strikes me as wrong. In the next section, I offer a contrast with painters for whom this kind of interpretation is apt in order to sharpen the differences. But worse than being wrong, the literal-mindedness of such interpretations of Bacon's figures leads spectators to neglect a defining feature of his art: his construction of impediments to the visibility of the spasm, the suffering, and so on: more generally, impediments to intimacy with his figures. My discussion of the *Study* will show that, at least in that painting, the impediment is essential to our encounter with Moraes. In a formula: to encounter Moraes we must encounter what is thrown up between her and Bacon, her and us. The impediment is thus in itself neither a barricade against the perception of the organic body (Bacon is not an abstractionist) nor the site of the abjection of the organic body (Moraes's distorted face is neither horrifying nor piteous). Instead, it serves as a screen on which the subject's face is remembered and reconverted into an image – a mask, to be exact – which is to say, on which it is phantasised as real. My leading question will then become yet more concrete: how does Bacon use impediments to intimate confrontation with Moraes to bring us face-to-face with the *material force of phantasy*?

## III    Presence and Irreality

*The methods by which [bringing somebody back] is done are so artificial that the model before you ... inhibits the artificiality by which this thing can be brought back.*
– Francis Bacon[7]

The treatment of Bacon as a painter of horror or pity – of destitute flesh – rests, I think, on a confused assimilation of him to other streams of figuration in twentieth-century painting. Admittedly, Bacon himself invites this confusion. His commitment to figuration, he once explained to Sylvester, rests on his view that figurative and abstract painting are the only live choices available to post-traditional painters. Naturally, this makes it seem that his artistic concerns must therefore be akin to those of other unwaveringly figurative artists.

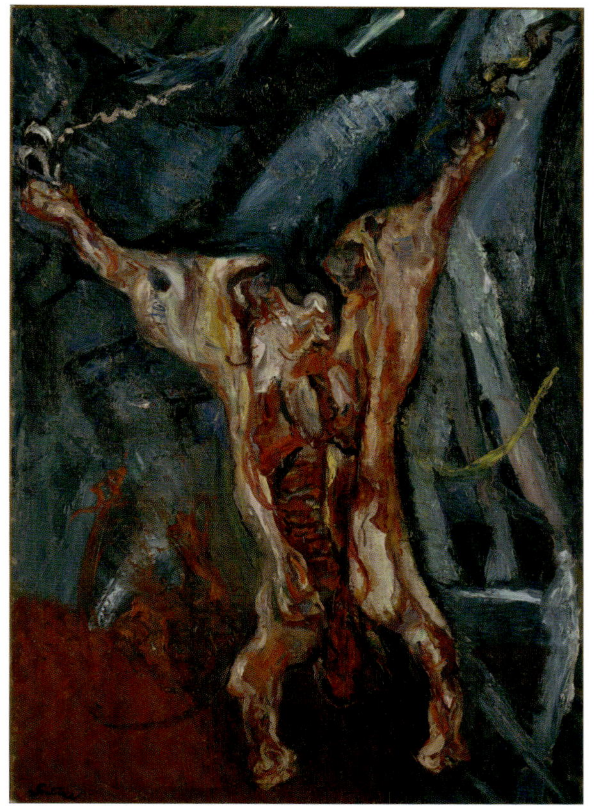

13. Chaim Soutine, *Carcass of Beef*, 1925

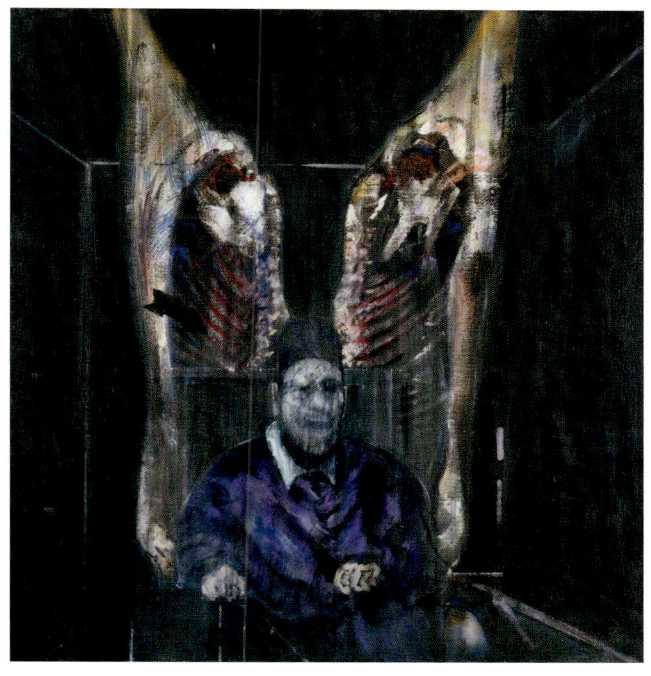

14. *Figure with Meat*, 1954

> Painters had a double role before. I think they thought they were recording,
> and then they did something very much more than recording…I think that
> now [recording] can be done better by other means on what I think is a
> more superficial level … I'm thinking about the direct photograph and direct
> recording … And I think that abstract painters, realizing this, have thought:
> why not throw out all illustrations and all forms of recording and just give the
> effects of form and colour? And logically this is quite right. But it hasn't worked
> out, because it seems that the obsession with something in life that you want
> to record gives a much greater tension and a much greater excitement than
> when you've simply said you'll just go on in a free-fancy way.[8]

Bacon's reflection on photography, recording, tension and excitement will prove of
additional interest to us shortly. Let us first consider, however, how assimilating
him to other kinds of figuration is misleading. Two contrasts towards this end. To
see Bacon as a painter of horror brings him near to Soutine, for whom the animal
body cut at its joints is flesh that has become meat, the blood and guts of which
Soutine's facture mimics and, in a way, eternalises. In Soutine, the having-suffered
of his subjects, the merciless exposure of their insides that were previously withheld
from sight, is what his technique directly evokes. Failing to sympathetically perceive
that suffering simply is failing to perceive the paintings. The contrast between
Soutine's *Carcass of Beef*, 1925, [13] and Bacon's *Figure with Meat*, 1954, [14] makes

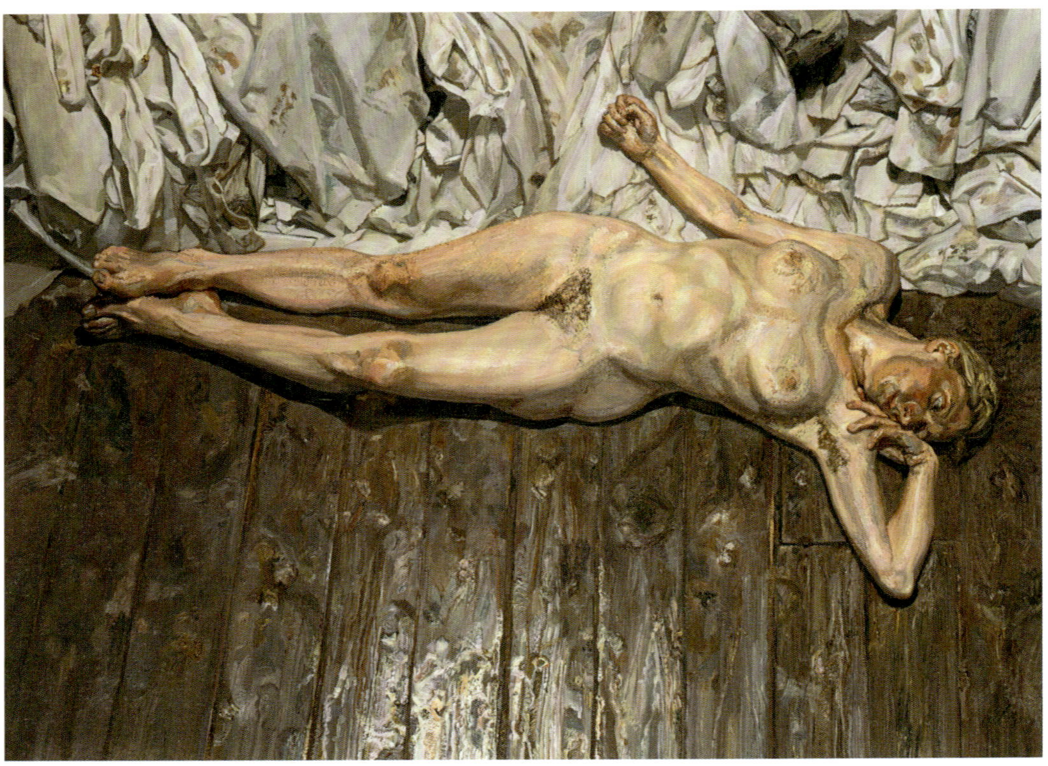

15. Lucian Freud, *Lying by the Rags*, 1989

vivid that Bacon is not that sort of expressive artist. The meat in Bacon's painting
does not glisten with life leaching away from it; its facture is dry, even scratchy, and
the interest in the carcass is not sympathetic but clinical. (In other words, Bacon
is more interested in the skeletal structure of the dead animal than in its viscous
remains.) But as different as he is from Soutine in both spirt and technique, Bacon is
equally unlike his close friend Freud. In Freud's work, the lubriciousness of oil paint
mimics the look and feel of flesh – not, as in Soutine, dead or dying flesh but flesh
that is abundantly alive. Freud's bodies are mounded, folded, cratered and creased;
their modelling encourages us to feel them with our eyes. Freud, while not a painter
of viscera, is nonetheless, like Soutine, a visceral painter. The contrast between, say,
Freud's *Lying by the Rags*, 1989, [15] and Bacon's earlier *Portrait of Henrietta Moraes*,
1963, [16] makes vivid that Bacon's figures, unlike Freud's, are not present to hand.
They are revenants.

    With this thought in mind, let us return to the impediments that Bacon
interposes between his figures and our perception of them. Consider again *Figure
with Meat*. If any picture might count as evidence that Bacon is a painter of horror,
this would be it. But note how Bacon simultaneously depicts and obscures the Pope's
face, which is built up of thick slabs of paint but also rendered hazy by the drag
of the brush. The face does not lose its expressiveness in the haze, but its grimace
becomes a rictus, as if frozen against a surface through which we see it. Those who
see this surface as a scrim behind which the Pope is posing must be imaginatively

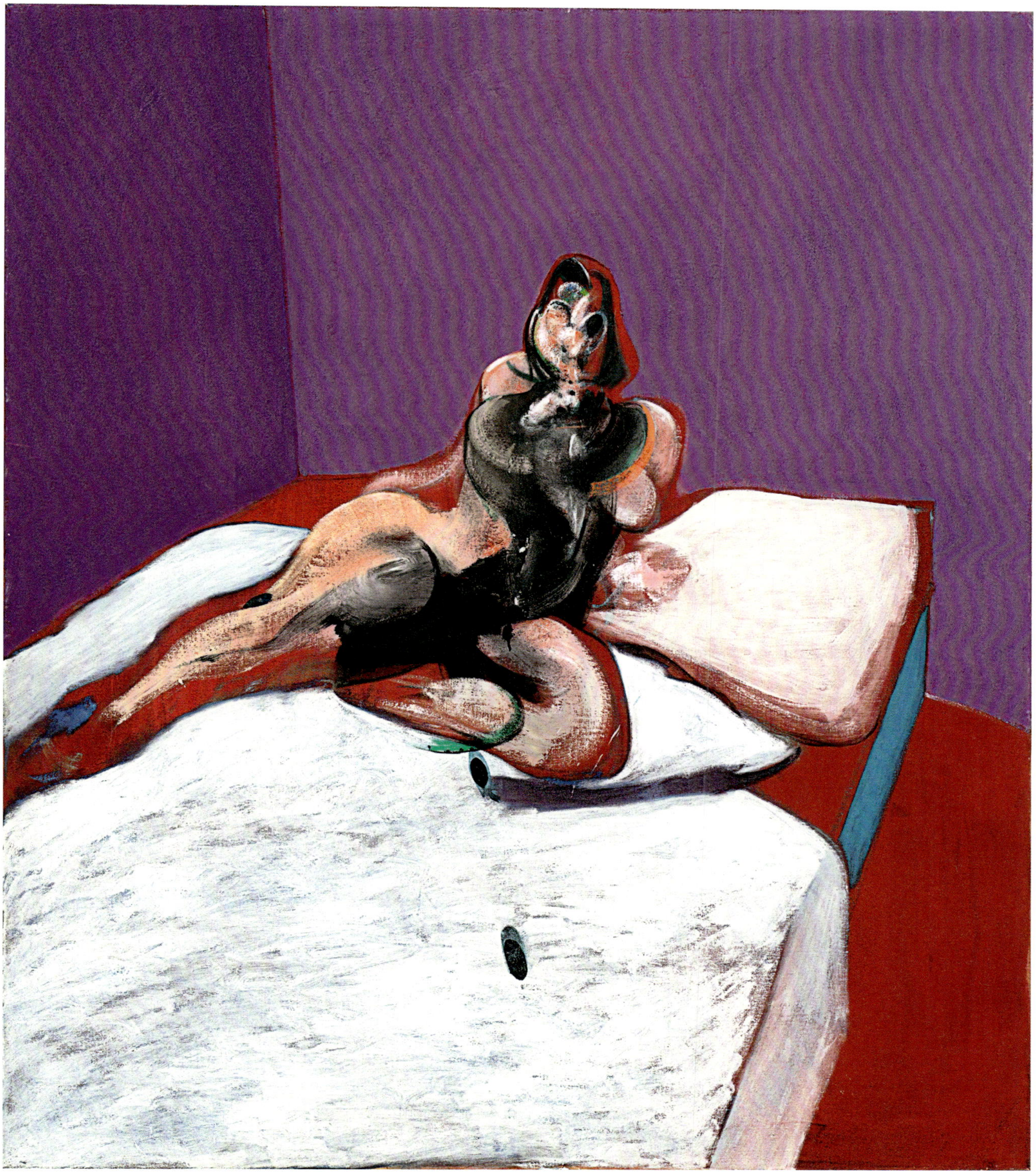

16. *Portrait of Henrietta Moraes*, 1963

seeing a figure trapped in a torture chamber, which Bacon then, in a moment of prim indirection, partially shades from us. But this perception of the figure as, first, horrifically present to sight, and then, after the fact, veiled, neglects the way Bacon paints the figure and its mantle simultaneously or, more exactly, the way he paints the figure by painting the mantle. Nothing, of course, could be more like Velázquez, for whom the idea would have been unintelligible that to paint Innocent X he first had to paint the Pope's body and then paint the finery in which it is draped. Making visible and making obscure happen not in two strokes but in one.

Not only, however, does the perception of the Pope as an integral body modelled and then muddled by Bacon err about his technique, it also cuts directly against his manner of working. As Bacon explained to Sylvester, he generally preferred to work not from live models but from photographs. That he did not work from a live model is plain in *Figure with Meat*, but even when he painted people he knew and whom he could paint from life, Bacon worked from recorded images. Having models in the studio, Bacon fretted to Sylvester, inhibited his imagination. Their presence made it hard to paint them. Bacon's use of photographs was not at all like later painters such as Richard Prince or Gerhard Richter, whom we may rightly think of as painters of photographs. Bacon was always a figurative painter, plain and simple, but one who needed the mediation of photographs to paint live figures. There is something uncanny about this requirement. Nothing in what Bacon himself calls the direct recording of photography is not also visible in the living subject of the photograph. What photographs seem to have made available to Bacon is not simply the preserved image of his models but assured distance from them. Photographs served him as both *aide-mémoires* and prophylaxis, direct recordings of his familiars that also provocatively – with tension and excitement – liberated him from the artistically disempowering presence of their bodies.[9] Photographs were both ghost images of what had been banished and means of banishing what would otherwise be all too present. The photographic memory-images that enabled Bacon to paint came to reside in a space in which he both could and had to recall the familiar life of the bodies that had been evacuated from it. Not, in other words, the mimesis of the living presence but of the living absence of what had been too-much-there is at work in Bacon's figuration. To return to the impediments, then: it would be more accurate to say not that Bacon interposes any sort of scrim between his models and our perception of them but that he begins to paint only when he is already enlivened by distance from his live models. Working from photographs, he began to paint when the irreality of his models was already assured. Not depicting them but impeding their absence – making them real again – is the driving ambition of Bacon's painting.

## IV   Face and Mask

*The crucial achievement in overcoming the depressive position is the infant's acceptance of his mother and other significant figures as really external and having an existence independent of himself.* – Hanna Segal[10]

Shortly after explaining to Sylvester his preference for working with photographs, Bacon turns aside the thought that his relationship with his models is emotionally ambivalent. He does not deny that conflicted feelings of love and hostility might rest behind everything in his life, but he denies that such emotions are artistically relevant. The distortions inflicted on his subjects, he says, are driven by one simple aim only: 'How do I feel I can make this image more immediately real to myself? That's all.'[11] While there is no general obligation to take an artist's account of his feelings and aims at face value, the fact that Bacon paints when already shielded by photographs from the embodied reality of his subjects suggests that whatever ambivalence he feels towards real people must be bracketed before he makes art. The scream is already split off from the horror, and Moraes's laugh from what her last husband, Dom Moraes, called its noisy, emphatic bray. Bacon paints faces and bodies not because they are compelling in all their messy psychological and bodily complexity, but in order that they may be called back to a reality that, as Bacon begins painting, they have already left behind.

Note that, in striving to make the image 'real', Bacon cannot mean anything as anodyne as 'convincing'. Convincing us of the rightness of a depiction is the province of what Bacon calls direct recording, the superficial this-looks-like-that by means of which photography enables the image to walk away from the body it depicts. Painting has no power to undo this hallucination and anchor the image once again in the body. This, as I understand it, is what Bacon means by calling himself a post-traditional painter, and why he rhetorically asks Sylvester, 'Who today has been able to record anything that comes across to us as a fact without causing deep injury to the image?'[12] To make an image real in the face of the division between it and the absented body that vouchsafes its meaning requires providing the painted body with a world to which, *post festum*, it must but can never properly belong. The task of overcoming the expulsion of the model from the studio must be not merely compensatory, then, as if the model had herself been injuriously denied something valuable in being expelled from the studio. (There is a political version of this thought that would take it in a different direction, but questions about the injuries inflicted by not painting excluded bodies are not among Bacon's concerns.[13]) No: the reality of the model is left in the safekeeping of her body. It is therefore precisely what is not to be painted. The painter, by contrast, is left with the irreality of the image, and it is Bacon's phantasy that painting can make a new world for what is irretrievably absent in the image. Kleinian psychoanalysts call the ethical imperative spun out of this phantasy 'reparation'. The painter provides not compensation for absence but the phantasy of an artificial world that will give the absence life.[14]

The painted worlds that Bacon invents to impede the absence of his figures are, as I said in section II, typically fantastical. Bacon's worlds contain his figures, but in the manner of cold prisons that lack reality to a degree suited to figures whose bodies are incapable of owning their own images. Yet there is something unusually intense about the *Study of Henrietta Moraes Laughing*. Bacon presents Moraes close-up and, as the painting is a mere 14 × 12 inches, barely larger than life-size. Her head is cradled in a halo that reads as bright yellow, almost gold, despite having touches of black in it where it shares edges with her hair. And while the halo bolsters Moraes's head, it also pitches it forward, so that, even though her face is just a smidgen bigger than is appropriate for a face-to-face encounter, it is overwhelming. This sense of Moraes as driven towards us is reinforced by the fact that her head is too big for

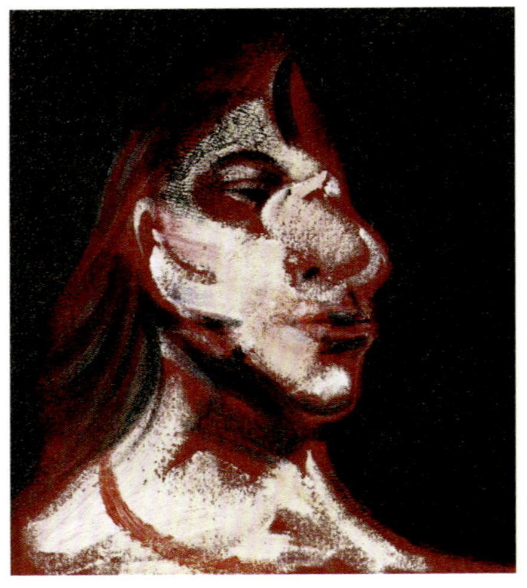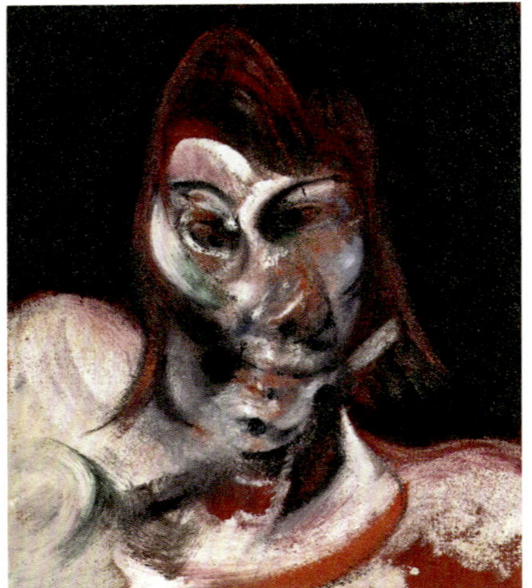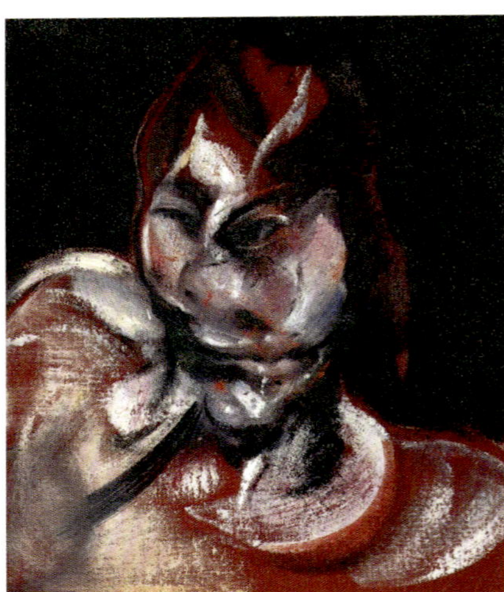

17. *Three Studies for Portrait of Henrietta Moraes*, 1963

the frame, which crops it at the top. One might expect Bacon to treat Moraes's face the way he does in an earlier picture of her, the triptych *Three Studies for Portrait of Henrietta Moraes*, 1963. [17] In that painting, Moraes's face does not loom; it is kept in check – at a distance – by the picture plane, which functions like a transparent pane of glass against which Moraes's face is flattened. That sort of impediment, with its whiff of fear or vengeance, is absent from the *Study*, where Moraes's face wins the struggle over the picture plane. In that sense, her face is not merely life-size, but emphatically so.

Emphatic, remember, is how Dom Moraes described Henrietta's domineering laugh. What, though, remains domineering about a laugh when its roar is bracketed? When it becomes, in other words, a merely visual phenomenon? Moraes's mouth remains wide open, to be sure, but in the still silence of the painting, her laugh comes to exercise power over the one who laughs. In other words, her mouth, not seen defensively from the perspective of those who hear the abrasive sounds coming from it, can be seen to explode the head to which it belongs. Bacon's depiction of Moraes's mouth records the ineluctable violence her laugh does to her own face. Her face thereby becomes a shattered mask for an invisible force.

Contrary to Bacon's painterly explanation of the general appeal of mouths to him, Moraes's mouth is not full of glitter and colour. It does not gape, and Bacon's colour palette, perhaps in consequence, is muted. But Bacon's interest in Moraes's mouth is no less painterly. What we get instead of colour and glitter as the call to painting, and perhaps even as its anticipation, is a mouth split in three: on the left, lips pulled back but not quite apart; in the centre, lips parted enough for the teeth to show; and on the right, a circular orifice painted in almost unmixed black and pointing away from the picture plane towards the right side of the painting. It is as if the familiar tripartition of Bacon's triptychs had collapsed into one image and Moraes's mouth became reaggregated. Problematically reaggregated, of course, since the three parts of Moraes's mouth do not add up to a whole. Moraes's face is a mask, but a mask of an explosion, a mask on which an explosion is splayed out, and Bacon does not try to force it back into an organic whole through the authority of painting.

Nor, I think, should we interpretively try to do so. The mask Bacon has painted is the impediment he interposes between Moraes and our encounter with her.

A mask covers the face, but it also invites projection. It is, one might say, a psychical worktable that functions to protect the face it covers precisely because we see it as face-like. (Unlike, say, a robber's ski mask, which counts as a disguise.) Here, I want to say, is the genius of the *Study*: Bacon takes Moraes's mask at face value. It is what her face must be if we are to apprehend the violence of her laugh, which is to say, the force of her character that it is the task of the portraitist to paint. We can only imagine Bacon in his studio with his silent pictures of Moraes, looking, wondering, asking where the laugh is. The condition of Moraes's being painted emphatically life-size is that her face be withdrawn from view, and simultaneously that the mask it disappears behind nonetheless impedes her absence. Not merely a death mask, then, but a mask enlivened by the unsatisfied phantasy of recalling what it hides back to life. The mask is the form in which Bacon pictures Moraes's disincarnation.

To be sure, Bacon's acceptance of her disincarnation is not passive. It is the reparative work of phantasy. Making the image real is a matter of letting the model go by recreating her. The dramatic push and pull of the painting of the *Study* is the record of Bacon's tense and excited struggle with the requirement to refigure Moraes's absence, as, for instance, in the seam which both splits and conjoins the two sides of her face, at the bottom of which there is a nose that both recedes into the painting and bulges tumescently from it. The work of making a mask of Moraes requires acts of both moulding and refraining from moulding.

No phantasy finally succeeds, of course, but that's because the work of phantasy is to endlessly reweave a world made of absences. (Another name for a fully successful phantasy is hallucination.) But that is not the thought with which to end. Rather, I wish to return us to Moraes's eyes. The question has been left hanging whether they are open or closed. The right answer, to my eyes, is both. Moraes's left eye is crossed by a lateral streak of black that suggests a drawn eyelid. But the streak is broken in the middle, where there is the suggestion of an orange pupil. In addition, highlights of white paint suggest a glint in that eye. Closed and open. Moraes's right eye has no suggestive streak of black through it to suggest an eyelid, but if it is open, it is nonetheless surprisingly blank. Open and closed. One might reasonably conclude that it is simply ambiguous whether Moraes's eyes are open or closed, but that way out of the puzzle suggests that there is visual evidence for both sides of what remain diametrical alternatives. In the *Study*, though, I think they are not alternatives at all. The eyes are open, as eyes behind a mask, and they are surfaces on which to paint. They are eyes and also the mask that covers them. There is a scrim of fine-nibbed blue marks that stretches from Moraes's left cheek to just above her left eye. These are scratches on Moraes's eye and on her mask, because Moraes looks out of the painting as a mask. This mask is Moraes's face, and on it Bacon scratches, endlessly in search of the eye that vouchsafes her absence.

# Endnotes


1.  David Sylvester, *Interviews with Francis Bacon* (New York: Thames & Hudson, 1980), p. 57.

2.  Martin Harrison, '*Study of Henrietta Moraes Laughing*', in *Francis Bacon: A Masterpiece from the Collection of S.I. Newhouse* (New York: Christie's, 2018), p. 35.

3.  Sylvester, op. cit., p. 57.

4.  *The Standard Edition of the Complete Psychological Works of Sigmund Freud*, ed. James Strachey, vol. 19, *The Ego and the Id* (London: Hogarth Press & the Institute of Psycho-Analysis, 1953), p. 26.

5.  Sylvester, op. cit., pp. 53–4.

6.  Gilles Deleuze, *Francis Bacon: The Logic of Sensation*, trans. Daniel W. Smith (Minneapolis: University of Minnesota Press, 2003), p. xxix.

7.  Sylvester, op. cit., p. 46.

8.  Ibid., p. 75.

9.  Ibid., pp. 45–6.

10. Hanna Segal, *Dream, Phantasy and Art* (London & New York: Tavistock/Routledge, 1991), p. 96.

11. Sylvester, op. cit., p. 46.

12. Ibid.

13. Every regime of representation is a regime of intelligibility. What we cannot represent, we cannot understand; what we cannot picture, we cannot see. From this point of view, to exclude a class of beings from the studio is a moral injury. This thought leads necessarily in the direction of a political critique of practices of exclusion. But Bacon is not a political painter in this sense. For him, exclusion is not the result of painting but its precondition.

14. Bacon surrounded himself in his studio not only with photographs of his official subjects but also with photographs clipped or torn from newspapers, magazines and books. This blizzard of photographic images is, we might say, the first artificial world in which even his official source images live. We know from his interviews with Sylvester that Bacon found the image of the screaming nurse from Eisenstein's *Battleship Potemkin* compelling early in his career – before, that is, he began to work on any of the many paintings in which that image came to serve as the scream motif. The ability of photographic images freely to establish relations among themselves also has direct bearing on Bacon's paintings of Henrietta Moraes. In the *Study* I am discussing here, as well as in the 1976 *Three Studies for a Portrait*, Bacon makes use of a film still of Emmanuelle Riva from Alain Resnais's *Hiroshima mon amour*. In the still, the desolate Riva is in the shower with Eiji Okada, and a strand of wet hair is crossed down her face. This strand of hair becomes a seam in Moraes's face. The film still offered Bacon a compositional device that he was at liberty to imaginatively intermingle with photographs of Moraes, the photographs themselves not offering him any resistance. We can sense that the photographs have no power to constitute a real world, in Bacon's sense of reality, not only from the free way he has with Riva's face, but also from his having torn the image across Okada's. One can think of this as a painter's indifference to his sources, but one might think of it instead as an avid effort to rescue Riva's look. The image of Riva, in other words, had already shed its history by the time Bacon saw it, which means ripping it from its photographic context is also in the service of making it real again.

    That Bacon used the still from Resnais's film is mentioned by Martin Harrison, in Martin Harrison, *Francis Bacon: Catalogue Raisonné*, vol. 3, 1958–71 (London: Estate of Francis Bacon, 2016), p. 924. An image of the studio document appears in Martin Harrison, In *Camera: Francis Bacon: Photography, Film, and the Practice of Painting* (London & New York: Thames & Hudson, 2005), p. 188. [Series editor's note: At the time the catalogue raisonné went to press the accepted title for the painting was *Study of Henrietta Moraes*, but subsequent inspection of the reverse of the canvas confirmed that Bacon had originally appended the word 'Laughing'; the longer title should henceforth be regarded as correct.]

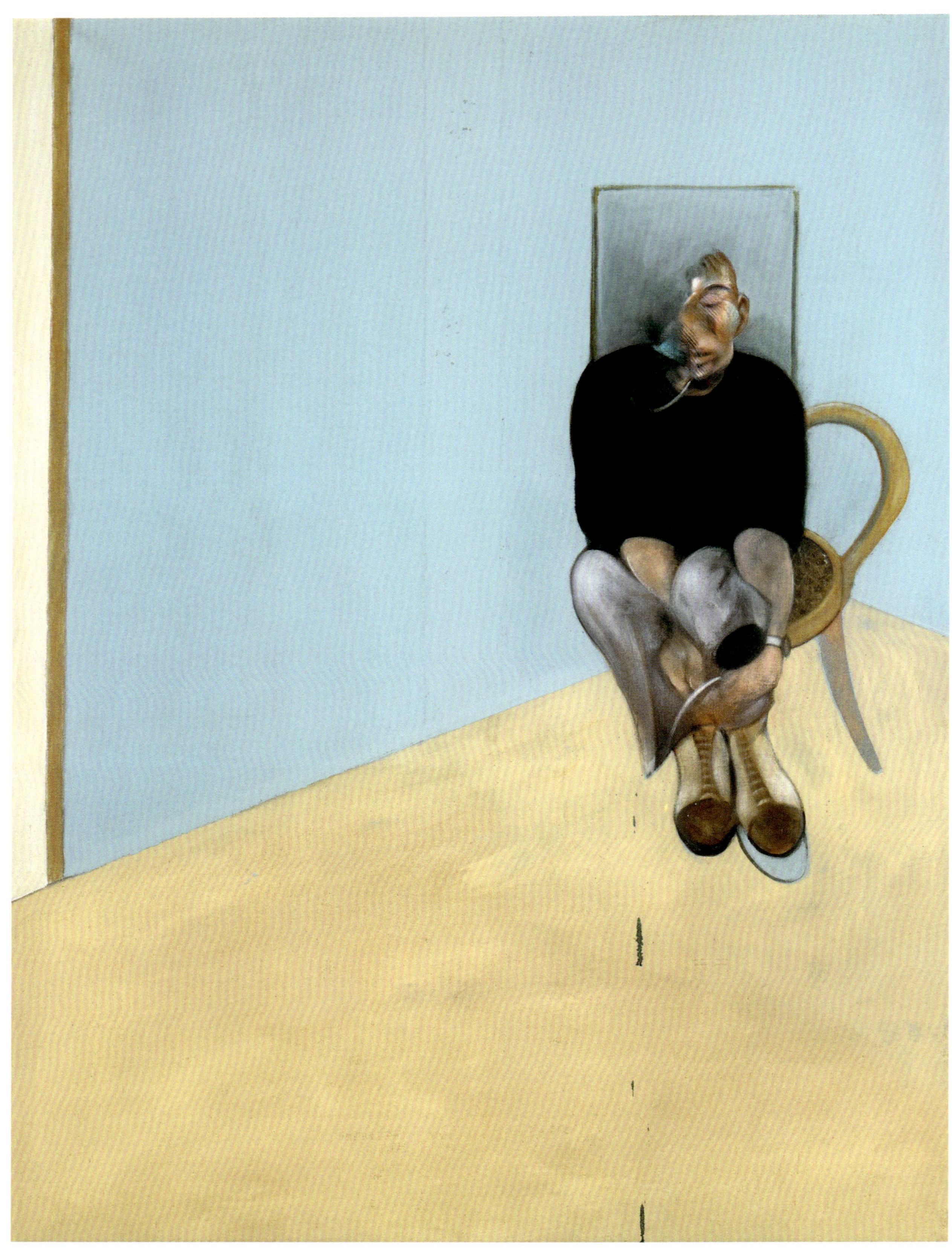

18. *Study for Self-Portrait*, 1982

# Revisiting the Mirror Phase

Darian Leader

In an earlier essay, I explored the question of Bacon's relation to several of the themes that are central to psychoanalysis: meaning, the body, repetition and the image.[1] Just as in the history of psychoanalysis we see a movement from broadly psychobiographical interpretations to what could be called 'sinthomatic' approaches to art and artists, so we see in Bacon's own pronouncements a rejection of narrative and meaning as frameworks for contextualising his paintings. Instead, we find iterated motifs which the artist was, to say the least, eager to dissociate from any set signification or hermeneutical grid.

This is no doubt one of the reasons for Bacon's popularity among psychoanalytically oriented exegetes, as it fits well the vogue for a devalorisation of meaning. The celebrated bodily excrescences, blurs and smudges which are so ubiquitous in his paintings are also nice illustrations of analytic ideas of the body's lack of containment in standard mirror frameworks and systems of representation. I have discussed these features of Bacon's work elsewhere, but in this chapter I would like to focus on something slightly different. Where psychoanalytic readings almost invariably evoke the mirror phase as a kind of spirit level to apply to Bacon's art – often with excellent results – perhaps we can find in his painting an invitation to revise the concept itself.

This is made all the more topical by the sheer omnipresence of the idea. Commentators on Bacon writing from a variety of different perspectives have used the mirror phase to explain questions of torsion, symmetry, reflection, identity and mirroring itself in the paintings, yet without problematising the theory of the mirror phase as such. If in my previous essay I had a lot of Bacon and a bit of psychoanalysis, here I will have a lot of psychoanalysis and only a bit of Bacon, but enough, I hope, to suggest ways of rethinking what we mean by the 'mirror phase'.

Lacan introduced his theory in 1936 at the Marienbad Congress of the International Psychoanalytic Association. Although no copy of the original paper survives, he was to write it up and publish a version in 1949, no doubt significantly changed due to his reading and experience in the intervening years. The background to the later paper includes late nineteenth- and early twentieth-century studies of mimicry, the sociology of the Chicago School and the work of neurologists, child psychologists and analysts in the 1920s and 30s.[2] The standard account of the mirror phase goes something like this: confronted with a state of motor helplessness and insufficiency, the infant identifies with an image of wholeness and completeness situated outside him or herself, provided by either the mirror or by the image of another, slightly older child. This is an 'alienated, virtual unity', and assuming it will have a number of consequences: if child A identifies with child B, then child A will want whatever child B wants. The field of competition and the value of objects are thus created simultaneously, together with an internal aggressiveness that will from then on characterise the human ego. The investment of the body image here is taken to be the primary route for the channelling of libido, marked initially by what Lacan calls a 'jubilation' at the mirror reflection.

The initial physiology of the infant here is one of prematuration. Unlike most other species, a human newborn is entirely dependent upon its caregivers for survival. We are born too early, and this prematuration – described and popularised in the theories of Louis Bolk – will have a number of consequences.[3] The infant will search for a means to overcome its motor helplessness and to transcend what Lacan calls the 'chaos' of its early physiological state. The mirror image offers a sort of solution, presenting a coherence that the infant can only anticipate, and exerting a gravitational pull in relation to the state of bodily discordancy. The infant's joy here lies in an 'imaginary triumph in anticipating a degree of muscular coordination which he has not yet actually achieved'.[4]

This basic theory would be reformulated in the early to mid-1950s with a new emphasis on symbolic as opposed to imaginary processes. The assumption of the mirror image would itself be dependent on how the parent situates the image for the child, the words they use to express the link to the image, and the other associations and connections that can be established by these moments.[5] Using a series of actual and thought experiments using mirrors, Lacan argues that the parental Other is the decisive agent in orienting the mirror and hence allowing the body image to be established. These considerations shed new light on clinical material, as they showed how it was possible for someone to become disconnected from their own image at moments when how they imagined they were perceived by the Other was put into question.

It was no longer just the child and the image now, but the child, the image and the parental Other who holds the child up to see the image and helps to solder it to them. The infant will always, Lacan says, turn to the adult for 'assent', to ratify the value of the image, and so our link to our own body image is dependent on a relationship.[6] Lacan uses the Freudian differentiation of ego ideal and ideal ego to theorise this dynamic: the ideal image that the child assumes is the ideal ego, whereas the parental point from which they see themselves as lovable is the ego ideal. The constitution of the ideal ego depends strictly on the ego ideal.

The next major revision to the mirror phase theory comes in 1963 in Lacan's seminar on dread. The issue here is the distribution of libido both within and outside the body, and although the body image remains the primary surface for investment, Lacan now focuses on an 'autoerotic' libido or 'autistic jouissance' which does not take the pathway of specular investment but remains rooted in the body.[7] This cannot be grasped in either imaginary or symbolic registers, and when it is touched on by certain disturbances in the framing of the body image, anxiety can result. The body image is written as i(a) and the autoerotic libido that resists transformation as (-phi) and then as (a).

So far so good. The theory is clear enough, and useful not only clinically but also to think about art and culture. The difference between the ego ideal and the ideal ego, for example, can help to explain certain changes in the sequence of Bacon's production, since whenever the ego ideal point is modified – through bereavement or separation – the ideal ego will be affected. Hence the repeated head portraits that emerge at precise points in Bacon's trajectory, as well as the efforts to sustain the body image at these biographical times. The painter needs to re-establish his image at the moments when the point from which these images are constituted is removed or undermined. The serial portraits of Dyer in the 1970s can thus be understood less as signs of Bacon's mourning his lost lover than as efforts to re-establish his own image.[8]

Similarly, the tension between i(a) and (a) can be seen as a basic matrix of Bacon's work, with a bodily excess, substantial shadow or surplus continually disrupting the surface of the mirror image and its derivatives. Bacon's painting, indeed, might be characterised as the impossible cohabitation of (a) and i(a). In biographical terms, one might evoke a problematic situating of i(a) in relation to the Ideal, leaving the painter condemned to a perpetual struggle to pin down his body image. His well-known attachment to mirror surfaces, from the famous single mirror that followed him from one address to another, to the oddly positioned mirrors at Limehouse to the mirrors of the Colony Room, is testimony to this.

If these considerations are helpful, let us turn now to what is more problematic about the theory of the mirror phase. To start with, many of the assumptions commonly made about the infant's behaviour are questionable. The mirror image is taken to be a source of partial mastery and the infant's encounter with it a source of elation. Yet in fact this is far from the case. The reflection in the mirror may be troubling, a source of anxiety and unease rather than jubilation. The child may back away from the mirror, hide from it, or become anxious. Likewise, the proposed chronology is slightly far-fetched. Lacan situates it between six or eight and eighteen months, when it is well known that there is both a much earlier interest in reflecting surfaces – from at least three months – and a much greater complexity within the time period evoked by Lacan.

The idea that a 'stage' or 'phase' can occur in infancy that lasts ten or twelve months does not really fit with clinical observation, and it is tempting to interpret this endlessly cited chronology as an example of exactly the false unity that Lacan thinks the child is searching for. This one nice bit of theory that can be clearly dated offers nothing less than a coherent image of the child's development, while in fact masking a much more complex sequence and a glossing over of a number of unanswered questions about the infant's body in its relation with its caregivers. To simply call the infant's state prior to the mirror phase a 'chaos', as Lacan does several times, shuts down a rich field of research on early symbolic, corporeal and affective processes.

The psychologists who have indeed attended to the developmental sequence have found diversity rather than unity here. In her well-known study, Beulah Amsterdam divided the early relation to the mirror into roughly four different phases.[9] From three to twelve months, the reflected image is seen as a playmate, generating sociable behaviour and smiling, sometimes including an expression of delight or what Henri Wallon termed the 'success feeling'.[10] The focus of attention here, however, may be less any idea of a 'whole' image than specific parts of the body and member movements. When Lacan describes 'the endless ecstasy when [the infant] sees that movements in the mirror correspond to its own movements', the qualifier is not entirely correct, as there may be a range of different responses.[11]

Amsterdam thought that the laughter and joy that occur later in this process around eight months may be less to do with any sense of self-recognition than of the discovery of another child in the mirror. As for the jubilation when the parent holds the child up to the mirror, which Lacan situates at six or eight months, this can occur in some cases but not in others, and it would be difficult to see this as a developmental signature for the supposed psychological process.

By one year, there is more curiosity, with efforts to touch the mirror surface, looking behind it and vocalisation. Yet very soon after this, infants seem more withdrawn, with crying, avoidance of their reflection and hiding. Some researchers ascribe fear and uneasiness to an earlier moment here, going back to at least eight months, with distress and withdrawal from their reflection actually preceding delight. From one year, 90 per cent of Amsterdam's subjects withdrew from the mirror, or, if they remained, would at times compare their own body parts in the mirror with those of their parents. Between fourteen and twenty months, there can be embarrassment, coy glances at the mirror and clowning. What had often begun as an experience of wonder has become troubling and unsettling.

These observations, and others, show how the relation to the mirror involves a complex process with multiple moments, rather than a single structural dynamic. Although the mirror phase is indeed often presented in this way, Lacan clearly discerns a sequence here, as we see in both the 1949 paper where he refers to its 'completion' and his commentaries in 1954 in the seminar on Freud's technical papers. The movement is from identification to transitivism, presented not as equivalent but as distinct moments. This is marked by a change in the libidinal charge: 'All of a sudden', he says, 'the behaviour changes completely.'[12] The key factor is the 'disappearance' around eighteen months of the jubilation that was present at eight months: now the mirror becomes just one more experience among others, indicating that a process of symbolic introjection has taken place.

But if the mirror phase starts at six or eight months with its 'fundamental feature' being the exaltation in relation to the reflected image, does it just suddenly change completely at eighteen months? The mirror phase, Lacan says, disappears at the moment of transitivism, when 'the image of the other's form is assumed by the subject' and the child becomes aware of him or herself 'as body'. So the sequence moves from the infant in jubilation at assuming a mastery which they have not yet attained, through 'the mediation of the image of the other', and an assumption of this mastery 'within himself', which is how we become aware of ourselves as body.

The mirror phase thus has an end point, and it is here that Lacan's chronology matches that of the psychologists. In the famous mirror mark test, a child has a mark made on its forehead or nose, sometimes while asleep, and then encounters a mirror. It is not before fifteen months that in most cases they will touch their own brow or nose after seeing their reflection, indicating to the psychologists that the image has been grasped as one's own. Although there is some disagreement here as to what exactly the turn to one's own body signifies, it is often taken to signal that the notion of self has been established. And where the mark test tends to be situated between fifteen and eighteen months, so Lacan gives eighteen months as the end date of his own mirror phase.

Yet curiously, the emphasis here is slightly different from Lacan's first conceptualisation. The mark test and the shifts in the infant's relation to the mirror

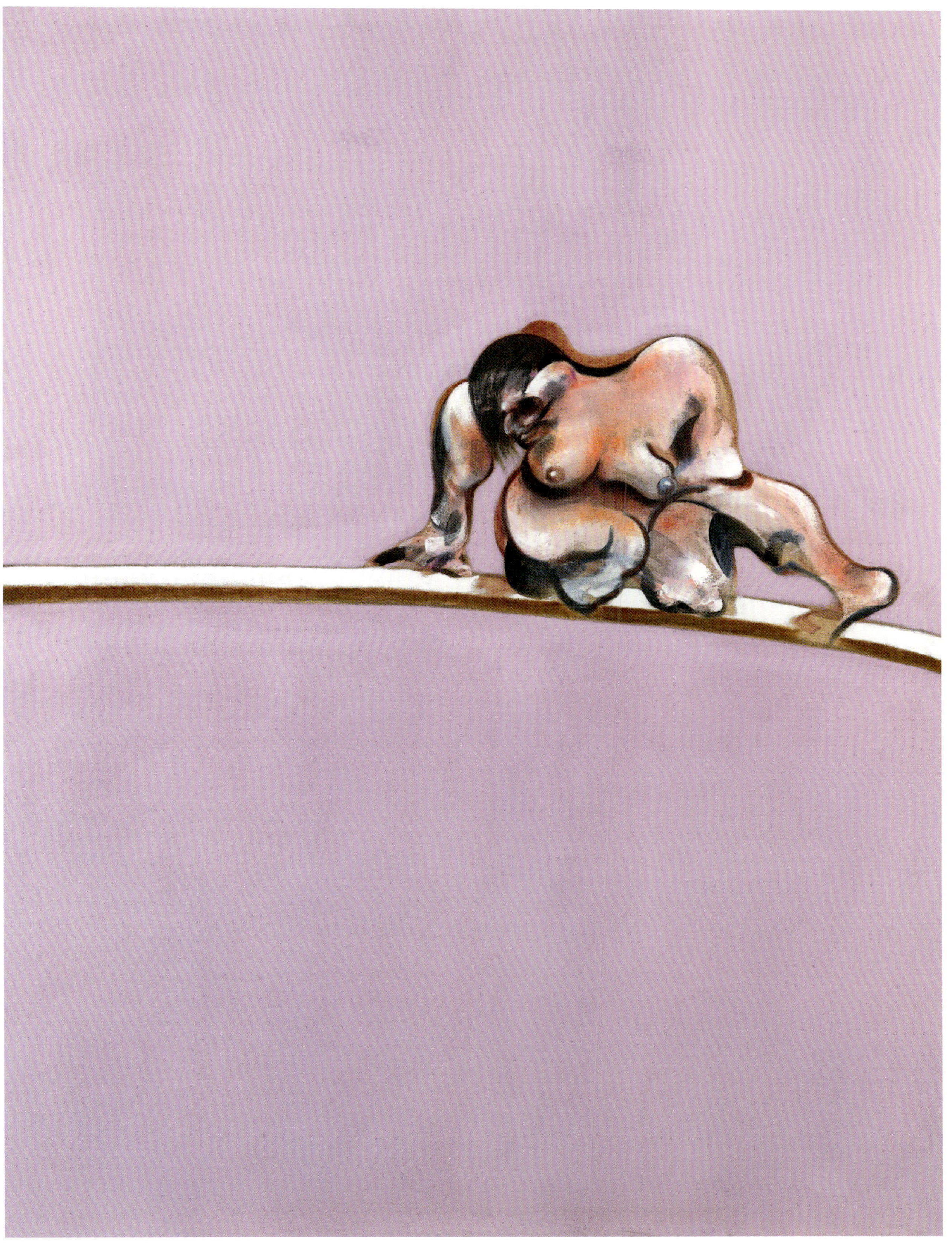

19. *Triptych – Studies of the Human Body*, 1970 (right panel)

suggest not simply an identificatory process but a recognition of the fact that one is visible to oneself as one imagines others see one. As Philippe Rochat comments, it is less that we succeed in identifying the image with ourself than the realisation that we exist in an intersubjective space, exposed and visible to others, and hence the squeamishness and wariness at the reflection that many observers have noticed.[13] In this sense, what we are witnessing here is the child's recognition that it has become an object of observation.

Whereas Lacan's initial focus is on the consequences of the identification in terms of an internal tension and the creation of rivalry, the psychologists and philosophers who studied these phenomena were interested in how we adopt the perspective of others in the moment of the constitution of self, thus seeing ourselves always as an other. As James Baldwin put it, the birth of the ego is simultaneously the birth of the alter ego.[14] Lacan's description certainly includes this idea, and it is developed in his later formulations, but these only come into perspective when we see the mirror phase as a sequence, and if we avoid collapsing together identification and transitivism, two processes that are almost invariably equated. In Lacan's schema, identification occurs first, with transitivism only taking place at the end of the mirror phase. From here, the only way out of the imaginary deadlock is through an act of 'transcendence', supplied by some symbolic agency or process. Without this, the infant risks remaining in a narcissism that Lacan qualifies as lethal, and that is clear once again in the observations of the psychologists: if the infant does well in the mirror mark test, they are just as likely at the same time to touch their own unmarked nose if they see that the nose of their mother is marked.[15]

Popular and scholarly accounts of the mirror phase tend to gloss over this inconsistency. The reflected image and the little other or counterpart are equated, yet the first little other that Lacan describes is in fact the mother. The child's 'lack of sensory and motor co-ordination', he writes, 'does not prevent the new-born baby from being fascinated by the human face, almost as soon as he opens his eyes to the light of day, nor from showing in the clearest possible way that from all the people around him he singles out his mother.'[16] And immediately after this, he states that 'It is the stability of the standing posture, the prestige of stature, the impressiveness of statues, which sets the style for the identification in which the ego finds its starting point and leave their imprint on it for ever.' The maternal imago thus seems to function as the true matrix of imaginary identification.

If we turn now to the question of libido and the mirror image, the standard formula is that the visual channel is the main pathway of libidinal investment, with a remainder of bodily libido resisting this transfer. This is equivalent to a lack in the image, and when this lack itself lacks, the result is anxiety. Without commenting on the theory of anxiety here, we can note that Amsterdam is herself drawn to discuss genital masturbation in her studies of the mirror in the early life of the child. She links this to shame and embarrassment regarding the image, and the idea that the genitals are now established as a 'separate entity', 'a distinct object', with the implication that there is a disjunction between the genitals and the body image.[17]

This echoes the famous example discussed by Karl Abraham, and commented on by Lacan, of the analysand who could 'only love her analyst, as her father's substitute, so long as the genital aspect was excluded',[18] an exclusion that he took to

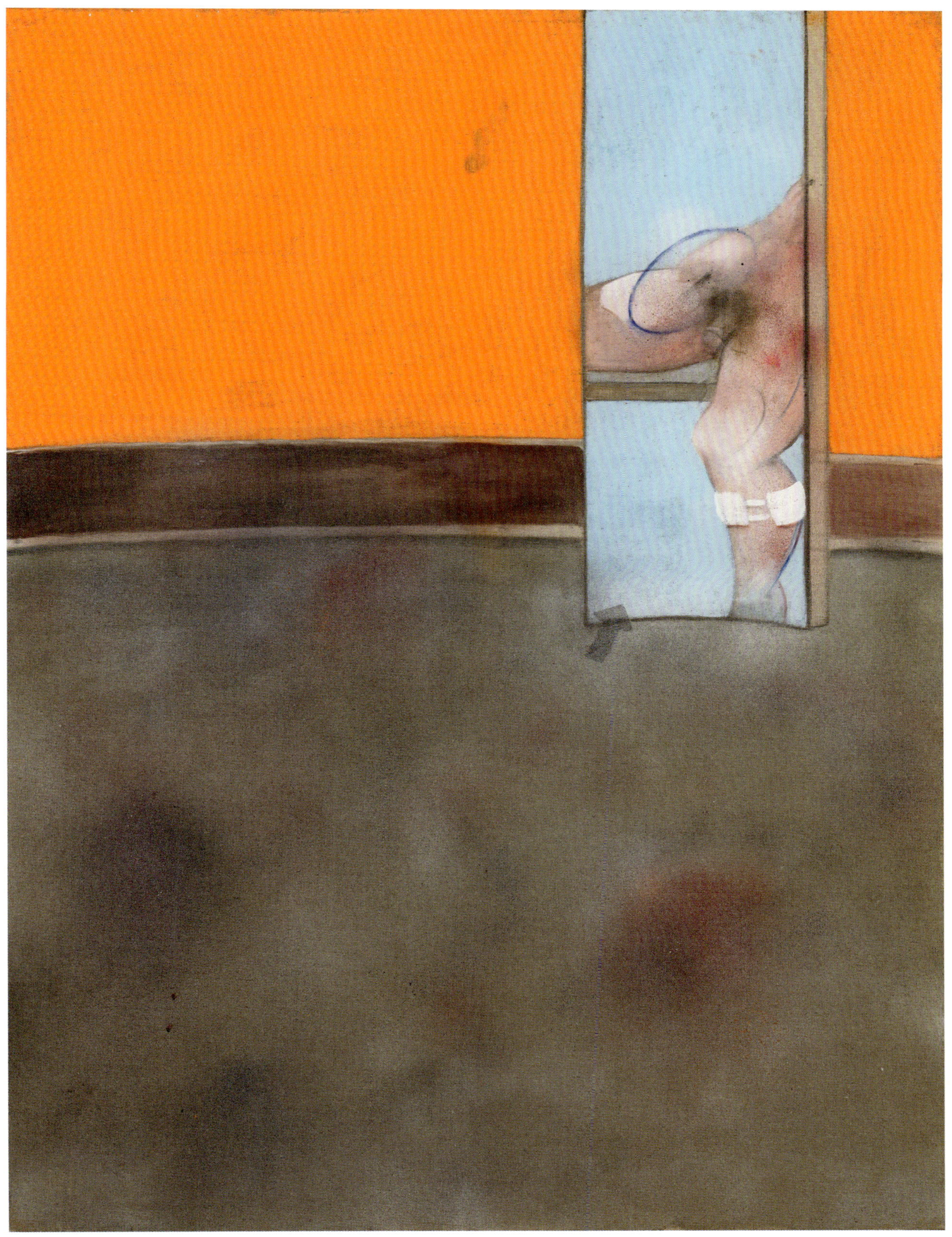

20. *Study of the Human Body*, 1987

affect the subject's own body as well. For Abraham, this means that the object cannot be loved completely because of the presence of the genitals, yet these will also be 'more intensely cathected by narcissistic love than any other part of the subject's body'. For Lacan, on the contrary, there is a difference between the libido that invests the specular body image and that which is 'preserved from this immersion, concentrating in itself the most intimate aspect of autoerotism'.[19]

But is the specular image really the primary pathway of libidinal investment? Does this not risk ignoring all the other infantile practices and activities that involve a distribution and generation of libido in the body? The fact that these are usually grouped together loosely under the term 'autoerotism' is unhelpful, especially when this is equated with infantile masturbation. As many analysts have noted, masturbation in the first years of life correlates with a withdrawal from the mother rather than an assimilation to her. The Parisian analyst who had a notice on his desk that stated 'No smoking, no masturbating – break the desire of the mother' was clearly misinformed. Genital masturbation implies a fracturing of the link to the mother, and is thus itself a relational process, as are most other activities lazily termed 'autoerotic'.[20] As Karin Stephen showed in her superb study, autoerotic practices are most commonly acts of revenge, reprisal, reparation and solicitude.[21] They are never confined, as it were, to the self.

And this brings us to one of the main problems of the mirror phase theory. Lacan evokes the motor helplessness and dependency of the infant, their state of 'organic disturbance and discord', and the consequent appeal to the image of wholeness promised by the mirror image. Through the imaginary identification, a vortex of aggression is created which requires the mediation of the symbolic as an exit plan. But what the theory leaves out here are the effects of the initial helplessness and dependency. What of the rage and destructive impotence that this in itself generates, long before any kind of assimilation to the image? To equate this with the aggression of the mirror phase is certainly not part of Lacan's conceptualisation, so what exactly happens to it? Is it repressed, forgotten, foreclosed, sublimated or sublated in the kind of *Aufhebung* that Lacan had at one point seen as characteristic of the developmental process?

Perhaps Bacon can help us here. Beyond the incommensurability of the mirror image and the body that he continually returns to, he presents us again and again with a body in pain: writhing, screaming, anguished, torn apart and torn open. This is clearly not a body situated in an imaginary field of rivalry and identification, and nor is it reducible to a bodily remainder inassimilable to the specular image. And yet at the same time the specular image is always referenced, be it in the form of a literal reflection, an absent reflection, a substantial fleshy mirror or a second-order representation, such as a portrait within a portrait. The reflected image is evoked without necessarily being appealed to here, and we could ask what is its correlate. What exactly is the image responding to?

If mirror identification has been taken by some psychologists to mark the birth of a self, and by Lacan to characterise the constitution of the human ego, the role of pain in this process has been largely ignored. Yet this is what Bacon's figures present to the mirror time and time again, as if to suggest that pain is less what disrupts the image than what allows it to be established in the first place. We know from clinical practice, indeed, that pain is precisely what both sharpens and defines

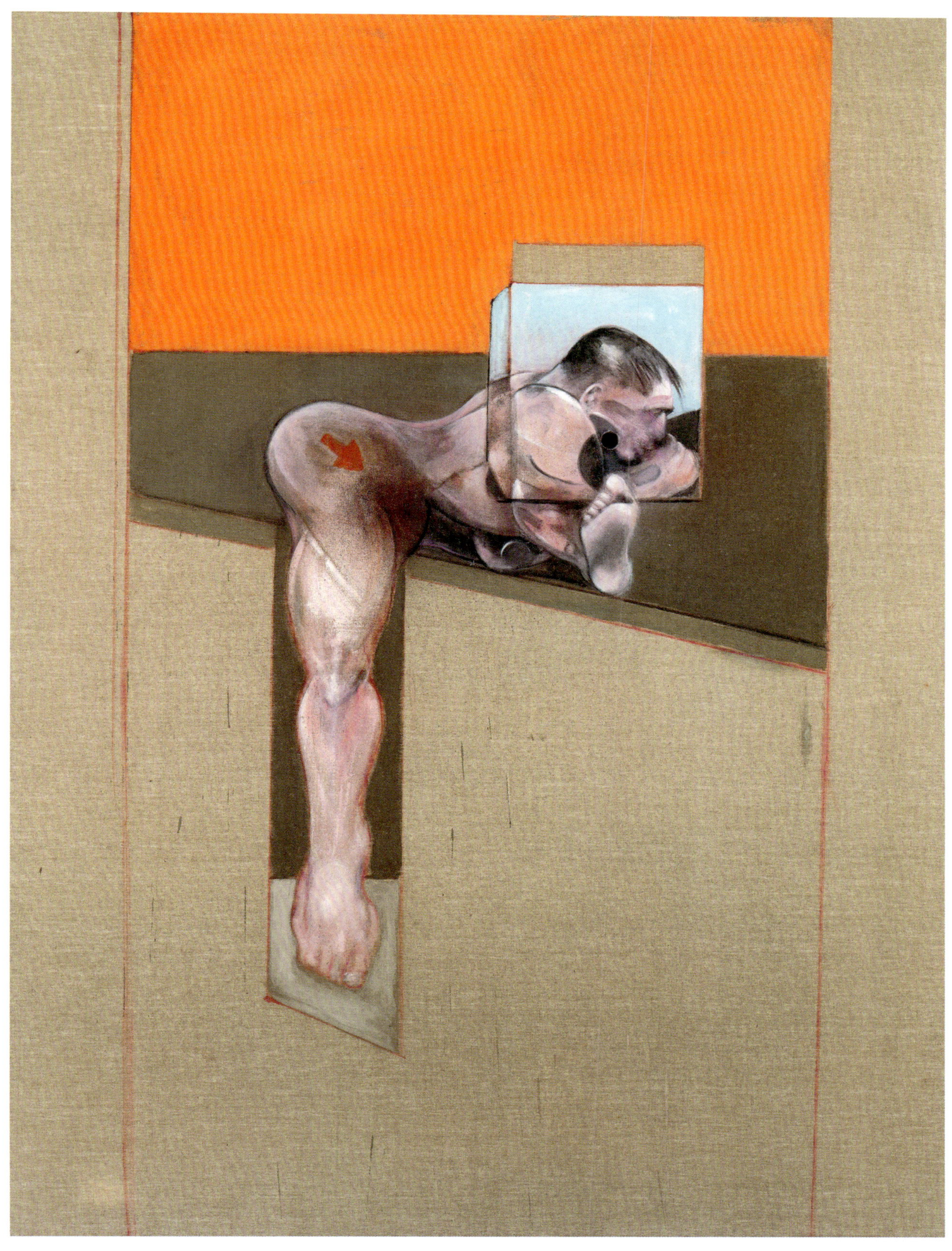

21. *Study for Human Body,* 1991

REVISITING THE MIRROR PHASE

bodily boundaries. Many people who cut or burn themselves explain that they do this in order to reconnect with their bodies and, more profoundly, with their sense of self. Hence the way in which the boundary between self-harm and the self seems increasingly difficult to demarcate.

If pain can serve to reconnect with one's image, we might guess that it plays a role in an initial connection. Lacan refers in his 1951 presentation of the mirror phase to the experience of the pain of phantom limb – what today would be distinguished from phantom limb as phantom pain – 'as if one caught a glimpse here of the existential relation of man with his body image in this relationship with such a narcissistic object as the lack of a limb.'[22] But should pain here be seen as an effect of the mirror assumption or as one of its conditions?

In his studies of the constitution of the infant's body, Willi Hoffer would argue that pain is indeed the earliest defining surface. Where Freud had introduced the tension between an archaic pleasure ego and what is rejected as alien to this, Hoffer argued that in addition there is a primary differentiating system of pain.[23] This idea responded to the problem that many of the early analysts had grappled with: what would stop the intense frustration and rage of the infant from being turned inwards, given the difficulty – at once both physiological and emotional – of directing it against the outside world, and especially against the agent of privation, the mother?

Citing some of the same ethological works that so fascinated Lacan, Hoffer evokes von Uexküll's valorisation of the pain barrier: 'pain forms one of the most powerful indicators of the subject's own body, and its chief duty is to prevent self-mutilation'.[24] The biologist observes how rats may devour their own legs if the latter's sensory nerves have been severed, and the brown dragonfly will chew at its own body if the hind part is placed next to the mouth. The tendency of some species to self-mutilate in order to save themselves was indeed discussed by both Ferenczi and Lacan, but for von Uexküll and Hoffer pain occupies a distinctive place here: it is only present when it has a function to serve. In the case of the human infant, this function is to prevent destructive rage from turning inward. A pain surface thus precedes an image surface.

For Hoffer, the actual libidinalisation of the body is secondary to this system, and will reinforce the archaic pain barrier. In his remarkable exposition, the infant's whole body becomes in fact a 'substitute' for the space of interactions with the mother: 'the infant finds a substitute for the first close attachment to the mother from which he must gradually be weaned. That is, he comes to love himself with a part of the love which was at first totally absorbed in his relations with his mother.' Libidinalisation, like pain, operates to deflect destructive reactions away from the self, although the body may still remain a space in which the autoerotic acts of relational cruelty and reprisal take place.

Libidinalisation of the body and pain will then function to move destructiveness outwards, from a system of boundaries that must be created and cannot be taken as a given. And just as the ideal ego will be affected by changes to the ego ideal, producing disconnects from the recognition of the body image, so too pain can be sought in order to set the body image back in place. Pain is thus necessary for an assumption of the body as one's own body, and helps to establish its limits. It can of course be filtered through phantasy structures and the scenarios that later events and experiences will forge, but perhaps we can see within them a trace of this primary function.

My aim here has been more to encourage a reassessment of the mirror phase
theory through an acknowledgment of the role of pain in fixing the image, rather
than to use it to interpret Bacon's work. Yet as an indication of its relevance we could
evoke what I have called the question of the first mark in the artist's sexual and
artistic practices.[25] Although Bacon's Soho is by now well known and documented,
his Earl's Court is more obscure, yet we know that this is where he would often go
on the way back from the West End in order to secure a beating. In Soho, this was
more difficult due to his celebrity, and his partners would hold back, a fact that
disappointed the artist.

To be struck is of course a key feature in two of the images that would haunt
the painter, the scene of the pram on the Odessa steps in Eisenstein's *Battleship
Potemkin* and in Poussin's *Massacre of the Innocents*. In both of these a soldier raises
a sword ready to strike. Bacon would often describe the formative effect of these
two scenes, and their link to both his art and his sexual life becomes clear when we
watch the 1985 interview with Melvyn Bragg from *The South Bank Show*. When Bragg
asks him what he aims at in his art, Bacon replies that he is trying to reach the first
stroke, the moment when 'the first mark' is made, when, for example, a wall has been
painted. This would usually be invisible, but his project is to return to this unique
and defining moment: and as he says this, he raises his arm and lashes his hand
outward with visible enjoyment. The first mark and the lash to his own body that he
would seek out with such tenacity thus share a common point.
    Echoing this, Bacon would date the start of his career as an artist with his
1944 *Three Studies for Figures at the Base of a Crucifixion*, [4] a factually incorrect
statement yet one which perhaps reveals a truth.[26] This is a scene, after all, of the
human body in pain, a suffering body, classically surrounded by onlookers. The
centrality of this suffering body to his subsequent art gives, for many viewers, a
religious dimension to Bacon's work, something that the artist would no doubt have
mocked, yet which one suspects would at the same time have somehow satisfied
him. However one chooses to interpret the pain of his figures – as existential, as
structural, as reactive to contemporary events, as autobiographical – the pain itself
is undeniable.
    The ascription of meaning to this pain was something that Bacon continually
rejected, and one can indeed read the many accounts from the 1950s until today as
illuminating social change rather than the art itself. The tortured figure signifies
the decline of faith, the horror of the concentration camp, the advent of the nuclear
age, a childhood trauma, and all of the preoccupations of the successive eras of
interpretation. Beyond these perhaps is a bedrock of bodily pain that we can use to
question our psychoanalytic concepts, and to bring the mirror phase into a
different focus.

# Endnotes


1. Darian Leader, 'Bacon and the Body', in Martin Harrison ed., *Bacon and the Mind: Art, Neuroscience and Psychology* (London: The Estate of Francis Bacon Publishing, 2019).

2. Jacques Lacan, 'The Mirror Stage as Formative of the I Function as Revealed in Psychoanalytic Experience' (1949), in *'Écrits*, trans. Bruce Fink (New York: Norton, 2006), pp. 75–81. See the discussion in Émile Jalley, *Freud, Wallon, Lacan – l'enfant au miroir* (Paris: Epel, 1998).

3. See Marc Levivier, 'La fœtalisation de Louis Bolk', *Essaim*, 26, (2011), pp.153–68, and for context Arnold Gehlen, *Man: His Nature and Place in the World* (1940) (New York: Columbia University Press, 1988).

4. Jacques Lacan, 'Some Reflections on the Ego', *International Journal of Psychoanalysis*, 34 (1953) pp. 11–17.

5. Jacques Lacan, *The Seminar of Jacques Lacan, Book I, Freud's Papers on Technique, 1953–1954*, ed. Jacques-Alain Miller (Cambridge: Cambridge University Press, 1988), p. 168, and 'Remarks on Daniel Lagache's Presentation 'Psychoanalysis and Personality Structure' (1960), in *Écrits*, op. cit, pp. 543–74.

6. Jacques Lacan, *The Seminar of Jacques Lacan, Book X, Anxiety* (1962–3), ed. Jacques-Alain Miller (Cambridge: Polity Press, 2014), p. 45, and *Écrits*, op. cit., p. 696.

7. Lacan, *The Seminar of Jacques Lacan, Book X, Anxiety*, op. cit., p. 32.

8. Leader, 'Bacon and the Body', op. cit.

9. Beulah Amsterdam, 'Mirror Self-image Reactions before Age Two', *Developmental Psychobiology*, 5 (1972), pp. 297–305.

10. Henri Wallon, 'Comment se développe chez l'enfant la notion du corps propre', *Journal de psychologie normale et pathologique*, 29 (1931), pp. 702–48.

11. Lacan, 'Some Reflections on the Ego', op. cit., p. 13.

12. Jacques Lacan, *The Seminar of Jacques Lacan, Book I, Freud's Papers on Technique*, op. cit., p. 168 and Lacan, *The Seminar of Jacques Lacan, Book X, Anxiety*, op. cit, p. 91.

13. Philippe Rochat and Dan Zahavi, 'The Uncanny Mirror: a Reframing of Mirror Self-Experience', *Consciousness and Cogntiion*, 20 (2011), pp. 204–13.

14. Baldwin, 'Imitation, a Chapter in the Natural History of Consciousness', *Mind* (January 1894), pp. 26–55.

15. Michael Lewis & Jeanne Brooks-Gunn, *Social Cognition and the Acquisition of Self* (New York: Plenum, 1979) and Philippe Rochat and Susan Hespos, 'Differential Rooting Response by Neonates: Evidence for an Early Sense of Self', *Early Development and Parenting*, 6 (1997), pp. 105–12. See also Joan Gay Snodgrass & Robert Thompson, eds. *The Self across Psychology: Self-Recognition, Self-Awareness and the Self Concept* (New York: New York Academy of Sciences, 1997).

16. Lacan, 'Some Reflections on the Ego', op. cit., p.14.

17. B. Amsterdam & M. Levitt, 'Consciousness of Self and Painful Self-consciousness', *The Psychoanalytic Study of the Child*, 35, (1980), pp. 67–83.

18. Abraham, 'A Short Study of the Development of the Libido Viewed in the Light of Mental Disorders' (1924), in *Selected Papers of Karl Abraham* (London: Hogarth Press, 1927), p. 494.

19. Lacan, *Écrits*, op. cit., p. 822.

20. Eleanor Galenson & Herman Roiphe, *Infantile Origins of Sexual Identity* (New York: Indiana University Press, 1981).

21. Karin Stephen, *Psychoanalysis and Medicine* (Cambridge: Cambridge University Press, 1933).

22. Lacan, 'Some Reflections on the Ego', op. cit., p. 14.

23. Hoffer, *Psychoanalysis. Practical and Research Aspects* (Baltimore: Williams & Wilkins, 1953), pp. 81–84.

24. Jakob von Uexküll, *Theoretical Biology* (London: Routledge, 1926), p. 145.

25. Leader, 'Bacon and the Body', op. cit.

26. Ronald Alley & John Rothenstein, *Francis Bacon, Catalogue Raisonné* (New York: Viking, 1964), p. 9.

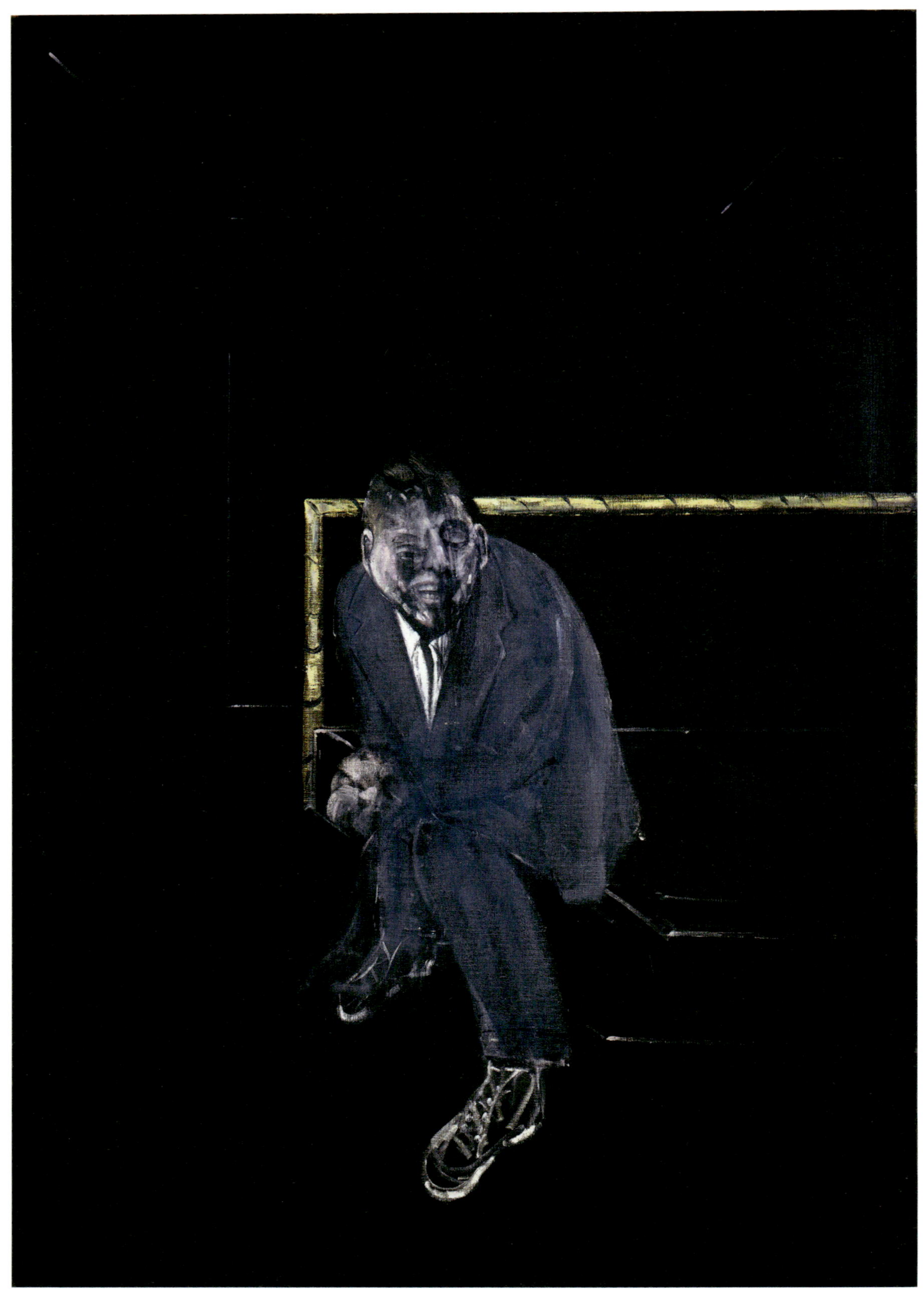

22. *Self-Portrait*, 1956

# From Deconstruction to Plasticity: Morphing Francis Bacon

Catherine Malabou

The notion of 'form' has been the constant target of philosophical deconstruction in the second half of the twentieth century. For a long time, the paradigm of inscription, or of the 'trace', has replaced it, and this not only in critical theory and philosophy, but also, in a predominant way, in art. I want to argue here, though, that Bacon is not a painter of the trace. I defend the idea that Bacon has brought to light a new, post-deconstructive approach to 'form' that has proved to be strikingly anticipatory of contemporary definitions of cerebral plasticity. Which does not mean that his painting can be considered a simple prefiguration of neurological discoveries. By distorting faces and bodies in a manner similar to certain brain diseases, Bacon has done a lot more than propose a simple pictorial translation of cerebral pathologies. Dismantling the philosophical 'anti-form' consensus and organising an incredible encounter between the most recent and the most traditional understandings of plasticity, Bacon has revealed the originary essence of form itself.

My demonstration then needs to find a way between two contradictory tendencies that have risked keeping Bacon prisoner of a false alternative. On the one hand, he has been regarded, by the tenants of the trace paradigm, as the painter of the irreducibility of the human face and body to mere 'forms'. On the other, and more recently, his work has been seen as an anticipation of contemporary brain imaging techniques. Exploring Bacon's relationship to form necessarily implies finding a way out of the irreducibility/reductionism dichotomy.

I

Human face and body have been said, by prominent contemporary continental philosophers, to definitely resist their representation as forms. Levinas called 'visage' what, in the human face, is according to him precisely irreducible to a form. The 'visage' reveals, in each subject, the withdrawal of subjectivity itself, thus letting the 'trace' of the Other appear and substitute for the 'I'. The Other is not 'present' in the face, he or she just appears in passing, leaving a pure mark of transcendence that prevents any closure of subjective identity on its own self. The trace is more ancient than any past. In this sense, it is 'the past of the Other' understood as an immemorial passage. 'The trace qua trace', Levinas writes, 'does not simply lead to the past but is the very passing toward a past more remote than any past and any future which still are set in my time ...'[1] The privileged images of this 'past', or 'passage' are those of displacement, crossing out, striating, all of which concord with the paradigmatic value of the line with no form: 'a scratch on a stone', or 'a footprint in the sand'.[2]

Transcendence — passage, transgression — necessarily breaks up form. This idea sustains Levinas's strong critique of the notion of plasticity, as well as the characterisation of art as 'plastic arts'. The Other is never the one who 'appeared in plastic form as an image, a portrait.' For the Other's beauty is the 'supreme presence ... breaking through its plastic form with youth ...',[3] for which it resists. Otherness can only '*break* [] *through* its own plastic essence.'[4] Otherness sits beyond form. It is a pure trace: 'this existence abandoned by all and by itself, a trace of itself, imposed on *me*, assigns me in my last refuge with an incomparable force of assignation, inconvertible into forms. Forms would give me at once a countenance.'[5] 'Form' remains assigned, for Levinas, to the field of sculpture, riveted to its function of both presentation and petrification: 'Form – incessantly betraying its own manifestation, congealing into a plastic form, for it is adequate to the same – alienates the exteriority of the other.'[6] Therefore, 'the face of the Other at each moment destroys and overflows the plastic image it leaves me ...'.[7] Or: 'a face is a trace of itself'.[8]

Contemporary art, painting in particular, should then dissociate itself from its plastic past – namely its mission of *shaping*. It should break from its sculptural memory, to the extent that the trace of the Other, always appearing as an excess, is irreducible to a definite contour or physical incarnation. The trace is inconvertible into forms.

Such an inconvertibility has long been considered a central feature of Bacon's portraits and heads. Isn't it obvious that the portraits of Lucian Freud, Isabel Rawsthorne or Georges Dyer, for example, make manifest an escape of their faces from themselves? A dissociation between their physical contours and the effect of transcendence that reveals the uncanny otherness of their identity? Bacon's famous declaration seems to confirm this view: 'When I look at you across the table,' he says, 'I don't only see you but I see a whole emanation, which has to do with personality and everything else. And to put that over in a painting, as I would like to be able to in a portrait, means that it would appear violent in paint. We nearly always live through screens — a screened existence. And sometimes I think, when people say my work looks violent, that perhaps I have from time to time been able to clear away one or two of the veils or screens.'[9] Isn't there a coincidence between this declaration and Levinas's description of the trace as what pierces the form of sameness in a face, thus letting the very personality of that face itself appear? Is not the 'screen', in Bacon's words, the equivalent of the 'plastic' form that occults, for Levinas, the welcoming essence of the subject? And is not this 'violence' Bacon is often accused of in reality an ethical gesture of disclosure?

Bacon is often associated with deconstruction ('Deconstruction of the Studio'[10]; 'Flesh and Body in the Deconstruction of Christianity'[11]), because his work appeared to many as one of the most convincing artistic versions of the Heideggerian *Destruktion* or *Abbau* of metaphysics, a movement that strongly influenced Levinas. *Destruktion* and *Abbau* were both translated by Derrida as 'deconstruction'. 'Deconstruction of metaphysics' designates the challenging of the privilege given, in the whole Western philosophical tradition, to presence, eternity and being over transience, becoming and finitude. The concept of 'form', *morphè* in Greek, is considered by the tenants of deconstruction the prominent expression of such a privilege. Ideas are forms. Substances are forms. Being, in its traditional sense, is a

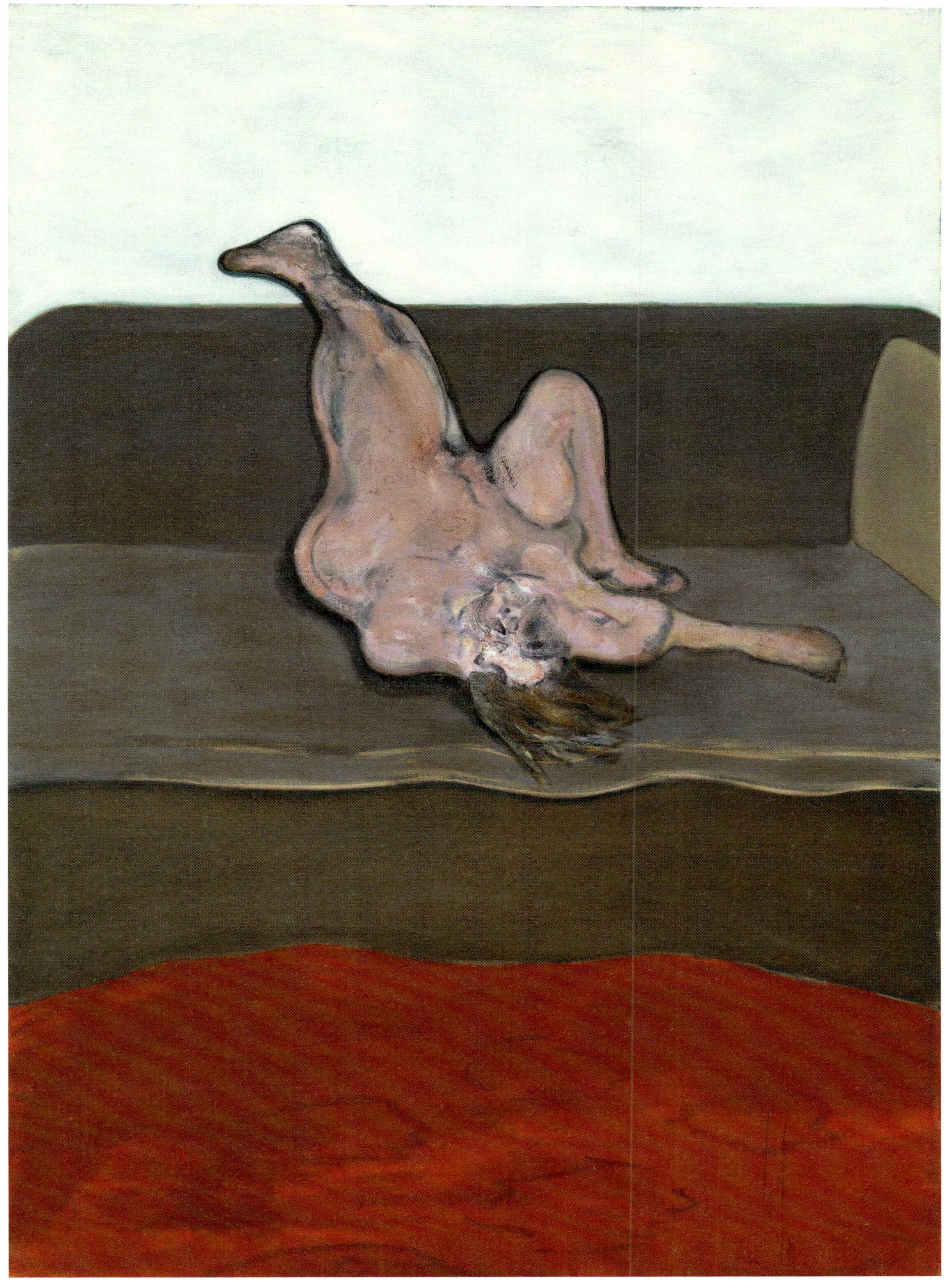

23. *Reclining Woman*, 1961

form. Becoming, on the contrary, cannot, according to the philosophical tradition, be contained in the rigid framework of a form or a shape.

In his text 'Form and Meaning', published in *Margins of Philosophy,* Derrida claimed that all notion of form, even that which believes it is criticising the traditional concepts of *eidos* or *morphè*, is forever prisoner to metaphysics.

> How could it be otherwise?' he asked. 'As soon as we utilize the concept of form – even if to criticize *an other* concept of form – we inevitably have recourse to the self-evidence of a kernel of meaning. And the medium of this self-evidence can be nothing other than the language of metaphysics. ... In truth, th[e] concept [of form] cannot be, and never could be, dissociated from the concept of appearing, of meaning, of self-evidence, of essence. Only a form is *self-evident*, only a form has or is an *essence*, only a form *presents itself* as such. This is an assured point, a point that no interpretation of Platonic or Aristotelian conceptuality can displace. All the concepts by means of which *eidos* or *morphè* have been translated or determined refer to the theme of *presence in general*. Form is presence itself. Formality is whatever aspect of the thing in general presents itself, lets itself be seen, gives itself to be thought.[12]

These remarks are of course also valid when it comes to art. The deconstructive artistic gesture is a 'dissemination', not a formation. Dissemination does not shape. It traces. The 'subject' of a painting is, once again, never 'present'. Painting always writes that which it displaces. Artistic displacements are 'breaks, re-inscriptions in a heterogeneous system, mutations, separations without origin'.[13] Derrida also called such displacements 'traits'. The relationship between traits, traces and painting is explicitly analysed in those terms: 'A trait never appears, never itself, because it marks the difference between the forms or the contents of the appearing. A trait never appears, never itself, never for a first time. It begins by retra(c)ting [se retirer]. (...) One space remains to be broached in order to give place to the space of painting. Neither outside nor inside, it spaces itself without letting itself be framed ... '.[14]

To open a space without appearing is a command to which plasticity cannot respond. Form and frame go hand in hand and have to be broached. Wouldn't it be possible, here also, to see Bacon's works as powerful versions of those dissociative gatherings that the traits are – traits that he calls 'free marks'?[15]

Form or trace: are they definitely incompatible, inconvertible, irreducible to one another? One might argue that Deleuze has proposed a way out of this dilemma. His famous book *Francis Bacon: The Logic of Sensation* is of course a perfectly autonomous and singular piece.[16] However, seen from the perspective of the present discussion, it appears as a compromise between the two tendencies mentioned earlier. The concept of 'figure', with which Deleuze chose to characterise Bacon's motifs, holds itself somewhere in between form and trace. It also holds itself somewhere in between philosophy and neurology, hence its considerable interest and value.

Some critics have argued that Deleuze was opposing Levinas about the centrality of the 'visage'. For Deleuze, as shown in *The Logic of Sensation*, the body would be more important than the 'face'. 'What Bacon constantly attempts to do', Jean Khalfa writes, 'is escape from representation, to return to a faceless head, a

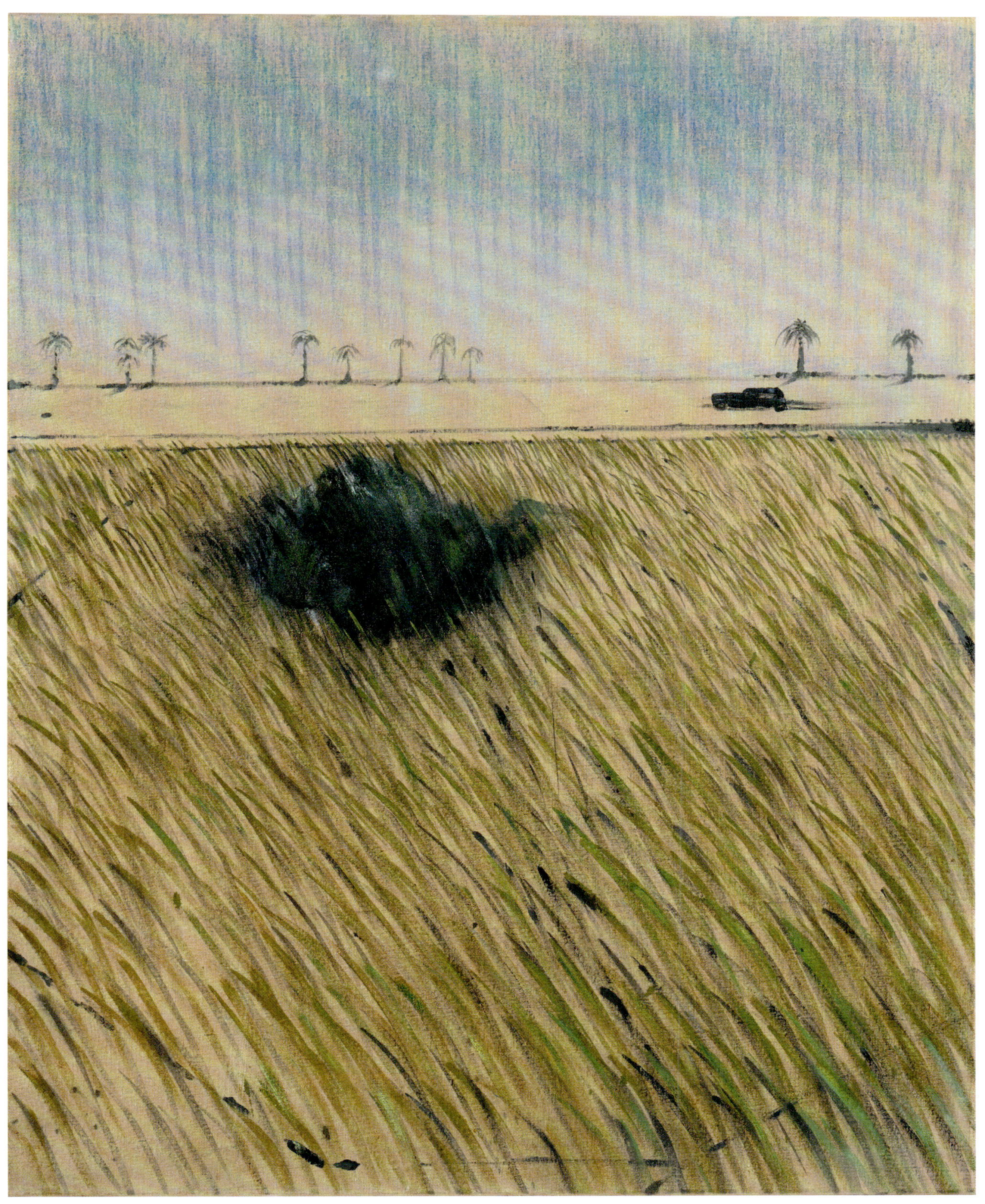

24. *Landscape, South of France*, 1952

body that effaces itself, or defaces itself, displaying, in negative fashion, the true characteristics of faciality and identity. It detaches itself, thus, from figuration towards the Figure ... '.[17] The face, then, seems to disappear without leaving a trace, allowing for the materiality of the body to appear. As Deleuze himself declares, 'The body is the Figure, or rather the material of the Figure. ... The Figure, being a body, is not a face, and does not even have a face. It does have a head, because the head is an integral part of the body. It can even be reduced to the head. As a portraitist, Bacon is a painter of heads, not faces, and there is a great difference between the two.'[18] The 'figure' would then characterise the new force of form once the (Levinasian) face is erased. The figure, as a body, through the body, reinstalls the face in its genuine form, gives it 'its true characteristics' back.

The Figure constantly tends to coincide with its 'material structure'[19], that is with its form. Deleuze is very careful to strictly distinguish between 'figure' and 'figuration', thus arguing that there exists a form that can escape representation, or abstraction, and remain, nevertheless, a form. 'Sensation' is precisely its name: 'The Figure is the sensible form related to sensation.'[20] Such a 'relation' is not a sublimation. Sensation does not transfigure what it touches, as the trace of the Other transfigures the face in Levinas. Bacon's paintings make manifest that there can be no possible distinction between human flesh and animal meat. The former never sublates the latter. Even if sometimes called 'formless' — in the sense of 'non-representative' — the meat bears witness to what can be done 'inside the same form'.[21] There is no way out of the form. Deleuze erases the trace as he affirms the dissolution of transcendence. Forms are deformed but not transformed (into something that would not be a form): 'this is why the problems Bacon faces are indeed those of deformation, and not transformation'.[22]

In Deleuze's book, the concept of form, as it appears in Bacon's painting, seems to have definitely lost its metaphysical heaviness, its charge of eternity and fixity, and it proves able to reveal the animality, precariousness and 'raw' misery of life. May one conclude that Deleuze's interpretation is already on its way to the 'reductive' one, according to which empiricality cannot be transgressed? Many passages seem to allow for such a conclusion. Referring several times to Bacon's desire to produce works that 'can make ... a direct assault upon the nervous system',[23] Deleuze affirms that the Figure is the form that 'acts immediately upon the nervous system, which is of the flesh'.[24] We know that Deleuze is one of the very few continental philosophers to have recognised the importance of the brain in all creative activities.[25] Is he, then, the philosopher who accomplished the transition from deconstruction to plasticity, and allowed for the convertibility of traces into forms?

We have to be extremely cautious in answering this question. The famous Deleuzian concept of the BWO (Body Without Organs) casts a powerful shadow over the empirical nature of the figure. I have always considered the BWO as the equivalent of the Levinasian 'face'. It is striking to see how Deleuze uses the vocabulary of the trace when characterising the BWO. All of a sudden, the lexicon of the line, of the wave, trait, furrow, invades the text. 'The body without organs', Deleuze writes, 'is opposed less to organs than to that organization of organs we call an organism. It is traversed by a wave that traces levels or thresholds in the body according to the variety of its amplitude.'[26] This 'wave' 'does not outline a form'.[27] Further: 'It is thus a line that does not cease to change directions, that is broken,

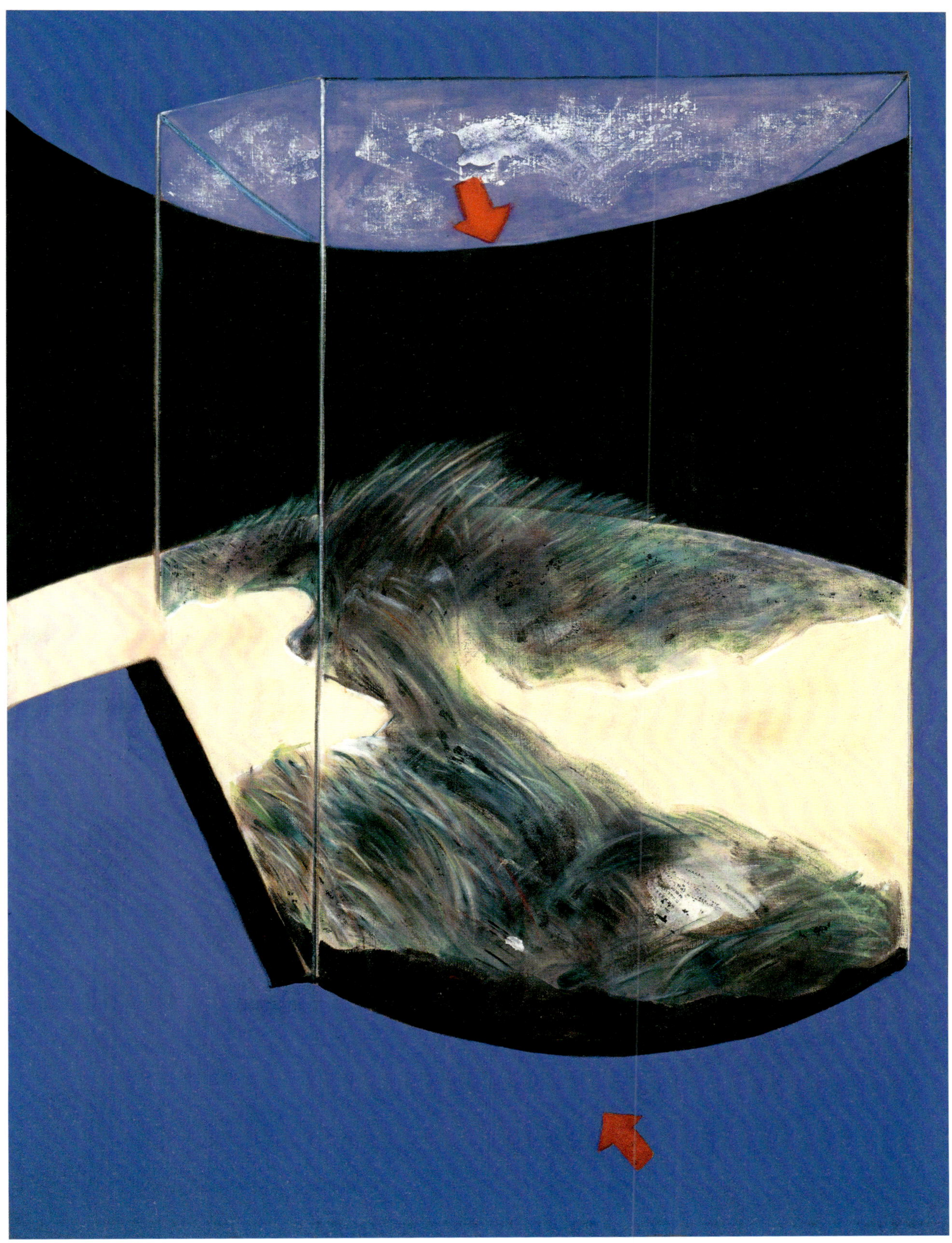

25. *Landscape*, 1978

FROM DECONSTRUCTION TO PLASTICITY

split, diverted, turned on itself, coiled up, or even extended beyond its natural limits, dying away in a "disordered convulsion". There are *free marks* that extend or arrest the line, acting beneath or beyond representation.'[28] Isn't this a way of saying that the trace is inconvertible into a form? What is a body when cut off from its biological being if not symbolic, transcendent, a-plastic glorious flesh? How could such an abstraction make a direct impact on the nervous system? Deleuze's book here reveals its strange ambiguity, as if written by two different persons: a philosopher of the form, and a philosopher of the trace and 'free marks'. According to the former, nothing is inconvertible, the symbolic can perfectly be at one with the biological. According to the latter, something of the flesh, of the meat, of the 'head', of the brain even perhaps, remains irreducible to the very plasticity of being. Is Bacon as ambiguous as Deleuze as far as 'form' is concerned? Are there two Bacons?

II

It is not certain that, despite his interest in the brain, Deleuze has rightly apprehended the revolution that occurred in brain science around the 1950s, and became manifest at the turn of the 1980s. This evolution brought to light the reality of neural plasticity. Far from being this rigid architectural organ described by traditional neurology, with determined functions localised in specific regions, the brain suddenly appeared as an ever-changing form, open to external influences, made of billions of connections variable in size and volume. Since this breakthrough, numerous 'neuro-disciplines' have emerged, and this not only in sciences but also in the humanities, like 'neuro-literature' or 'neuro-aesthetics'. The neurological revolution allowed for a new approach to art, and consequently also to the concept of form.

Many articles, at the turn of the twenty-first century, have attempted to explain *in concreto* Bacon's declaration about the relationship between his painting and the nervous system. One of the most interesting among them, called 'The "Visual Shock" of Francis Bacon: An Essay in Neuroesthetics',[29] recently proposed to scientifically analyse the possibility of the 'assault' of painting upon the brain. Using the recent data provided by brain imaging techniques, as well as the results of cognitive psychology in the domain of visual perception, the authors of the article, Semir Zeki and Tomohiro Ishizu, explain how Bacon's painting succeeds in hitting 'the nervous system (...) violently and poignantly'.[30] Visual perception of faces and bodies, they recall, cause specific effects on the brain that are totally different from those produced by perception of objects, namely that of man-made artefacts ('such as houses, chairs, cars'). This is because the two types of perception do not activate the same cerebral regions. Starting from there, the article develops the following hypothesis: 'we argue', say the authors, 'that Bacon succeeded in delivering his "visual shock" because he subverted the normal neural representation of faces and bodies, without at the same time subverting the representation of man-made artifacts.'[31] Bacon would have in a certain sense redoubled the discrepancy between the treatment of faces and that of artifacts by subverting the former while respecting the usual and normal process of the latter. The 'visual shock' would then pertain to the effects produced on cortical activity by the contrast between the distortion of faces and bodies and the preserved familiar, habitual aspect of objects.

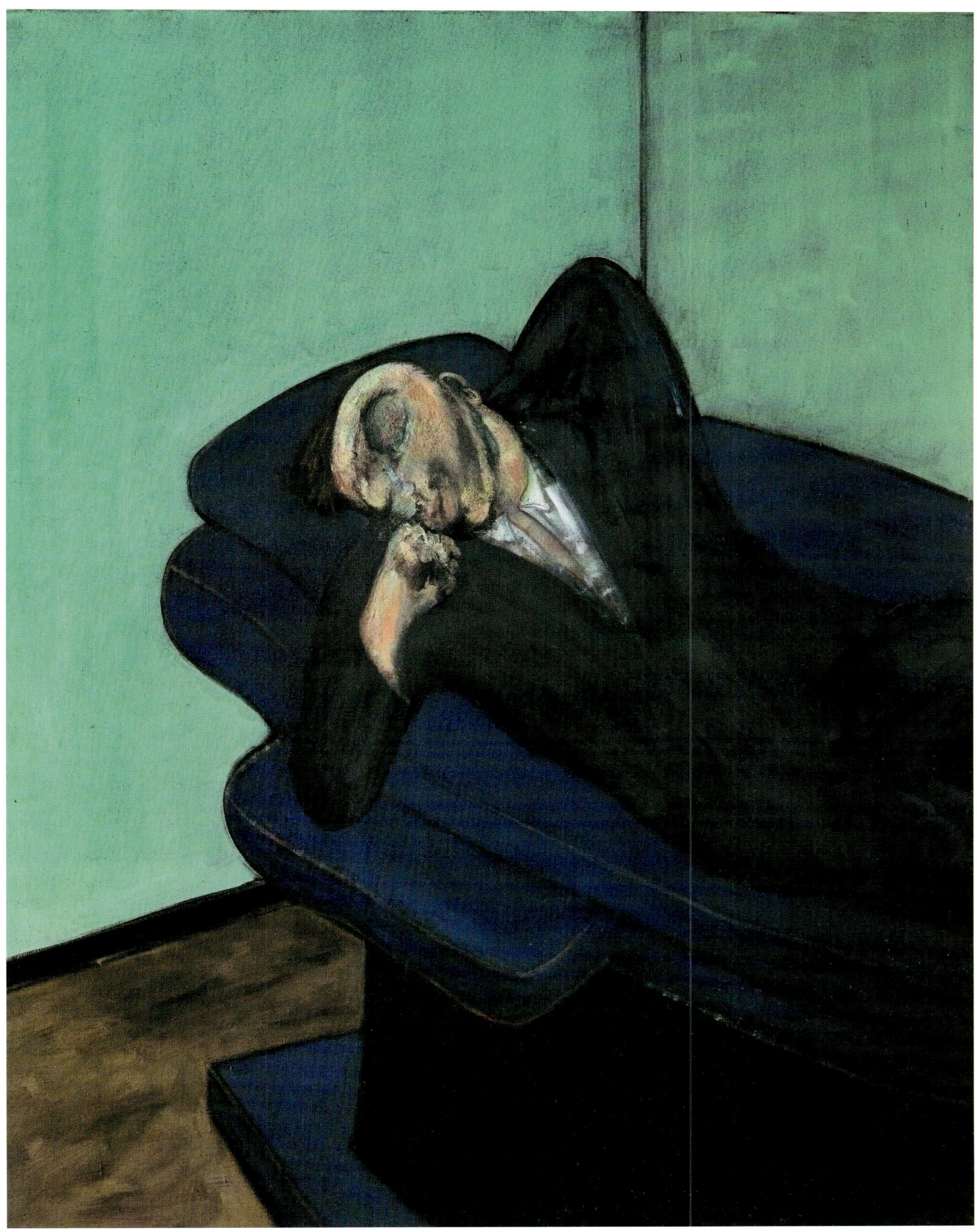

26. *Lying Figure*, 1958

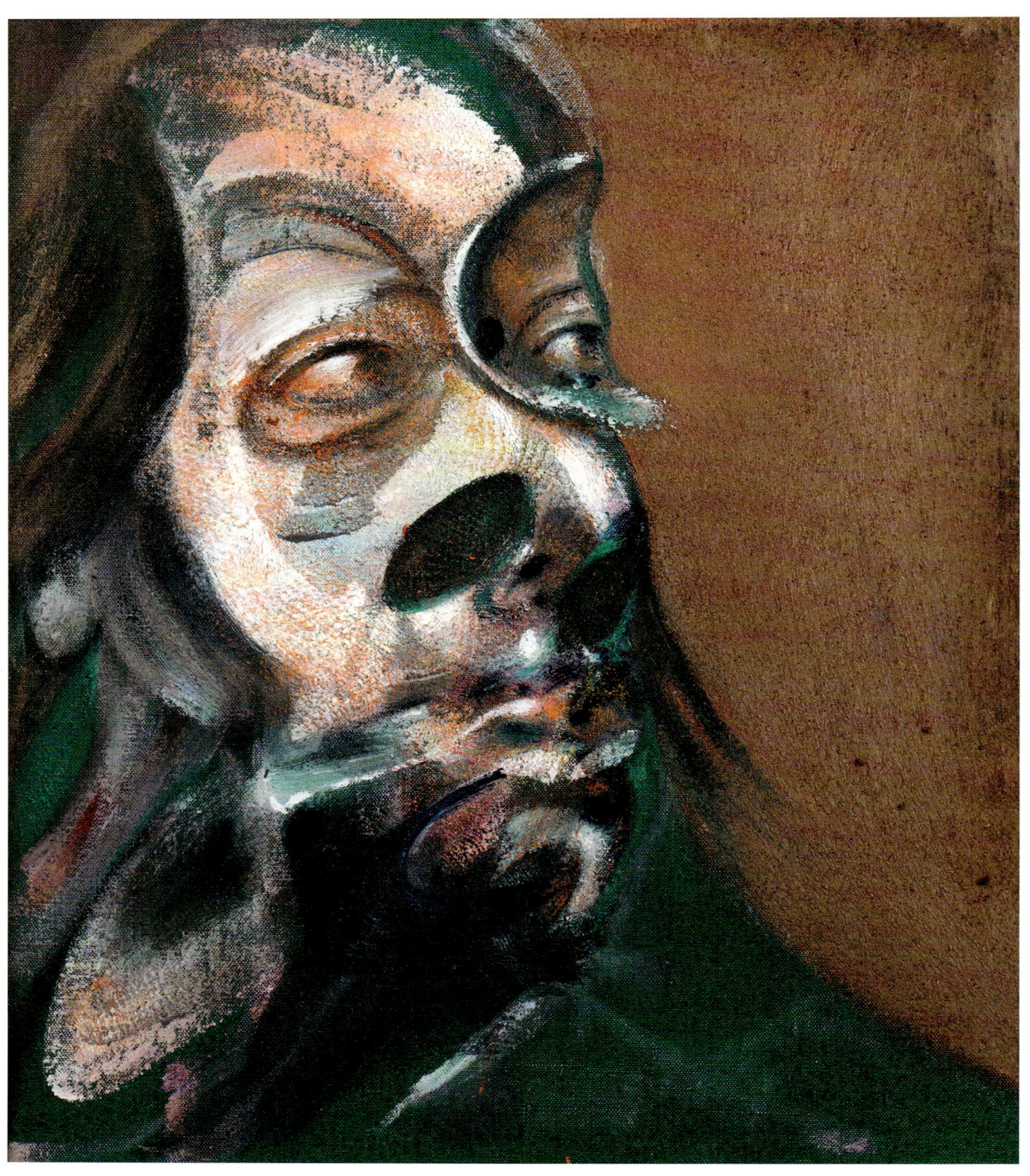

27. *Study of Isabel Rawsthorne*, 1966

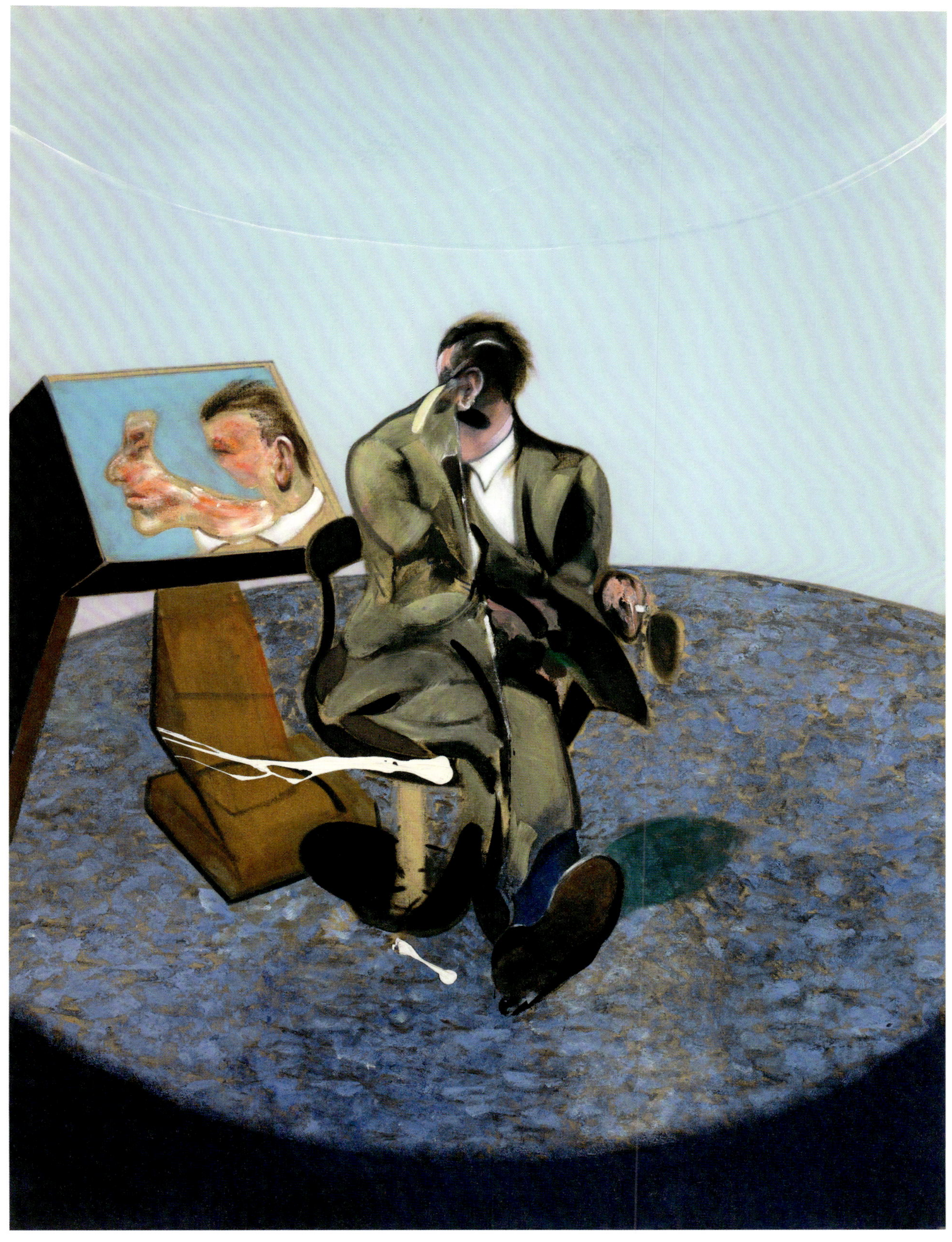

28. *Portrait of George Dyer in a Mirror*, 1968

The article explains that there exists a dramatic difference between inherited and acquired brain concepts. 'Faces and bodies', the authors declare, 'are examples of the former and there is reasonable evidence to suggest that the recognition of faces and bodies, though not of their identity, is at least facilitated through inherited concepts that are present at birth.'[32] The difference between the two concepts pertains to the fact that inherited concepts are 'robust, stable, and do not change with time or do so insignificantly, and are common to all humans'. By contrast, 'acquired concepts to which that of houses, cars and other human artifacts and situations belong, are malleable and change with time and acquired experience, and are culture dependent.'[33]

Bacon's painting would precisely have inverted the properties of the two concepts, so that the objects would appear unchangeable, faithful to their normal features, while faces and bodies found themselves systematically distorted due to their secret mutability. 'The means that Bacon employed to project his acquired concepts in his paintings was to subvert the brain's inherited concepts of what faces and bodies should look like.'[34] Further: 'Bacon … violated and subverted deliberately the brain template for registering faces and bodies.'[35]

How did Bacon proceed to obtain such a result? Inherited concepts can only be altered pathologically, as it happens in certain relatively rare brain diseases like prosopagnosia, also called facial imperfection, an incapacity to recognise not only familiar faces, but faces in general.[36] 'Special areas of the brain appear to be critical for the recognition of faces and bodies,' the authors write, 'like an area located in the fusiform gyrus and known as the fusiform face area (FFA).'[37] Damage caused to this area causes prosopagnosia. 'The brain also appears to devote special cortical areas to the representation of human bodies, even headless ones. One of these is the fusiform body area (FBA).'[38] The areas critical for body recognition lie in close proximity to those for facial recognition.

The distortion of faces and bodies systematically operated by Bacon strikingly resembles those caused by prosopagnosia. Bacon's way of painting is the artistic equivalent of determined cerebral lesions. Clearly, for the authors, both create forms out of the impairment of forms. Such a creation out of destruction is the work of what I have called 'destructive plasticity'. Destructive plasticity is the site where the arts and the brain meet. Let's recall that the term 'plasticity', in its nominal form, is etymologically linked to two older words, the substantive 'plastic' and the adjective 'plastic'. All three words are derived from the Greek *plassein*, which means 'to model' or 'to mould'. 'Plastic' in its adjectival sense has two meanings. On the one hand, it means 'to be susceptible to changes of form' or 'to be malleable'. Clay, by virtue of its capacity to receive form, is 'plastic'. On the other hand, 'plastic' also means 'having the power to bestow form'. In the expressions 'plastic surgery' or 'the plastic arts', plasticity refers to the capacity to assign form. The term 'plasticity' describes the nature of that which is plastic, capable both of receiving and of giving form. The very meaning of plasticity itself appears to be plastic, mapped somewhere between two extremes. On one hand, plasticity describes the crystallisation of form (as is suggested both by the substantive uses of the term and by the expression 'plastic arts'). On the other hand, plasticity appears diametrically opposed to form, describing the very annihilation of concrete form, suggested by the unstable and destructive character of 'plastic explosives'. Neural plasticity can be both formative

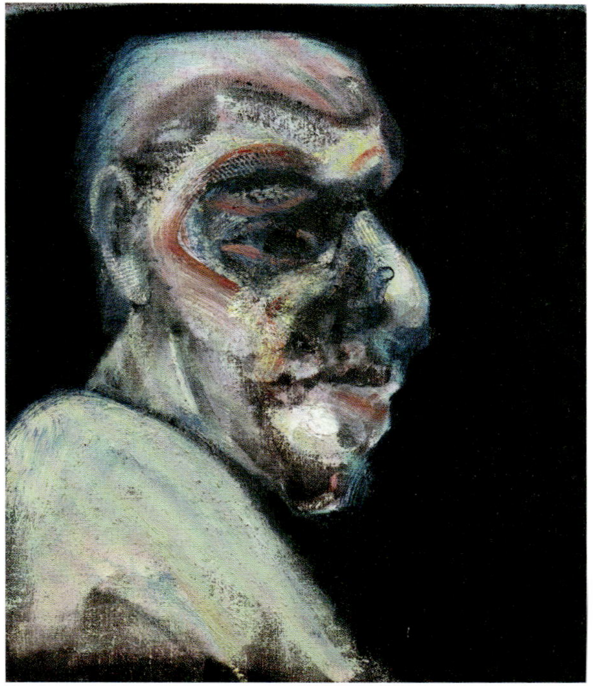

29. *Head of Man,* 1960

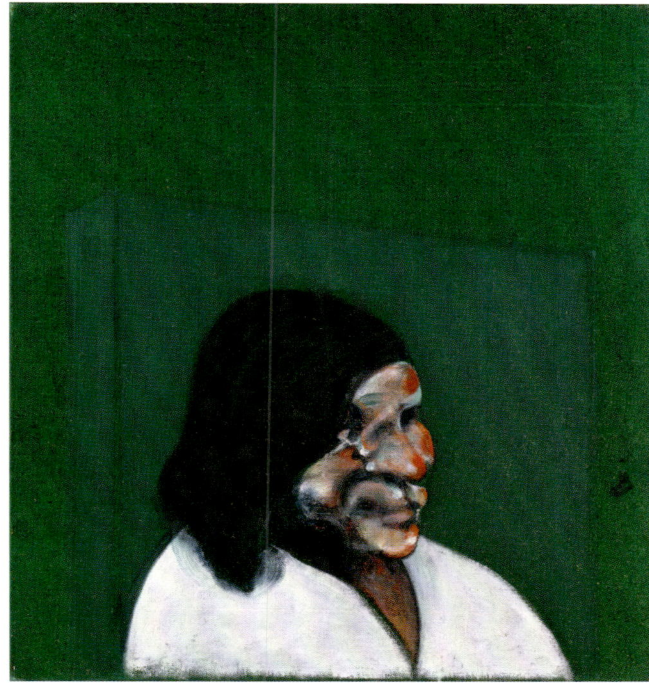

30. *Head of Woman,* 1960

and constructive, it creates forms and structures through education, training, pleasure. It can also produce new forms of identity out of destruction of the previous ones. In my book *Ontology of the Accident*, I wrote: 'No one thinks spontaneously about a plastic art of destruction. Yet destruction too is formative. A smashed-up face is still a face, a stump a limb, a traumatized psyche remains a psyche. Destruction has its own sculpting tools.'[39] If I allow myself to refer to this book, it is because Bacon so often insisted upon the importance of accidents in his painting. He has subverted something very privileged in visual perception, altering the templates for face and bodies that are not modifiable unless by accident, or, which is the same, out of pathological causes.

Modifications at that level are always modifications of forms. Zeki and Ishizu highlight the fact that the recognition of faces and bodies depends on a series of brain processes that constitute 'the form system'. They write: 'The form system in the brain is commonly thought to be derived from the orientation selective cells of the ventral temporal cortex and consists of a single hierarchical pathway which uses the orientation selective cells to build up more complex forms.' Bacon worked at altering this form system, while at the same time maintaining a general holistic representation of the context. This by preserving the immediate recognisability of objects and human artifacts: light bulbs, shoes, syringes, spectacles, tables, chairs, wash basins, toilet seats ... Once again, mutability (of the object recognition neural templates) and immutability (of faces and bodies recognition templates) find themselves inverted, and the subtle mix of creative and destructive plasticity constitutes Bacon's inimitable signature on forms. Of course, a lightning of transcendence, so to speak, can always happen that opens a crack in the form and

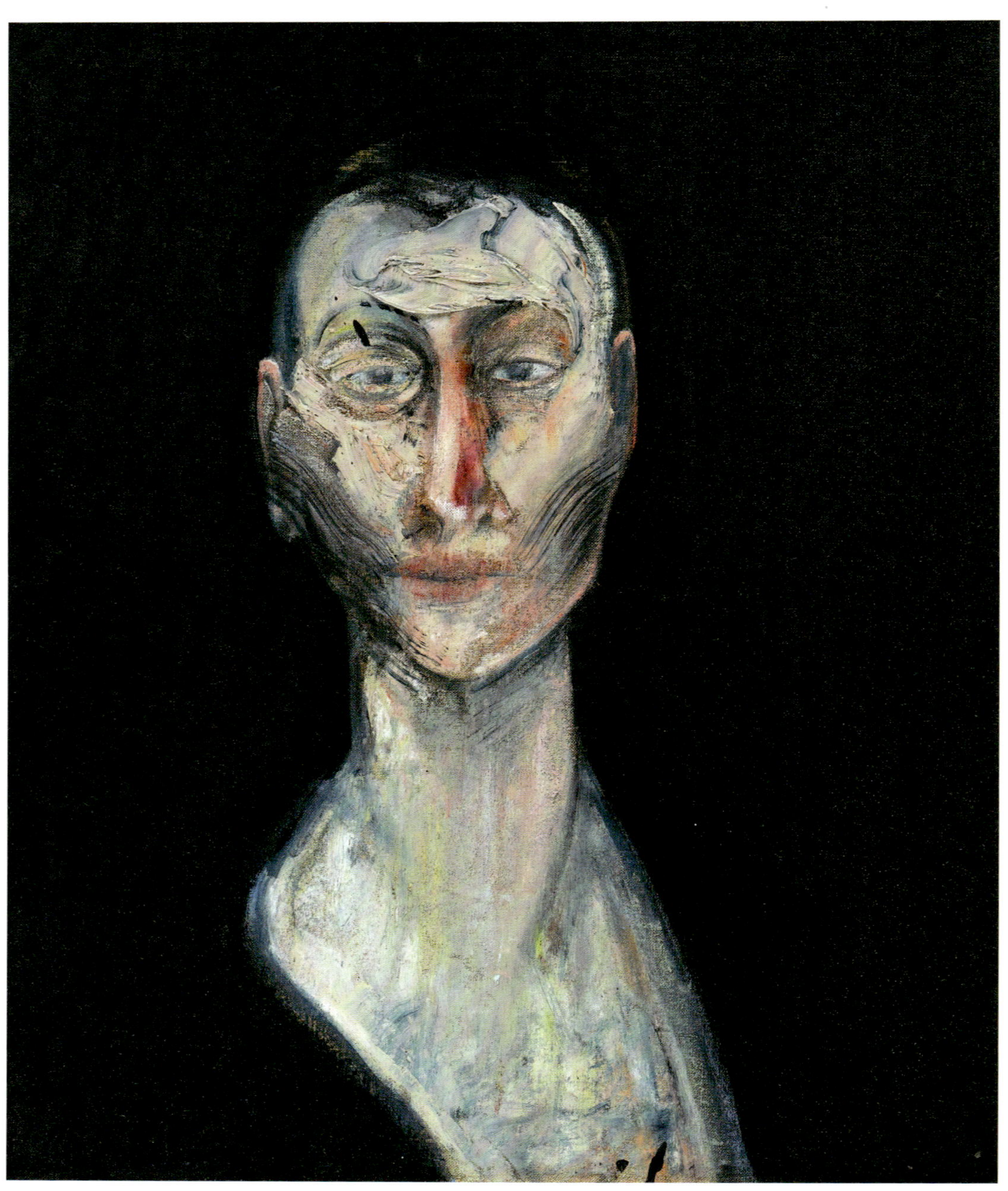

31. *Portrait of Lisa*, 1957

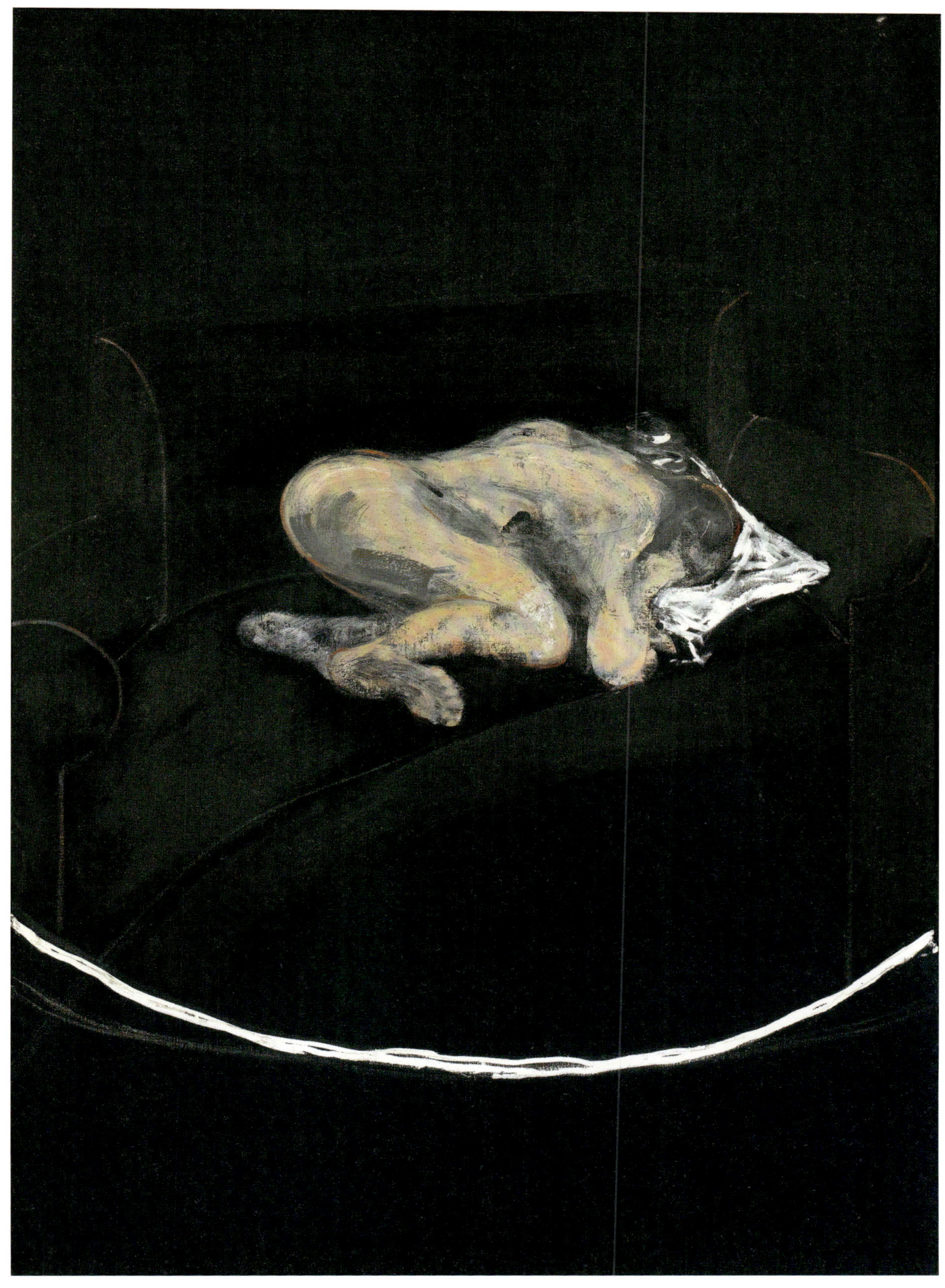

32. *Study for Portrait of P.L. No.1*, 1957

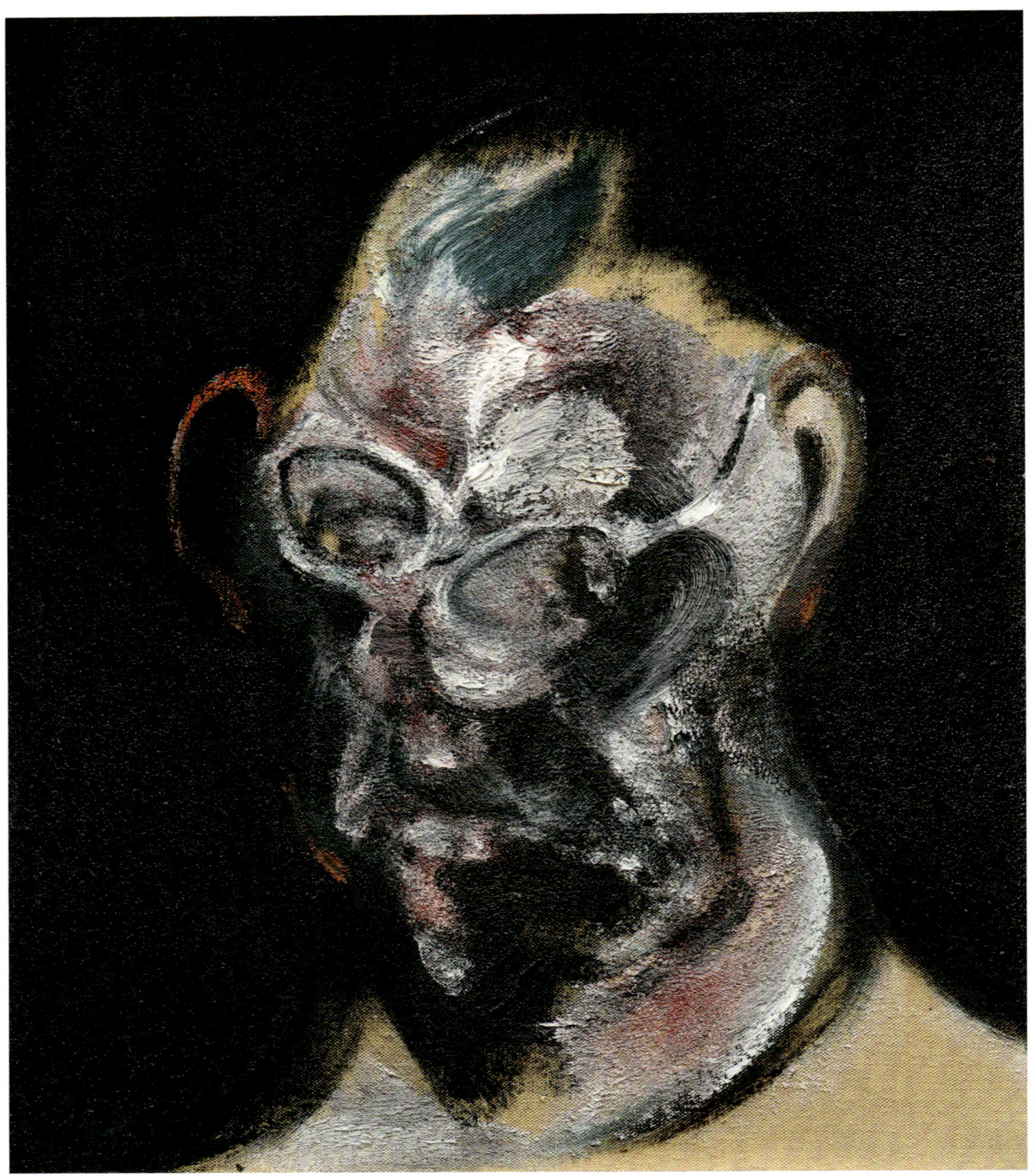

33. *Portrait of Man with Glasses II*, 1963

exposes it to something like its meaning, or utter otherness. However, what Bacon's painting shows is that the destruction of the form still is a form, the distortion of the organic is never without organs, and a symbolic escape from raw materiality is impossible. There is no such thing as a body without organs; there are, rather, 'organic forms that are not bodies', or organic forms that are not faces. When distorted, faces and bodies, far from revealing their irreducibility to their biological texture, disappear in this texture itself, thus revealing that they were never anything else than contingent life forms.

**III**

As announced earlier, it would be illegitimate to reduce Bacon's painting to a mere illustration of neurological theses. Through his remarkable pictorial apprehensions of brain plasticity – both constructive and destructive – Bacon also accomplished a re-elaboration of the concept of form that brought it very close to its Greek origins. Let's go back to deconstruction of metaphysics. It is true that Heidegger, who initiated it, was the first to notice that the concept of form has been the privileged instrument of the metaphysical domination – the domination of presence. Nevertheless, Heidegger also distinguished – which has been much more seldomly acknowledged, if at all — between two understandings of form. The first constitutes the traditional one, that is the *eidos* as the fixed and immutable contour of being; the second is a more originary one that has been covered and occulted by the former. This originary concept of 'form' is inseparable from movement; it is 'metabolic' and is at work in the heart of the ancient Greek thinking about change (*metabolè*).

There is a metabolic understanding of form bound up with the vision of appearing. Heidegger proposes therefore translating *morphè* no longer as 'form' but as *Gestellung*, 'installation', or, more precisely, 'installation in the aspect [*Gestellung in das Aussehen*]'.[40] Such an 'installation' is the unity of a movement of throwing in which something shoots out, a flash that makes a face visible. Form, in this case, designates not only the result of an installation, but the very constitution of the thing, the movement that consists in coming to be lodged in an aspect the way one settles in a nest.

To install or to install oneself is to find a place, but a kind of place that invents what there is to install in it. What form designates is precisely the emergence of what is installed – a face or aspect – in the very act of its localisation. Form is a 'composition', one that holds together and installs the essence and the particular thing that lodges in it not for ever but only for awhile: the face 'installs *itself* into a given thing that is 'there for a while' (the 'appearance' 'table', for example, that puts itself forth into this table here). We call an individual thing das *Jeweilige*, 'that which is there for a while,' because as an individual thing 'it stays for awhile' in its aspect and preserves the 'while' (the presencing) of this appearance, stands forth in and out of it—which means that it 'is'.[41] In that sense, form is the very expression of finitude and transience, not their opposite.

Heidegger shows that there is a conflict at the heart of Greek philosophy between this *mobile-form* and the *idea-form*. Form, understood as idea, is a seal that imprints its mark onto movement and stops it in order to render it thinkable. The mobile form on the contrary expresses the movement of installation of everything, not only the face, not only the body, into its transient shape. 'Installing in the aspect' is movedness, the cinematic prelude to ontology.

I could not help thinking of Bacon's fascination with Muybridge and his photographs of movement when reading those passages by Heidegger. Bacon explained that, in Muybridge's photographs of figures in motion, 'animal movement and human movement are continually linked in my imagery of human movement ...

I think of the contours of those bodies that have particularly affected me, but then they're grafted very often onto Muybridge's bodies. I manipulate the Muybridge bodies into the form of the bodies I have known.'[42]

A painting like *After Muybridge – Woman Emptying a Bowl of Water and Paralytic Child on All Fours,* 1965, [34] of course lets appear all the face and body prosopagnosic distortions I have referred to earlier. But it also expresses something from the ancient metabolē and *kinesis,* according to which every being is constituted by different regimes of mobility all at once. The Greek notion of 'schema', in its originary sense of 'gesture', might express such a unity between different occurrences of motion. This unity is, precisely, the form.[43] Undoubtedly, Bacon's forms are kinetic structures owing their distortion to the combination of the main Greek kinds of motion: rectilinear movement, augmentation, diminution, generation, corruption, rest. Deleuze rightly talks about 'the co-existence of [different] movements' in Bacon's painting, adding: 'the painting *is* this coexistence'. About Muybridge's photographs again, Bacon declared: '... they are the alterations of the muscular structure of the body but then every movement of the body has another intonation because every way that a person moves, stands, moves their arms or anything else has not only its movement but, you may say, all the implications of that movement as well.'[44]

Now, is there a way to manifest the solidarity between the neurological and ontological forms? Let's turn to Heidegger one last time as he shows us the way to the answer. This solidarity expresses itself as and in *pain.* In his address to Jünger in 'On the Question of Being', Heidegger declares: 'When in your work *The Book of the Sandclock* (1954), you say, "*Gestalt* (form) is confirmed in pain [*im Schmerz bewährt sich die Gestalt*]," then, so far as I can see, you retain the fundamental configuration of your thinking, but let the fundamental words "pain" and "*Gestalt*" speak in a transformed sense'.[45] 'This would be the place to go into your treatise *On Pain* [Über den Schmerz],' continues Heidegger, 'and to bring to light the intrinsic connection between 'work' and 'pain.'... [T]he Greek word for pain, namely, *algos,* would first come to speak for us. Presumably *algos* is related to *alego,* which as the *intensivum* of *lego* means intimate gathering. In that case, pain would be that which gathers most intimately.'[46] This passage is fundamental. It effectively enables us to understand that pain and suffering maintain an originary bond with the *logos,* the movement of gathering, of installing in the aspect. Here, also, I think that Bacon's works resonate in a profound way with Heidegger's words. 'We are born with a scream,' Bacon affirms; 'we come into life with a scream, and maybe love is a mosquito net between the fear of living and the fear of death. That was one of my real obsessions. The men I painted were all in extreme situations, and the scream is a transcription of their pain. Animals scream when they are frightened or in pain, so do children. But men are more discreet and more inhibited. They do not cry or scream except in situations of extreme pain. We come into this world with a scream and we often also die with a scream. Perhaps the scream is the most direct symbol of the human condition.'[47] It is as if – through the death of George Dyer, and the different studies for Crucifixion, [35] and the carcasses – the fusion of brain plasticity with metabolic and kinetic classical schemas had become visible, for the first time and for ever.

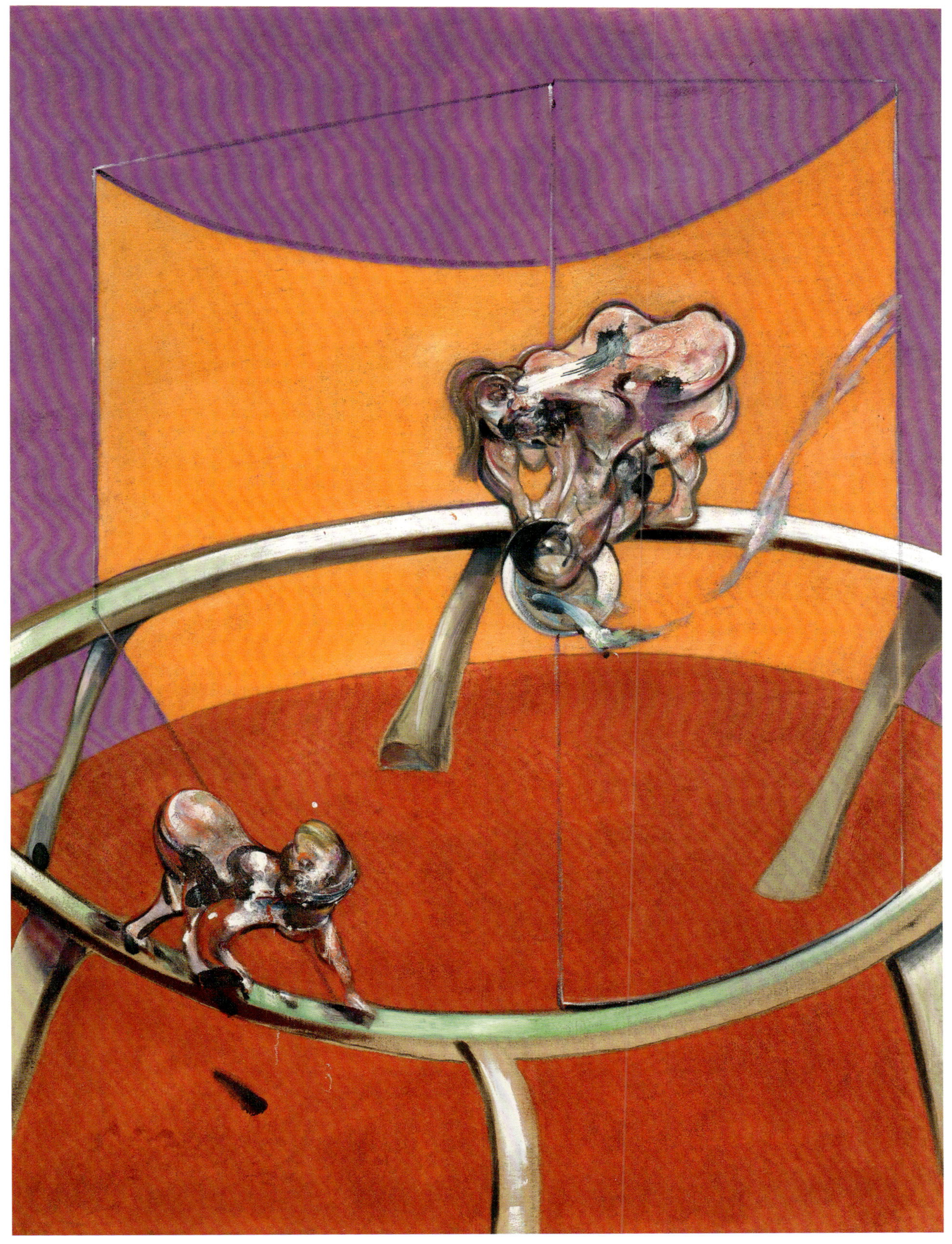

**34.** *After Muybridge – Woman Emptying a Bowl of Water and Paralytic Child on All Fours,* 1965

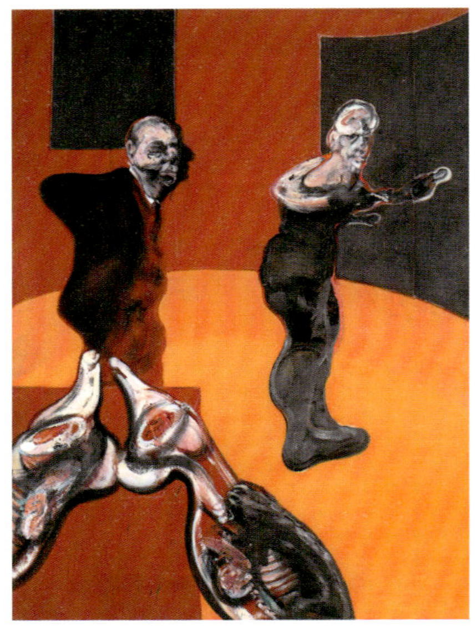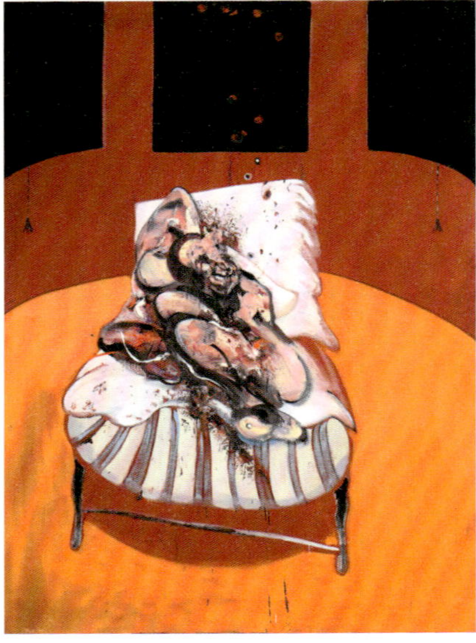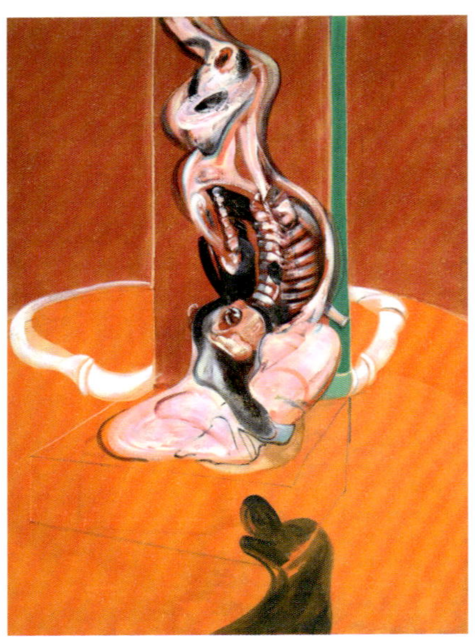

35. *Three Studies for a Crucifixion*, 1962

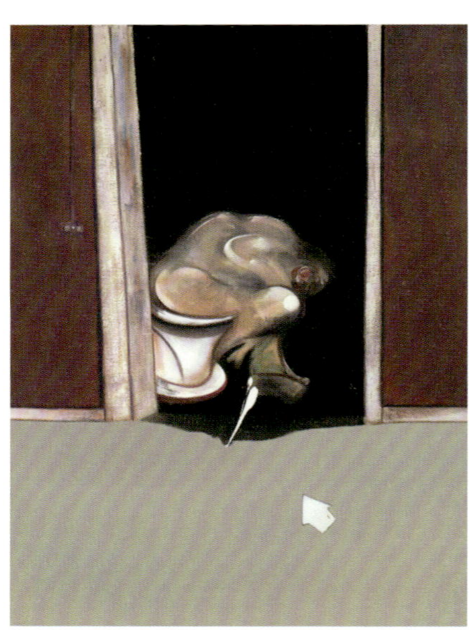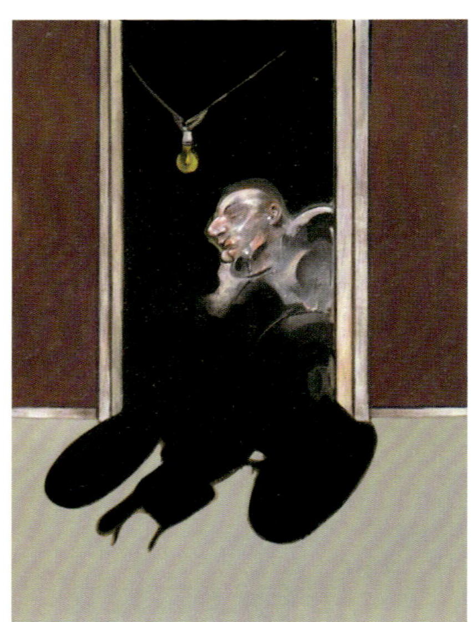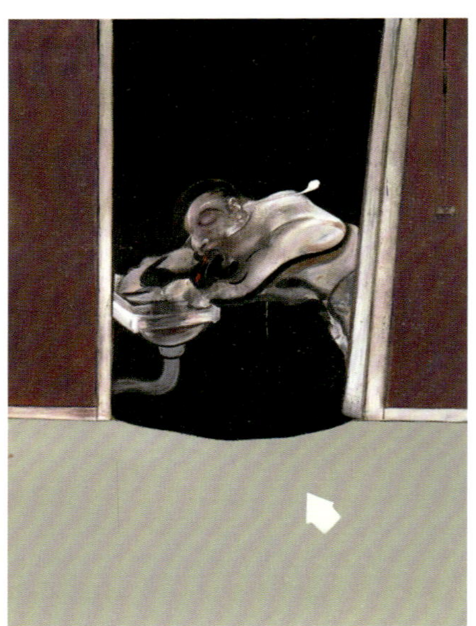

36. *Triptych May–June 1973*

IV

It is increasingly clear to me that form cannot be 'undone' without calling on the support of form, including the aid of its power of explosion. There is no exceeding of form that does not assume the plasticity of form, and hence its convertibility. If I insisted upon the divide between the trace and the form, it is because this divide pertains to the possibility or impossibility of exchangeability and desacralisation.

To affirm the existence of something that remains inconvertible, whatever this may be, is to affirm that this very something does not enter into the game of substitution, remaining outside of the circle, holding itself separate from the economy of exchange. If the trace is considered to be absolutely inconvertible, utterly resistant to circulation, then it becomes substantial. It is no longer a trace, but a substance. It then bears all the characteristics it was supposed to challenge: presence and immutability. If the trace does not play into the hands of its own conversion, in a certain sense, it resists its own effacement. This contradiction remained unperceived by Levinas and even also perhaps by Derrida and Deleuze themselves.

Bacon's painting, in a manner that prevents the trace's non-deconstructed sanctification, makes manifest that there is nothing inconvertible, that the human face and body do not have any transcendent characteristics, and that forms, out of their kinetic, metabolic and synaptic power, ceaselessly undermine their inevitable fetishisation.

# Endnotes


1.  Emmanuel Levinas, 'Meaning and Sense', *Emmanuel Levinas: Basic Philosophical Writings*, ed. A.T. Peperzak, S. Critchley & R. Bernasconi (Bloomington: Indiana University Press, 1996), p. 63.
2.  Ibid.
3.  Ibid., p. 90.
4.  Emmanuel Levinas, *Collected Philosophical Papers*, ed. A. Lingis (Pittsburgh: Duquesne University Press, 1987), p. 96.
5.  Ibid.
6.  Ibid., pp. 90–91.
7.  Emmanuel Levinas, *Totality and Infinity: An Essay on Exteriority* (Dordrecht: Kluwer Academic Publishers, 1991), pp. 50–51.
8.  Ibid.
9.  David Sylvester, *The Brutality of Fact: Interviews with Francis Bacon*, (London: Thames & Hudson, 1987), p. 82
10. Brian Clarke, 'Deconstruction of the Studio', Francis Bacon, The Estate, online publication, 2006.
11. Roberto Esposito refers to Bacon in his article 'Flesh and Body in the Deconstruction of Christianity', in 'Franco-Italian Political Thought', special issue, *The Minnesota Review*, n. 75 (Fall 2010), pp. 89–99, p. 89.
12. Jacques Derrida, 'Form and Meaning: A Note on the Phenomenology of Language', tr. Alan Bass, in *Margins Of Philosophy* (Chicago: Chicago University Press, 1982), pp. 157–58.
13. Jacques Derrida, 'White Mythology', ibid., p. 215.
14. Jacques Derrida, *The Truth in Painting*, trans. G. Bennington & I. McLeod (Chicago: Chicago University Press, 1987), p. 11.
15. David Sylvester, *Interviews with Francis Bacon* (London: Thames & Hudson, 1987), p. 61 ff.
16. Gilles Deleuze, *Francis Bacon: The Logic of Sensation,* trans. Daniel W. Smith (New York: Portmanteau Press, 1992; London: Continuum, 2003).
17. Jean Khalfa, 'An Impersonal Consciousness', in *Introduction to the Philosophy of Gilles Deleuze*, ed. Jean Khalfa (London: Continuum, Bloomsbury, 1999), p. 82. We also find the idea of an opposition of Deleuze to Levinas in Gavin Rae, 'The Political Significance of the Face: Deleuze's Critique of Levinas', in which Bacon plays a central role. *Critical Horizons*, 17:3–4 (September 2016), pp. 1–25
18. Deleuze, op. cit., p. 11.
19. Ibid., p. 20.
20. Ibid., p. 34.
21. Ibid., p. 160.
22. Ibid., p. 59.
23. Francis Bacon, 'Matthew Smith: A Painter's Tribute', in *Matthew Smith: Paintings from 1909–1952*, exh. cat., Tate Gallery, London, [Sept.–Oct.] 1953 (London: Tate Gallery, 1953). We find ten occurrences of this declaration in Deleuze's book.
24. Ibid., p. 34.
25. Cf, for example, the concluding chapter of Gilles Deleuze, Félix Guattari, *What Is Philosophy?,* trans. Hugh Tomlinson t G. Burchell (New York: Columbia University Press, 1994).
26. Deleuze, *Francis Bacon: The Logic of Sensation,* op. cit., p. 45.
27. Ibid., p. 46.
28. Ibid.
29. Semir Zeki, Tomohiro Ishizu, 'The "Visual Shock" of Francis Bacon: An Essay In Neuroesthetics', *Bacon and the Mind: Art, Neuroscience and Psychology* (London: EFB Publishing, 2019); the authors declare, 'seeks inspiration and insight from works of art and from debates in the humanities to try to get some insights, however small, into the working of the brain.'
30. Ibid.
31. Ibid.
32. Ibid., p. 2.
33. Ibid.
34. Ibid.
35. Ibid.
36. 'Prosopagnosia is an incapacity to recognize a face while sparing the ability to recognize its constituents, like the eyes or the nose.' Ibid., p. 6.
37. Ibid, p. 4.
38. Ibid.
39. Catherine Malabou, *Ontology of the Accident*: *An Essay on Destructive Plasticity,* trans. Carolyn Shread (Cambridge: Polity Press, 2012), p. 4.
40. Martin Heidegger, 'On the Essence and Concept of *physis*: Aristotle's *Physics* B', tr. Th. Sheehan , in *Pathmarks* (Cambridge: Cambridge University Press, 1999), translation modified, p. 211.
41. Ibid.
42. Sylvester, op. cit., p. 116.
43. Cf, on that point Alex C. Purves, *Homer and the Poetics of Gesture* (Oxford: Oxford University Press, 1972), pp. 4–5, where a parallel is drawn between Homer's description of movement and Muybridge's 'Chronographs'.
44. Interview by Gavin Millar, *Francis Bacon: Grand Palais 1971*, a film for BBC Television, London, 1971.

45.  Martin Heidegger, 'On the Question of Being', in *Pathmarks,*
     op. cit., p. 305.

46.  Ibid.

47.  'The Last Francis Bacon Interview – On Violence, Meat
     and Photography', *The Art Newspaper*, 137 (June 2003),
     pp. 28–29. [Series editor's note: Neither the authenticity
     of this interview is confirmed nor the accuracy of its
     transcription, although Bacon may have expressed views
     similar to these.]

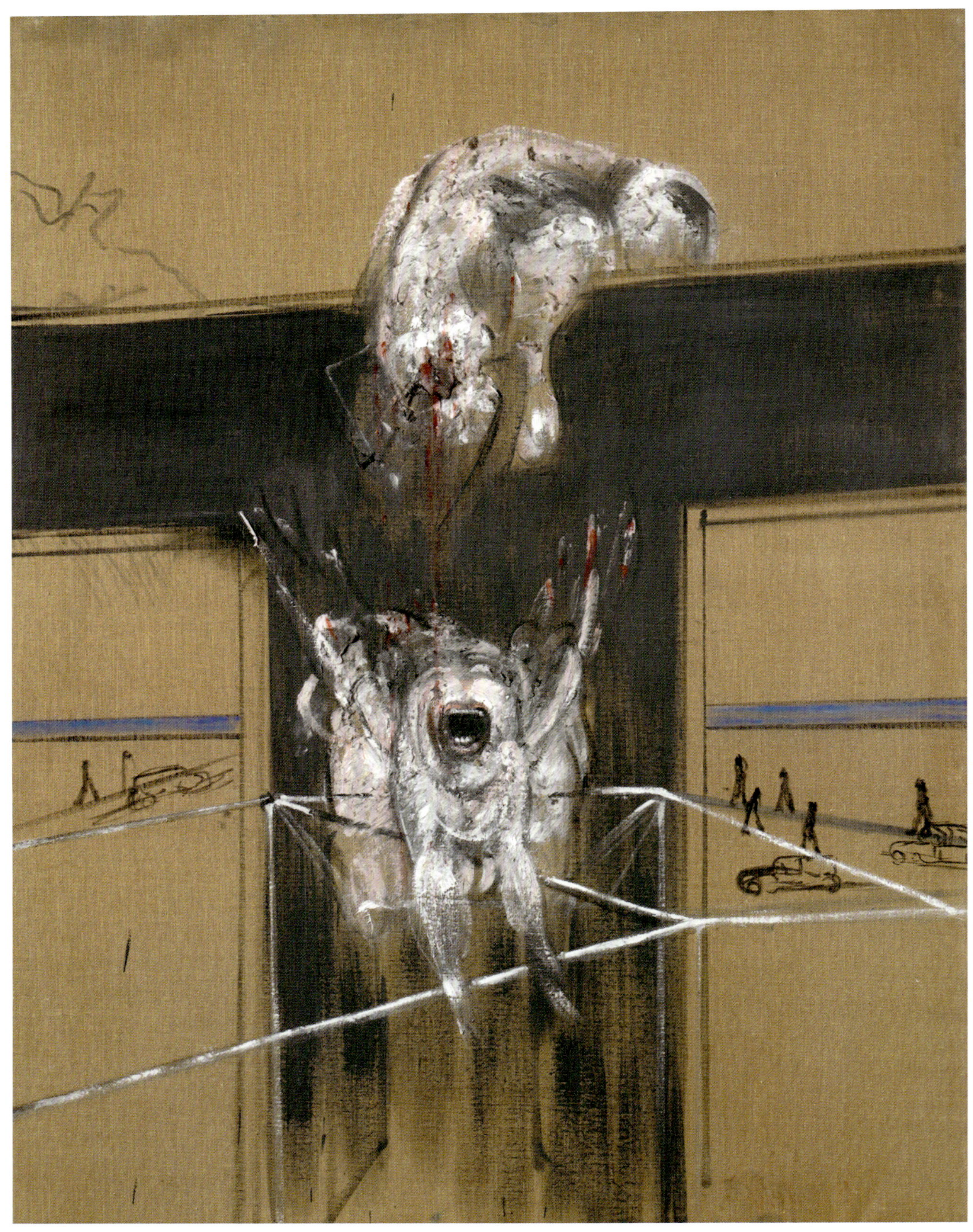

37. *Fragment of a Crucifixion*, 1950

# From Sense to Sensation:

# Bacon, Pasting Paint and the Futility of Lacanian Psychoanalysis

Dany Nobus

*Brother Francis, and whoever may in the future be in leadership*
*of this way of life, promises obedience and reverence*
*to our Pope Innocent and to all of his successors.*
– St Francis of Assisi

*There is no excellent beauty that hath not some strangeness in the proportion.*
– Francis Bacon, Baron Verulam

*[Painting] will only catch the mystery of reality if the*
*painter doesn't know how to do it.*
– Francis Bacon

*Who am I to judge?*
– Pope Francis I

## Prologue

Some four-and-a-half years before he would devote a year-long seminar to James Joyce, Jacques Lacan composed a short essay titled 'Lituraterre' for a special issue of the newly created journal *Littérature*, on the confluence between psychoanalysis and literature.[1] In it, he revised the deep-rooted connections between Freud's brainchild and literary cultures, and firmly reclaimed the primacy of the signifier over the letter, thereby tacitly responding to Jacques Derrida's critical exposition of the distinctly logocentric tradition in Western philosophy and in Lacan's own, purportedly Freudian restoration of psychoanalysis.[2] Glossing his peculiar spooneristic title, Lacan reminded his readership in the opening paragraphs of his text how Joyce had once played on the near-homophony of 'letter' and 'litter', and how the writer's 'littering of the letter' (*faire litière de la lettre*), as a persistent work-in-progress, had effectively allowed him to recuperate, within the space of his creative imagination, Thomas Aquinas's famous final judgment on the quality of his voluminous oeuvre: *sicut palea* (like straw).[3] Most provocative, however, was Lacan's claim that Joyce would not have gained anything from the psychoanalytic treatment with Jung, which had at one point been recommended to him by his wealthy benefactor Edith Rockefeller, because in this very game of making litter of the letter he had allegedly moved straight 'to the best one may expect from psychoanalysis at its end'.[4]

As always, Lacan did not explain himself on this point, so we are left with more questions than answers.[5] What does it mean exactly for the ideal outcome of a psychoanalytic treatment process to coincide with a 'littering of the letter', or whatever the equivalent of it at the level of the analysand's speech may be? If littering is the outcome, then how are we to understand the (clinical) process leading up to it? How does this conception of the end of analysis relate to or differ from the various other formulas Lacan had articulated over the years to capture the anticipated direction, the ultimate goal and the endpoint of a psychoanalytic journey, such as the 'traversal of the fantasy' and the 'destitution of the subject'?[6] If, as Lacan intimated, the (beneficial) effects of a psychoanalytic treatment may also be induced through a particular process of creative writing, and thus by means of an artistic endeavour that bypasses the operative function of a psychoanalyst, might this principle be extrapolated to other art forms, such as music, sculpture, cinema and painting? If so, what would be the equivalent of Joyce's 'littering of the letter' in these other artistic practices, bearing in mind that the notions of 'litter' and 'littering' contain the highly charged semantic ambiguity of being newly born, offering comfortable bedding and having the status of a disruptive waste-product? What could it possibly mean, for example, for visual artists to create detritus or, better still, for them to engage in acts of sustained creative destruction leading to the emergence of artistic objects that are simultaneously extraordinarily valuable as innovative works of art and utterly disposable as serviceable products? How does an artist engage in this process? Where does it begin and how does it end? What does it reveal about the relationship between the artist and his own work? And what is there to be learnt from this alternative, 'artistic' process of psychoanalysis that can be of benefit to a reconsideration of the conventional, clinical encounter between an analyst and her patients?

In the three panels of this essay, I shall take up Lacan's challenge, without thereby offering robust answers to all the questions above, and propose that the psychoanalytic impact of 'littering the letter' is by no means restricted to a process of experimental, modernist writing, but may also be identified in other creative pursuits. More specifically, I shall argue that Joyce's psychoanalysis by means of writing, or what may be designated as his 'writing cure', meets its pictorial counterpart in Francis Bacon's lifelong attempt to capture, with no other means than canvas and paint, the absolute truth of the human appearance. Joyce's 'littering of the letter' will show itself to be identical, here, to Bacon's 'pasting of the paint', in the dual meaning of paint being applied to flat, receptive surfaces (the canvas as well as other planes in the artist's studio) and it simultaneously being moulded, softened up, demolished and transformed into a shadow of its former reality. I should emphasise that this exercise has nothing to do with psychoanalysing Bacon, neither the man nor his work, but is purely geared towards eliciting a certain understanding of his creative process, which may shed as much light on his paintings as it does on the practice of psychoanalysis itself.[7] And much like Bacon's triptychs, the three panels of my essay could in principle be read from left to right and from right to left, despite the inescapable diachrony of the textual image imposing a linear sequence in which one panel will be seen to take priority over the other.

**Left Panel: Study for a Perfect Self-Portrait**

Even though he had painted quite a few pictures before World War II, some of which were shown in the 1962 Tate retrospective of his work, Bacon insisted that the Grand Palais exhibition in Paris, which opened on 26 October 1971 and which would galvanise his reputation as the greatest living painter, should start with his 1944 triptych *Three Studies for Figures at the Base of a Crucifixion*. [4] Indeed, from that moment onwards the artist would vehemently object to all works from his 'early period' being included in shows or reproduced in monographs.[8]

Many Bacon scholars have noted that it was not until the 1944 triptych that the young painter managed to break into the contemporary art scene as a major new talent, which might in itself suffice as an explanation for his subsequent insistence that it should be considered the only starting point of his artistic career. Yet a comparison of this work to the earlier paintings that have survived also indicates that the 1944 triptych definitely constituted a new beginning, if not in subject matter (biomorphs, crucifixion), most perceptibly in colour scheme (cadmium orange), in spatial organisation (the geometrical armature), in style of presentation (large triptych), and in pictorial focus (the gaping mouth). Looking back at the composition in light of the painter's later work, the 1944 triptych is instantly identifiable as a 'Bacon', even if some of its most conspicuous features (the gaping mouths and the contorted bodies) would subsequently be exchanged for other types of figurative distortion. Hence, in more than one way, it makes sense to say that with his 1944 triptych Bacon was born, made his first appearance, and first entered the world that he would come to occupy so prominently and intensely for almost fifty years. And like all newborns, Bacon arrived on the scene of the world with the emblematic sign of life — a gaping mouth.

On various occasions, Bacon himself pointed out that his obsession with the open mouth was conditioned by two poignant images — the mother's cry in Nicolas Poussin's *Massacre of the Innocents* and the nanny's cry at the very end of the Odessa Steps sequence in Eisenstein's *Battleship Potemkin* — and that he always aspired to make the best painting of the human cry in the history of Western iconography.[9] Of course, what sets these images apart from other famous representations of the human cry, such as Edvard Munch's *The Scream of Nature*, is that they were not identified as such by the artists themselves and that they were both utterly silent – the clamour of the nanny's cry in *Battleship Potemkin* only accentuated by Edmund Meisel's thundering timpani. Looking at Poussin's mother figure and Eisenstein's bloodied face of the nanny, we can see what their scream looks like, but we can only imagine what it sounds like, and this extraction of sound from the image makes the representation much more ambiguous and open to interpretation. When Bacon re-created the gaping mouth in the 1944 triptych and in numerous subsequent variations, including some of his most captivating portraits of Pope Innocent X (after Velázquez), he exponentially augmented the gaping mouth's sensory ambiguity by either reducing the figure's eyes to dark shadows merging with the background, or cutting the rest of the facial expressions altogether. [37], [38], [55] In painting little more than a gaping mouth in a human body or biomorph, colourful as the latter may be, and without providing much in the way of context, the meaning of the scream thus evaporates to the point where just one meaningful unit remains, notably that of meaning itself. We shall never know whether Bacon's scream represents despair, anger, anguish, agony, sexual ecstasy or gasping for air; what we do know is that the scream screams for interpretation, and that the only possible way to respond to it is with a question: 'What do you want?'[10]

Francis Bacon thus arrived on the scene like all human beings enter the world, yet he also endeavoured to ensure that his very own 'primal scream' would be stripped as much as possible of each and every unequivocal meaning, devoid of a clear sense, so that it could erupt from the canvas as a pure sensation of lived experience, as unadulterated life force. In the 1944 triptych, this evacuation of meaning is to some extent obstructed by the work's title, because it situates the three screaming biomorphs 'at the base of a crucifixion'. The spectator's interpretative actions are thus directed towards a set of embodied responses to the horror of an execution, whose representation clearly lies outside the painting but which is nonetheless assimilated within it on account of its invocation. As his art progressed, Bacon exchanged suggestive titles for neutral designations such as 'study' and 'portrait', occasionally accompanied by the name of the person represented or an anodyne description of the painted object, such as 'seated figure' or 'man talking'.[11] It is important to emphasise, however, that Bacon's artistic journey from sense to sensation, and from meaning to nonsensicality, was never complete, and only came to a pragmatic end when his own body abandoned him and he was reduced to simple fleshy substance, maybe with his mouth wide open and notably at the base of a crucifixion.[12] In 1962, he conceded that he was always hoping 'to paint the one picture which will annihilate all the other ones, to concentrate everything into one painting', yet that he had 'never yet been able to make the one image that sums up all the others'.[13] I would be surprised if Bacon ever visited the Monastery of San Juan de los Reyes in Toledo, but if he did he would undoubtedly have been struck by the alluring inscription on one of its walls: 'Travellers, there are no trails – all there is, is travelling.'

Bacon's obstinate search for the one picture, balanced against his desire (or his mental need) to carry on painting, already demonstrates how much of himself he was compelled to invest in his work. In this sense, and given how I am trying to understand here how Bacon might have pursued a lifelong psychoanalytic 'painting cure', I would be prepared to say that, irrespective of their subject matter, Bacon's entire body of work is part and parcel of a massive unfinished self-portrait. Even when he was painting biomorphs, friends and lovers, popes and heads, landscapes and seascapes, he was only ever painting himself. Strange as it may seem, if only because entire series of images were explicitly designated as self-portraits (with the ostensible implication that all the others are not), my point can be further substantiated on the basis of two key observations.

Firstly, throughout his career, Bacon was enthralled by the letters of Vincent van Gogh, and in particular by a letter in which the Dutch master had stated: '[R]eal painters do not paint things as they are, after a dry and learned analysis. They paint them as *they themselves* feel them to be.'[14] Applied to Bacon's artistic practice, the implication of Van Gogh's testimony is that the distorted yet truthful reality as it would appear on the canvas could only ever be Bacon's own psychic reality. Bacon's vehement and endlessly repeated attempts to get access to the absolute reality of an appearance is tantamount to a continuous struggle with his own appearance and a perpetual search for his own subjective truth, and this

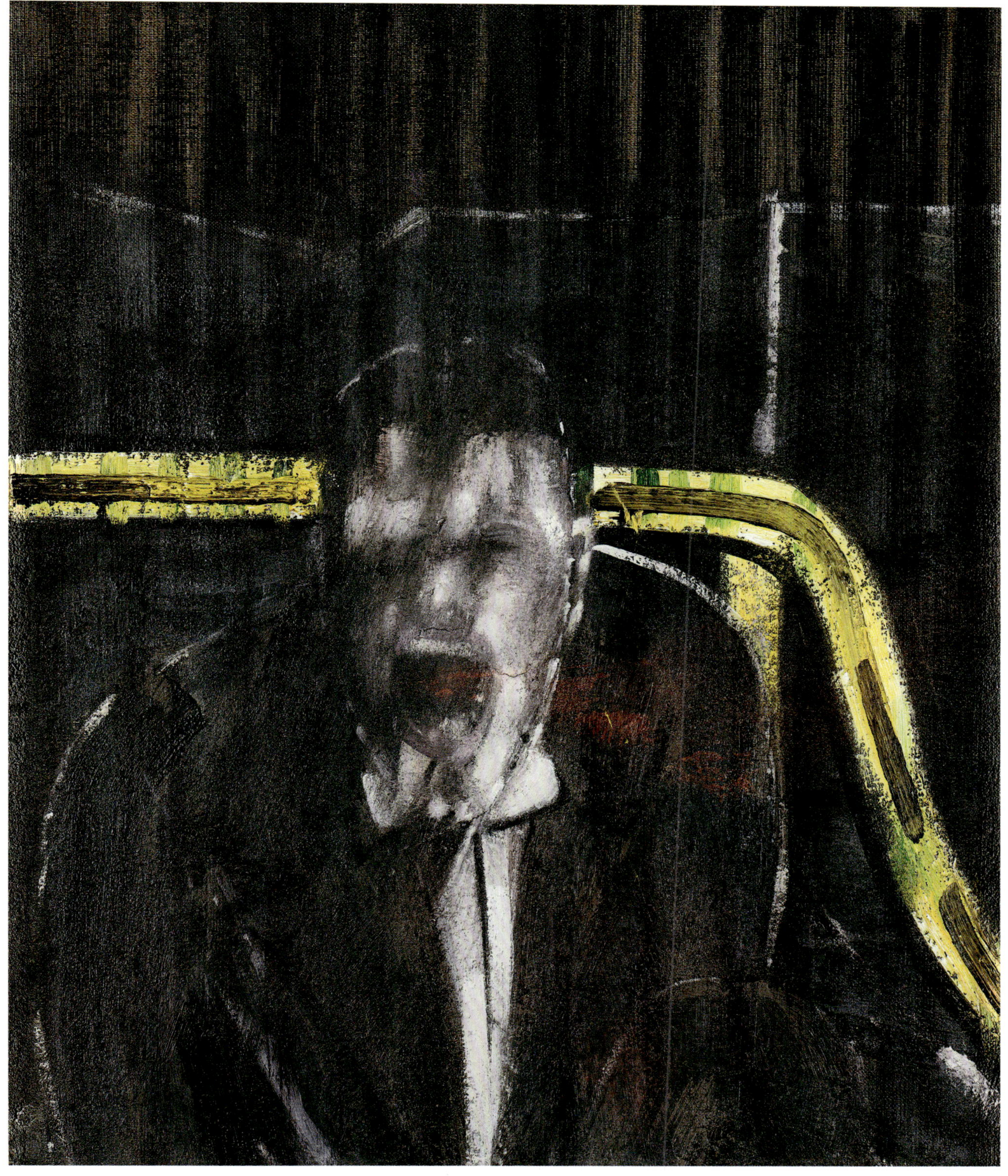

38. *Study for Head*, 1952

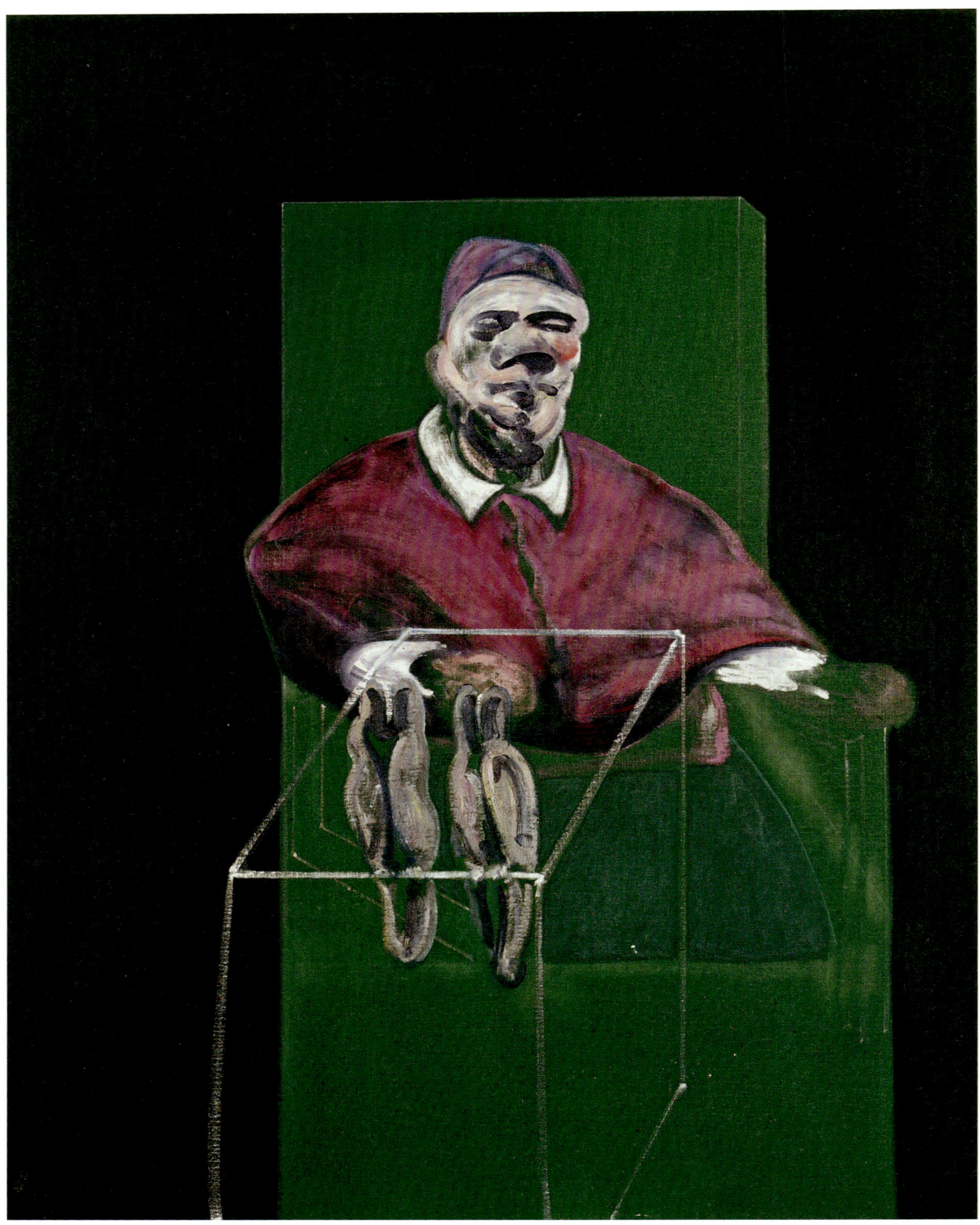

39. *Pope No. 3*, 1960

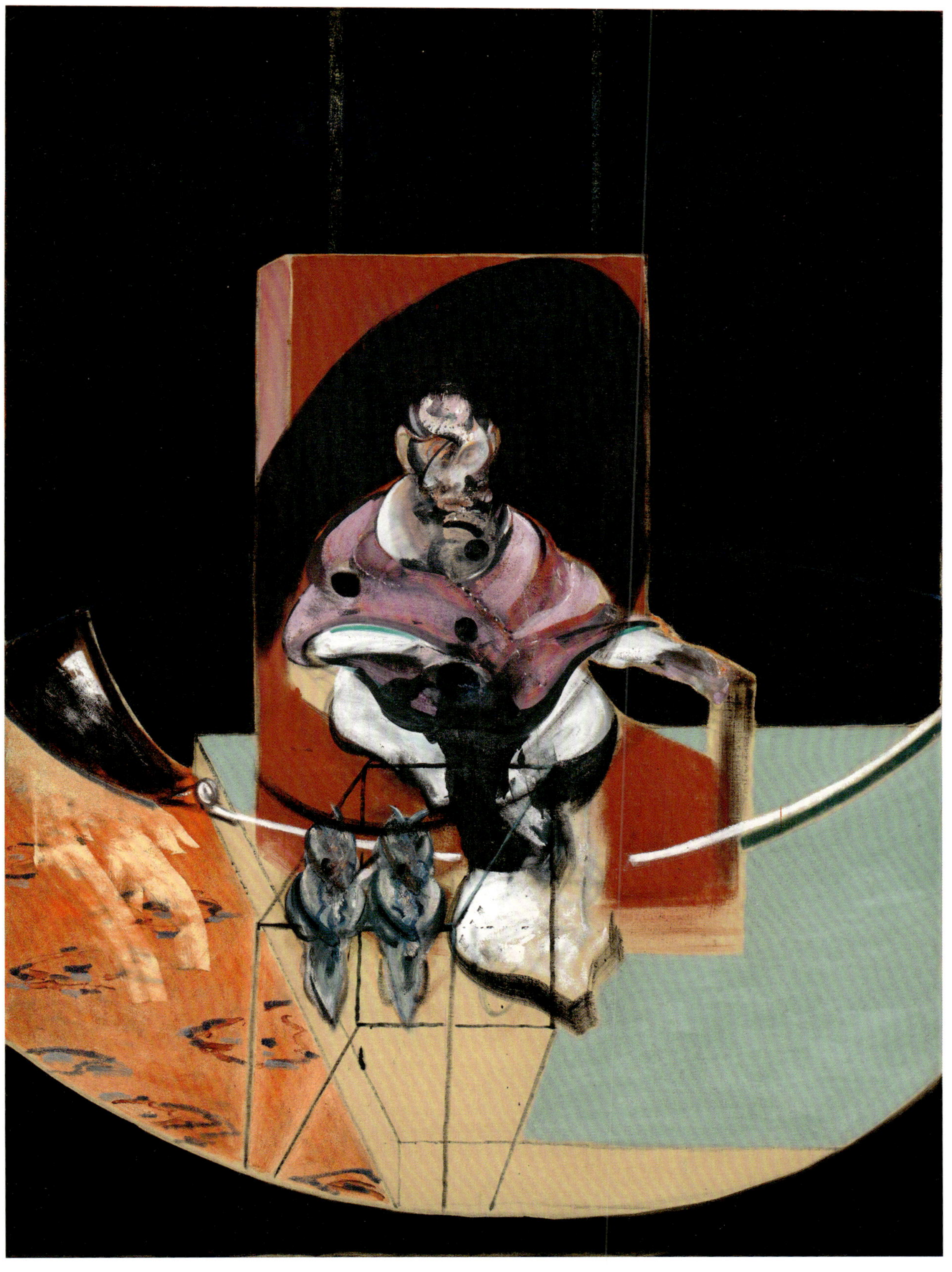

40. *Study for Portrait (with Two Owls)*, 1963

principle applies equally to the paintings of biomorphs, popes and landscapes as it does to the self-portraits.

Secondly, speaking to David Sylvester in 1975, Bacon acknowledged that in trying to capture the reality of an appearance he could never extract himself from the picture: 'Every form that you make has an implication, so that, when you are painting somebody, you know that you are, of course, trying to get near not only to their appearance but also to the way they have affected you, because every shape has an implication.'[15] Although Bacon's admission, here, clearly resonates with Van Gogh's statement, it enters much deeper into the mind of the artist, or into his 'nervous system' as Bacon would call it. The appearance unlocks the painter's 'valves of sensation' and the painting process employs the appearance as a conduit for exploring and giving shape to these sensations.[16] Whereas Van Gogh's radically impressionistic concept of the real painter may still be adjusted to the artist's conscious intentionality, the attempt to render figuratively an appearance's subjective implication on the painter is a much more subliminal, unconscious endeavour, although the net result reconfirms the ineluctable presence of the painter's self-image in the frame(s) of the painting. In Lacanian terms, one might say that the painted images are an index of the 'subject of the statement' (*sujet de l'énoncé*), which may very well represent the artist *qua* depicted figure but may also represent anything else, yet that the act of painting coincides with the enunciating subject (*sujet de l'énonciation*), which is driven by an unconscious desire (the desire to paint, but also the desire as it has been triggered and stimulated by the external appearance), and which runs through each and every aspect of the painting – the process as much as its result.[17] In so far as painting is in itself a type of language, Bacon thus speaks about himself and others in his work, but always only about himself through it – hybrid, overdetermined and intractable as this point of enunciation may be.[18]

**Centre Panel: The Labour of Rejection**

At the start of his technical paper 'On Beginning the Treatment', Freud famously compared the psychoanalytic treatment process to a game of chess. It is not that the analyst and the analysand are trying to outwit one another with a series of clever, unexpected moves, and that the game ends either in checkmate or stalemate, but that the opening tactics and the endgame can be described fairly exhaustively, whereas what happens in between, and what constitutes the kernel of the game, cannot be laid down in rules and strategies, on account of the 'extraordinary diversity of the psychical constellations, the plasticity of all mental processes and the wealth of determining factors'.[19] Looking at Bacon's artistic practice as a psychoanalytic 'painting cure' runs into similar problems. Whereas I can confidently explain how he arrived on the scene portraying himself as an open mouth which screams for nothing but interpretation, I am less reassured by the picture of his own work-in-progress, which in this case has nothing to do with the evolving themes, variations, iterations, scansions and punctuations in his paintings, even less with how he came to terms with his infatuation with alcohol, his love of low-lifes and his sexual predilections, but much more pertinently with the logic of the creative mechanisms underpinning his art. Owing to this, the centre panel of my triptych will be inevitably more abstract than its left and right panels.

Nonetheless, a certain insight into Bacon's artistic practice is provided by the man himself in the extensive interviews he granted to art critics and journalists over the years. Four separate elements deserve to be highlighted here. One, Bacon always reiterated that his work was predicated upon a fruitful combination of 'instinct' and 'chance', 'intentionality' and 'accident', an initial excitation (and an associated image) and the unexpected stroke of the brush, a rough outline and an unforeseen adventure.[20] Second, throughout his career, Bacon radically opposed all references to narrative structure, whether in the succession of images from one period to another, in the sequential variations on a particular theme, or in the three constitutive panels of a triptych. Although he remained generally immune to critics detecting a palpable storyline in his work, he was adamant that the telling of a coherent story was the furthest removed from his artistic aspirations. In Bacon's view, narrative painting was purely illustrative, and only served the purpose to record, register and document reality, which is something photography had already accomplished, and in a much better way.[21] Third, to exorcise the spectre of narration and its intrinsic dimension of meaning (sense), Bacon was at great pains to situate his paintings outside the temporal framework of linear chronology. Even though the creation of a painting would evidently require a certain time-investment, and would sometimes be the result of work carried out over longer periods of time, the finished product would have to be appreciated in all its immediate intensity, as a sudden unitary 'assault on the nervous system'.[22] Fourth, Bacon intermittently highlighted how his work – the process and the act of painting rather than the painting itself – revolved around a tension and conflict between the 'subject matter', that is, his mental idea and rough outline of what would appear on the canvas, and the physical matter of the paint, whereby he would intimate that the medium (and the tools to apply it) is simultaneously necessary, impossible and full of contingencies.[23] The paint is a necessary substance for giving shape to the subject matter, even when the process of shaping involves the deconstruction and distortion of the appearance: '[T]he violence of paint … [has] to do with an attempt to remake the violence of reality itself, … but it's the violence also of the suggestions within the image itself which can only be conveyed through paint.'[24] However, paint is also impossible, because it only ever seems to allow for a mediocre approximation of the truthful reality that lies buried in the subject matter, so that the perfect, ideal image that would render all the others futile can never be accomplished: 'The longer you work, the more the mystery deepens of what appearance is, or how can what is called appearance be made in another medium.'[25] It is, moreover, also full of contingencies, because the paint may suddenly take the artist into hitherto unknown directions and previously unexplored spheres. As he said to Sylvester some time during the early 1970s: '[Paint] is such an extraordinary supple medium that you never do quite know what paint will do.'[26] As beacons of Bacon's artistic process, these four elements are extremely precious signposts for developing an understanding of the artist's psychoanalytic 'painting cure', and they resonate with some of Freud's (admittedly sparse) insights into the mechanisms of the clinical journey called psychoanalysis, as it unfolds between the opening tactics and the endgame.

    Bacon intermittently referred to his painting activities as a work of making, a labour of construction, with the proviso that the making would always entail a constant remaking, and that this sustained act (or game) of remaking would not be a cumulative process, but rather a battle of continuous rejection, a struggle towards creative excoriation (my term rather than Bacon's), in an attempt to trap or lock down the appearance at those points where it may emerge in its brutal reality.[27] Were we to replace the matter of paint with 'signifying matter' here, that is to say the series of acoustic images an analysand generates during a psychoanalytic session, we would arrive at an excellent definition of what Freud once designated as 'working-through' (*Durcharbeiten*), and which he described as 'the work which effects the greatest changes in the patient and which distinguishes analytic treatment from any kind of treatment by suggestion'.[28] Perhaps inevitably, Freud was better at underscoring the significance of this working-through than at articulating a proper definition of it. In their seminal volume *The Language of Psycho-Analysis*, Laplanche and Pontalis remained equally vague: 'Working-through is taken to be a sort of psychical work which allows the subject to accept certain repressed elements and to free himself from the grip of mechanisms of repetition.'[29] As to Lacan, at the very end of his 1964 seminar on *The Four Fundamental Concepts of Psychoanalysis*, he rekindled Freud's notion in the context of a discussion of the 'traversal of the fantasy'. Working-through appeared, here, as the process whereby an analysand would mentally travel through his signifying structures a sufficient number of times for the drive to be liberated from its fantasmatic setting.[30] As such, the process involves neither a radical disintegration of the fantasy nor a deactivation of the drive, but rather a cutting and removal of the umbilical cord that binds them together, which would bring about a greater degree of freedom to the analysand and a certain cleansing of her psychic window onto the world.

Yet Bacon does not just inadvertently offer a fine definition of psychoanalytic working-through; the four components of his practice detailed above also provide us with a terrific insight into the pillars upon which this most important of psychoanalytic assignments is built. In proclaiming that his artistic labour was entirely driven by a combination of instinct and chance, he perfectly echoed Freud's dualistic conception of human development, which the founder of psychoanalysis explained most lucidly in a lengthy footnote to another of his technical papers, this one on 'The Dynamics of Transference': 'We refuse to posit any contrast in principle between the two sets of aetiological factors; on the contrary, we assume that the two sets regularly act jointly in bringing about the observed result. Δαίμων καὶ Τύχη [Endowment and Chance] determine a man's fate – rarely or never one of these powers alone'.[31] As regards Bacon's mordant objection to any type of narrative structure, and his concurrent suspension of chronological order, this too resonates with how Freud described the threefold (triptychal) stratification of unconscious psychic materials around a central nucleus of (traumatic, pathogenic or repressed) memories, whereby the third arrangement would generally be the most important one, in so far as it would overrule and subdue the two other layerings, its dynamic concatenation of mnemic materials taking precedence both in the way a patient would present her symptoms and in her subsequent analysis of them. Whereas the first type of organisation entails a strictly linear, chronological sequence of mental representations, starting from the nucleus and moving forwards in the patient's developmental history (or vice versa), and the second type represents a thematic or concentric arrangement, every mental representation being linked by a common quantum of resistance vis-à-vis the nucleus, the third (and most important) stratification is entirely conditioned by an overdetermined, yet highly individual logic. 'What I have in mind', Freud wrote,

> 'is an arrangement according to thought-content, the linkage made by a logical thread which reaches as far as the nucleus and tends to take an irregular and twisting path, different in every case. ... The logical chain corresponds not only to a zig-zag twisted line, but rather to a ramifying system of lines and more particularly to a converging one. It contains nodal points at which two or more threads meet and thereafter proceed as one; and as a rule several threads which run independently, or which are connected at various points by side-paths, debouch into the nucleus'.[32]

The principal implication of this third arrangement is that conventional (chronological or thematic) narration is replaced with a proto-modernist stream of (un)consciousness. Within this stream, (variations on) thematically linked subjects are juxtaposed with chronologically connected representations in such a way that both temporal and spatial logics are superseded by a complex network of loosely related sensory impressions whose meaning, if there is one, cannot be reduced to one or the other type of organisation, and thus gives way to a 'violent', multi-sensory experience of direct sensation. This, in a sense, is also what Deleuze tried to theorise, although without any reference to Freud or psychoanalysis, in his landmark 1981 volume on Bacon, which allegedly prompted the painter to react with the words: 'It's as if this guy was looking over my shoulder when I was painting my pictures.'[33]

Finally, there is the matter of the paint itself – necessary, impossible and contingent. In various interviews with Sylvester, Bacon commented that the surprise and excitement of trapping the true reality of an appearance can only 'come about in the working'.[34] The labour, here, is primarily a manipulation of the physical matter of the paint, and this paint is always in conflict with the 'subject matter' that triggered the initial concept of the painting, because it is both the only way to access it and a material tool that is made of a completely different substance, much like the signifier simultaneously creates and annihilates 'the thing' by rendering it in symbolic terms. Hence, the subject matter and the matter of paint are always there when the artist enters his studio, and the best he can hope for when adopting his position in front of the canvas is that he will be able to work and rework the paint so much that he may have an unexpected rendezvous with the core reality of an appearance. Whether this meeting takes place does not depend on the artist's conscious search for it, nor on his awareness of the subject matter or his technical expertise, but purely on his receptiveness to the paint's inherent capacity to surprise. In his first interview with Sylvester, Bacon already pointed out: '[I]n my case all painting ... is accident. So I foresee it in my mind, I foresee it, and yet I hardly ever carry it out as I foresee it. It transforms itself by the actual paint ... [I]n the way I work I don't in fact know very often what the paint will do, and it does many things which are very much better than I could make it do'.[35] Four years later, in 1966, he reiterated: 'If anything ever does work in my case, it works from that moment when consciously I don't know what I'm doing.'[36] And during the early 1970s: '[Painting] will only catch the mystery of reality if the painter doesn't know how to do it ... I know what I want to do but don't know how to bring it about.'[37] Hence, the artist

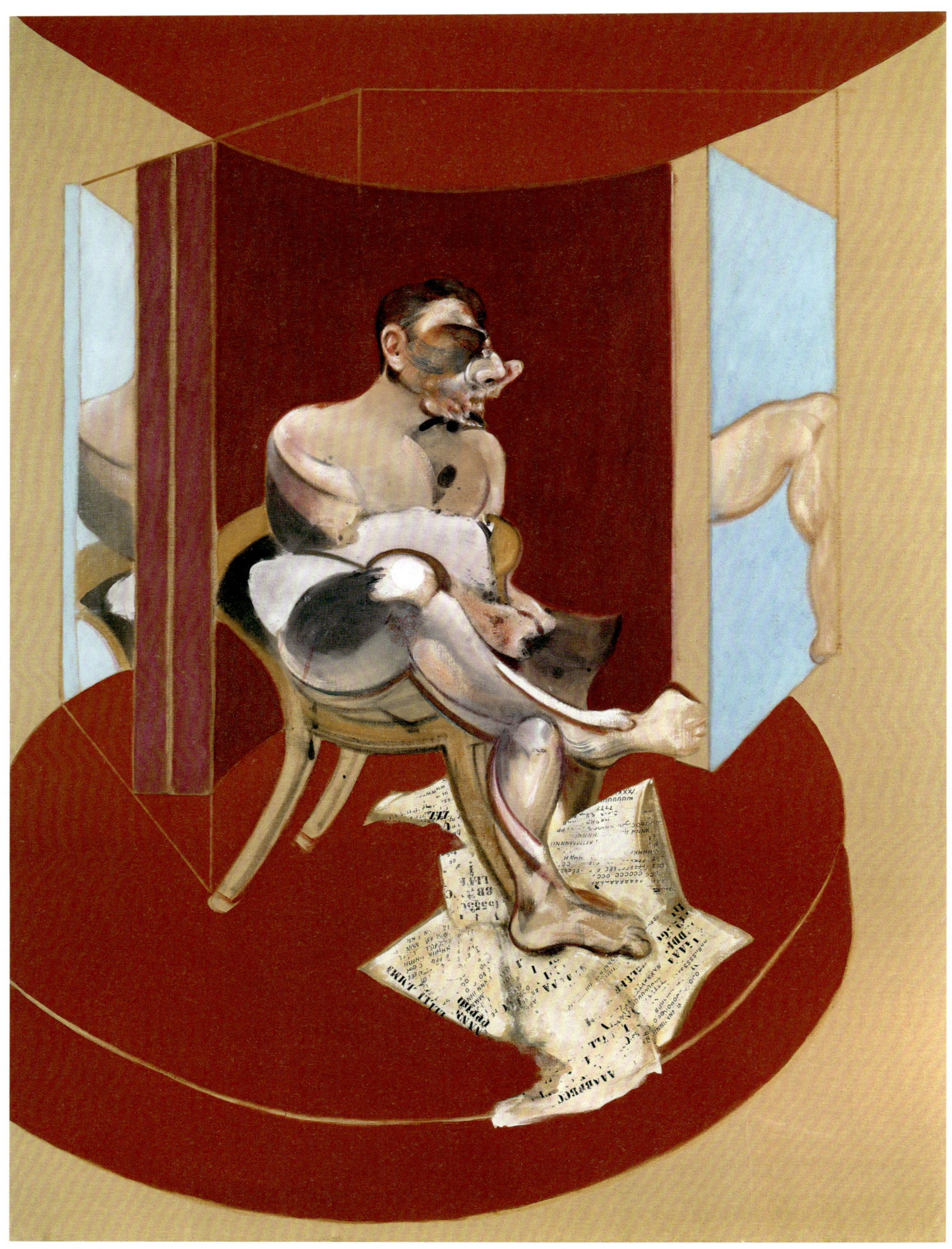

41. *Study of George Dyer*, 1971

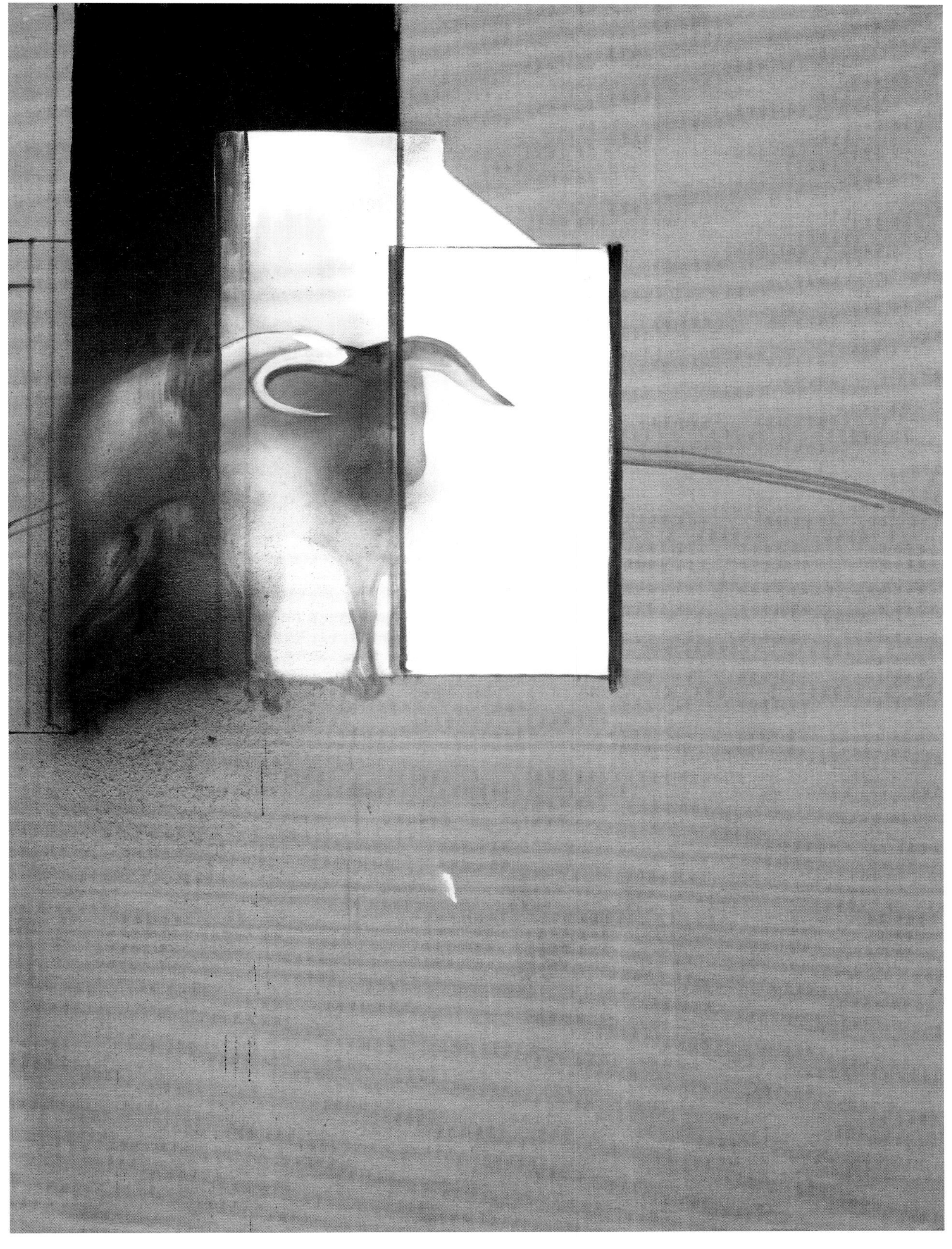

42. *Study of a Bull,* 1991

can only expect an encounter with an unexpected conjunction of elements if he allows himself to suspend his conscious set of representations as to what the painting should be about and how the paint should be technically employed with a view to obtaining the desired result. Although working in a completely different idiom, the American jazz pianist Keith Jarrett has described this unconscious receptivity most poignantly as 'a discrimination against mechanical pattern, for content, against habit, for surprise, against easy virtuosity, for saying more with less, against facile emotion, for a certain quality of energy, against stasis, for flow, against military precision, for tactile pulse. It is like an attempt, over and over again, to reveal the heart of things.'[38] Again, were we to exchange paint and musical texture for the signifier here, the explanation of what is required for the painting or the music to work would not be too far removed from how Freud's psychoanalytic ground rule of free association was intended to allow the patient to suspend her conscious mind, so that the acoustic images of speech could take her in new, unexpected directions – generating sudden collisions of sound and facilitating access to the repressed heart notes of her psychic reality.

**Right Panel: Study for an Artificial Destruction**

During the early 1980s, Bacon accorded a series of interviews to the French novelist and essayist Franck Maubert, who came to visit him in his studio at 7 Reece Mews. 'You know', Bacon opined, 'my life is a complete disaster. I've never succeeded in what I wanted.'[39] Seemingly unfazed by this candid remark, Maubert continued: 'In your own way, you're practising a self-analysis . . .'.[40] To which Bacon responded: 'Maybe it's true that I'm ultimately doing a long, permanent analysis on myself (*laughs*). It reminds me of "*le dérèglement des sens*" Arthur Rimbaud was talking about. So yes, maybe that's what I'm putting into practice. I'm working on myself.'[41] At that point, we are led to believe that the conversation moved in a different direction, but here we had Bacon comparing himself to Rimbaud's oracular vision of the poet, who can only become a seer by virtue of a complete deregulation of the senses, which in this case applies as much to the sensory organs as it affects the channels of meaning.

Having arrived on the scene as an insatiable gaping mouth screaming for nothing but interpretation, and having worked his way through an endless sequence of proteiform self-portraits by pasting the paint on the canvas and pasting (as in demolishing) both the paint and the canvas as fossilised traces of a prolonged labour of rejection and subtraction, Bacon nonetheless continued on his journey, looking for the sparks of sensation behind sense, and trying to capture the true reality of the subject behind its appearance. What is of cardinal significance, in this context, is that the entire process does not entail a steady accumulation of insights that might one day crystallise in the realisation of some form of absolute knowledge, but rather a persistent abrasion, or decortication of obstinate layers of meaning, so that pure sensation may prevail. The (finished) painting is what falls out of the (work of) painting, here, like the canvas of a seashore might temporarily register and display the imprints of the living creatures that have travelled through it. Voicing Bacon's thoughts in an interview from the early 1970s, Sylvester posited:

'The motivation to do it [painting] is the doing of it, the excitement of solving
problems, but problems of a kind that can only be solved through actually
making something, so that, at the end of the process, there's this thing, the
residue of the activity. Now, once having made that thing, the artist really
might as well destroy it, but usually he seems to prefer to let it go on existing.'[42]

Bacon did not disagree, presumably in full awareness of the fact that he himself had
destroyed countless paintings of his own, but could only come up with two reasons
for keeping the residue: it may sell for a good amount of money, and may gratify the
artist's vanity. The key point, however, is that the artistic process of pasting paint
results in the sporadic emergence of painted remainders with no use-value other
than their functioning as reminders of the labour that has been undertaken.

As the process and its outcomes go, this is not radically different from how,
during the 1960s, Lacan would have conceptualised the end of a psychoanalytic
treatment. What is at stake is not the reintegration of the patient's life history (as
Lacan had presumed earlier on in his career), much less the induction of subjective
autonomy in those places where alienation would have formerly reigned supreme,
or even the facilitation of the patient's renewed sense of authenticity, but rather
a deactivation of nodal (master) signifiers, the recalibration of the patient's
subjective experience against the ineluctable flow of the symbolic register in
which he is embedded.[43] Put succinctly, what the patient stands to gain from her
psychoanalytic experience is directly proportional with what she is prepared to lose.
Much like Bacon's 'pasting of the paint', the patient's free associative speech acts,
as punctuated by the analyst's interventions, do not lead to more truthful (self-)
knowledge or a more accurate battery of meanings, but to a dismantling of the
pathogenic meanings that had already been manufactured around his suffering (and
indeed his entire life history), so that the signifiers can acquire new sonorities and
new affective qualities. Much like Bacon's intensive labour of remaking and creative
rejection, (Lacanian) psychoanalysis is an iterative cycle of mental construction
and reconstruction, whereby the most important elements, in a 'therapeutic' sense,
are those signifiers that fall out of the process, as irrecoverable and indivisible
remainders. Where Joyce is busy littering the letter and Bacon is preoccupied with
pasting the paint, the psychoanalytic patient is shedding the signifier.

Looking at Bacon's creative labour as a progressive destabilisation of meaning
(sense) in favour of the appearance as pure sensation, it is also remarkable how this
work of rejection, distortion and destruction of form initially relies quite heavily on
the artifice of the geometrical armature (the famous Baconian 'cage') and gradually
starts to operate more freely, without the necessary support of the surrounding
framework. In his first documented interview with Sylvester, from 1962, Bacon
commented: 'I use that frame to see the image – for no other reason ... I cut down
the scale of the canvas by drawing in these rectangles which concentrate the image
down. Just to see it better.'[44] Bacon went on to say that he did not think it was a
particularly satisfactory device, that he tried to employ it sparingly, but that it was
nonetheless necessary from time to time. Be that as it may, other than the series
of heads, very few paintings that have escaped Bacon's hand of destruction portray
figures without some form of support, armature or framing, which is represented
in a wide array of different forms: imaginary cage, 'papal' chair, bed, chair,

sofa, doorway, window, table, mirror, carpet, and so on. [39], [40], [41], [43] Some paintings even display figures with more than one supporting framework. Taking into account that Bacon would always prefer his paintings to be exhibited in solid frames, and under glass, his consistent recourse to additional frames to trap the image (the subject matter) in the paint not only demonstrates how the structures of artificiality are an essential prerequisite for seeing, locating and capturing the truth of an appearance, but also (and perhaps more crucially) how sensation cannot be relayed as a violent (immediate and intense) assault on the nervous system without an artificial, and to some extent fictive, holding environment. Being exposed to the famous *Study after Velázquez's Portrait of Pope Innocent X,* 1953, [61] in an art gallery or exhibition essentially means that the violent sensation of the pontiff's gaping mouth – which makes his *sedia gestatoria* look more like a *sedia elettrica* – is transmitted to the spectator via no less than a quintuple armature: the glass covering the painting, the frame surrounding the painting, the frame of the canvas itself, the cage-like extension of the papal chair, and the *sedia* upon which he is seated. If truth is always embedded in a structure of fiction, as Lacan would proclaim, then Bacon's true reality of the appearance could definitely only appear, here, by virtue of a complicated, superimposed set of fictive structures.[45]

Yet towards the end of his career, in what could be called his 'late style', the cages, armatures and containers seem to become lighter, if not less frequent at least less conspicuous and less imposing, as if he had somehow found a way to trap the image without having to first delineate the contours of its appearance on the canvas. In light of this, although the argument could no doubt also be made on the basis of other features of his 'late work' such as the sections of raw, unpainted canvas, Bacon's 'painting cure' is also a journey towards greater economy, simplicity and minimalism.[46] [21], [42] What started off as a portrait of the artist as a scream screaming for interpretation from inside, or on top of an artificial holding frame, develops into a self-portrait of a distorted, yet largely self-composed figure in a state of physical tranquillity and relative equilibrium. In this respect, Bacon's life may not have been a complete disaster after all.

**Epilogue**

Sometime during the late 1990s, shortly before Francis Bacon's studio at 7 Reece Mews would be relocated to the Hugh Lane Gallery in Dublin, John Edwards, his closest friend during the autumn of his life and the sole beneficiary of his estate, invited the British documentary photographer Perry Ogden to capture the inside of the artist's long-standing home and workplace in a series of close-up images for posterity.[47] When the book of photographs was published in 2001, it hardly contained any text and presented Bacon's living quarters in almost unbearably bright, stark-naked detail, from a smudged black-and-white picture of George Dyer in oversized white underpants to the hastily scribbled phone numbers on the noticeboard above a kitchen tablet, and from the chaotic jumble of caked brushes and rags littered around the studio to the relatively organised assemblage of books, records and photographs in the bedroom-cum-living space.

To many, the pictures of the studio, which make up more than half of the book, would have been the most interesting, even though numerous images of

Bacon's workspace had entered the public domain over the years. Personally, I have always been more intrigued by the pictures of Bacon's bookcase, and the stacks of reading materials on the Boulle commode in his living room and on the mahogany chest of drawers next to the bed. An image of the lower two shelves of the bookcase shows, for example, that Bacon owned a copy of Peter Gay's biography of Freud as well as Richard Ellmann's biographies of Oscar Wilde and James Joyce.[48] Even more interesting are the books on the bedside chest of drawers, which range from Joyce's *Dubliners* to A. J. Ayer's 1986 volume on Wittgenstein, and also include copies of Nietzsche's *Twilight of the Idols/The Anti-Christ* and *Beyond Good and Evil*. Sharp and well lit as Ogden's photograph may be, the titles are not always easy to discern, yet in one case the identity of the book is unmistakable, if only because it is placed horizontally and the black lettering of the title on its spine contrasts well with the plain silver grey of the cover. Partially obscured by a white table fan yet within easy reach from the bed lies a clean copy of Alan Sheridan's English translation of Lacan's selected *Écrits*, originally published in hardcover in 1977 and subsequently released in a customer-friendly paperback edition during the mid-1980s.[49] How, when and where Bacon acquired Lacan remains couched in mystery. More intriguingly, the online catalogue of Bacon's books on the webpages of the Hugh Lane Gallery has no trace of *Écrits*, although it contains most of the books on the chest of drawers as shown in Ogden's photograph, including the Michelin guides to regions of France and a rather lovely volume on champagne cocktails. When John Edwards moved into 7 Reece Mews he wanted more space and so a large number of books were moved to Edwards's other house in Suffolk. Maybe the Lacan volume was part of this clear-out alongside the other books on the chest of drawers, yet unlike its companions it appears to have gone missing, then, when the Suffolk-based books were sent to Dublin with the remaining volumes from the kitchen, bedroom and living space at 7 Reece Mews. Maybe the Lacan volume never made it to Suffolk in the first place, or maybe it was stolen, borrowed or destroyed in one or the other location.[50]

Needless to say, just because Bacon owned a copy of Lacan's selected *Écrits* does not necessarily mean that he also read it. I know quite a few people whose bookshelves contain *Écrits* without them ever having read it, the notorious impenetrability of Lacan's baroque style often deterring the casual reader from moving beyond a few introductory lines. But let us imagine for a moment that Bacon had not just purchased a copy of the book because one of his French intellectual friends had spoken to him about Lacan's innovative surrealistic take on Freudian psychoanalysis. Which of the nine papers in the collection would have drawn his attention? Which pages could have excited him to the point of imbuing his nervous system with fresh images, new subject matter and perhaps a renewed desire to paint? In the absence of Bacon's copy, we may only speculate as to where exactly he delved into Lacan, yet I would not be surprised had he been struck, trapped and captivated by p. 313. In the middle of that page there is a drawing of the third stage of Lacan's graph of desire, which he also dubbed 'the bottle-opener of desire', on account of the visual resemblance between its singular armature and the standard shape of a heritage cap bottle-opener, and which projects onto its outer layers the only phrase with which one can respond to the Other's desire when it screams for interpretation: '*Che vuoi?*', 'What do you want?'[51]

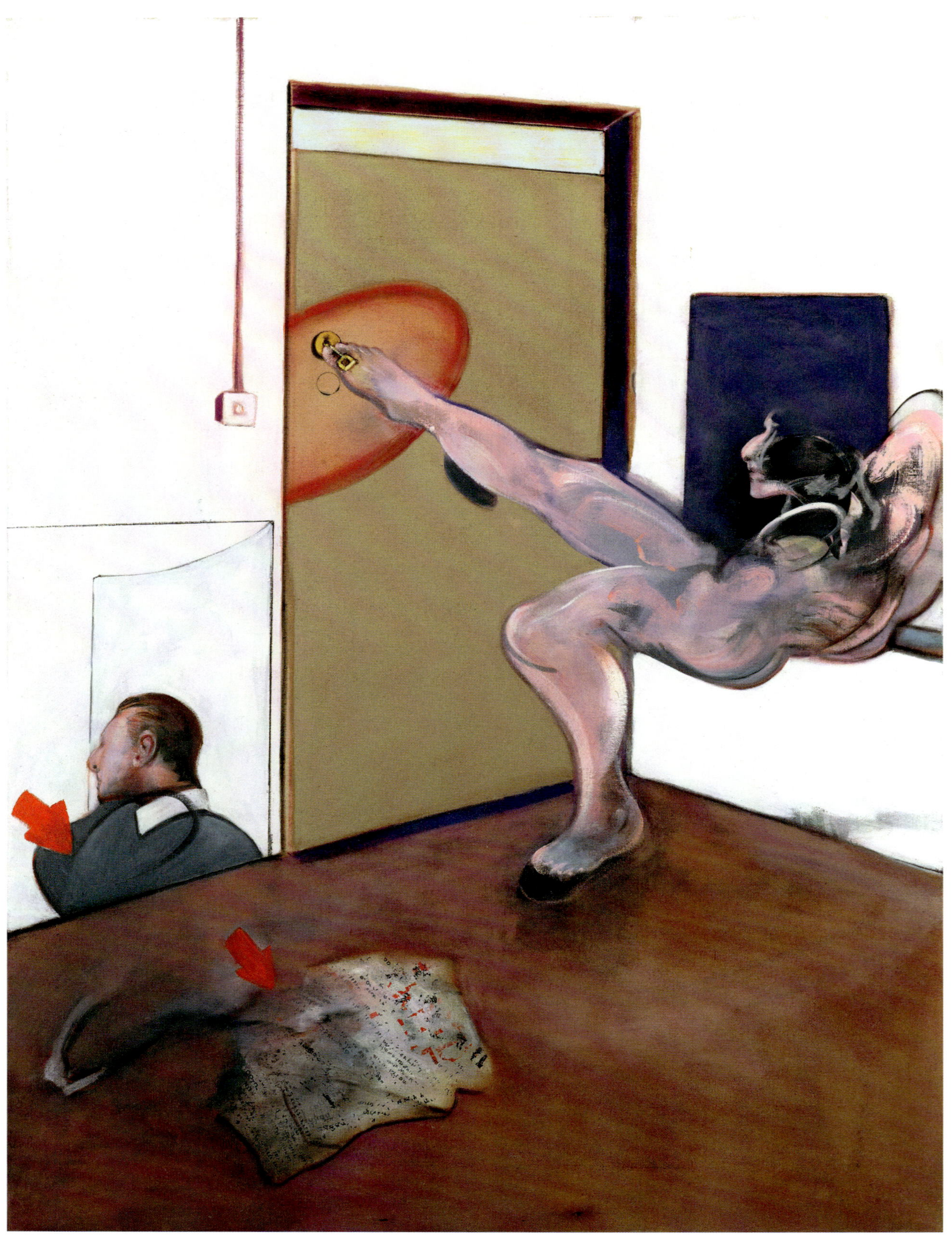

43. *Painting,* 1978

Who knows, while 'pasting his paint', Bacon may have allowed his fingers to take a walk on Lacan's graph, marking the intersections on the circuit with arrows, and painting an imaginary self-portrait on top of the psychoanalytic bottle-opener. As he said to Sylvester in 1966, when Lacan's written text on the graph of desire was first published: '[T]he marks are made, and you survey the thing like you would a sort of graph. And you see within this graph the possibilities of all types of fact being planted ... [I]f you think of a portrait, you maybe at one time have put the mouth somewhere, but you suddenly see through this graph that the mouth could go right across the face.'[52] Lacanian psychoanalysis may have been futile for an artist of Bacon's calibre, because in pasting the paint he moved straight to the best one may expect from psychoanalysis at its end, yet this should not have stopped him from transposing his gaping mouth onto the psychoanalyst's graph of desire.

# Endnotes


1.  Jacques Lacan, 'Lituraterre', trans. D. Nobus, *Continental Philosophy Review*, 46:1, (2013), pp. 327–34.

2.  For Derrida's critique of the privileged position bestowed upon speech (the signifier) in psychoanalysis, and especially in Lacan's famous 'return to Freud', see, for example, Jacques Derrida, 'Freud and the Scene of Writing', in *Writing and Difference*, trans. A. Bass (London & New York: Routledge, 1978), pp. 196–231.

3.  In *Finnegans Wake*, Joyce produced the exclamation 'The Letter! The Litter!', yet in all likelihood Lacan borrowed the example from 'A Litter to Mr James Joyce', a diabolically parodic response to Joyce's *Work in Progress* by a certain Vladimir Dixon, in a 1929 collection of critical essays. See James Joyce, *Finnegans Wake* (London: Faber & Faber, 1939), p. 93; Vladimir Dixon, 'A Litter to Mr James Joyce', in *Our Exagmination Round his Factification for Incamination of Work in Progress* (London: Faber & Faber, 1929), pp. 193–94. On Aquinas's dismissal of his own work, see, for example, Kenelm Foster, *The Life of St Thomas Aquinas: Biographical Documents* (London: Longmans, Green, 1959), p. 109.

4.  Lacan, op. cit., p. 327; Richard Ellmann, *James Joyce*, New and Revised Edition (Oxford & New York: Oxford University Press, 1983), p. 466.

5.  Lacan briefly invoked Joyce's wordplay again in his 1975 opening address to the 5th International Joyce Symposium, but he did not return to it in the seminar on Joyce that would commence five months later. See Jacques Lacan, 'Joyce the Symptom', in *The Seminar. Book XXIII: The Sinthome* (1975–76), ed. J.-A. Miller, trans. A. R. Price (Cambridge & Malden, MA: 2016), pp. 141–48 & p. 145 in particular.

6.  For 'traversal of the fantasy', see Jacques Lacan, *The Seminar. Book XI: The Four Fundamental Concepts of Psychoanalysis* (1964), ed. J.-A. Miller, trans. A. Sheridan (Harmondsworth: Penguin, 1994), p. 273. For 'subjective destitution', see Jacques Lacan, 'Proposition of 9 October 1967 on the Psychoanalyst of the School', trans. R. Grigg, a*nalysis*, 6 (1995), p. 8.

7.  Although the secondary literature on Bacon is gargantuan, psychoanalytic scholarship is still relatively meagre, especially from a Lacanian perspective, and those source materials that do exist either tend to highlight similarities between some of Bacon's obsessions and prominent Lacanian themes (such as the mirror stage), or unashamedly generate (implicitly pathologising) psychobiographical readings of one or the other aspect of the artist's life and works. For thought-provoking, Lacan-inflected studies in English, see, for example, Parveen Adams, 'The Violence of Paint', in *The Emptiness of the Image: Psychoanalysis and Sexual Differences* (London & New York: Routledge, 1996), pp. 109–21; Nicholas Chare, 'Regarding the Pain: Noise in the Art of Francis Bacon', *Angelaki*, 10:3 (2005), pp. 133–43; Nicholas Chare, 'Passages to Paint: Francis Bacon's Studio Practice', *Parallax*, 12:4 (2006), pp. 83–98; Brenda Marshall, 'Francis Bacon, Trash and Complicity', in *Francis Bacon – New Studies: Centenary Essays*, ed. M. Harrison (Göttingen: Steidl, 2009), pp. 209–31; Nicholas Chare, *After Francis Bacon: Synaesthesia and Sex in Paint* (London & New York: Routledge, 2012). For additional, proto-psychobiographical Lacanian readings, see Hervé Castanet, 'Ni beau, ni laid, ni indifférent mais plus "réel" ou la peinture selon Monsieur Francis Bacon', *Barca!*, 11:17 (1996), pp. 229–42; Jean-Paul Charancon, 'L. Freud, F. Bacon ou la rencontre avec l'existentiel', *Abords—Bulletin de l'ACF Aix-Marseille*, 10:6 (1996), pp. 19–23; Nicole Desury, 'Réflexion sur la peinture de Francis Bacon ou l'art de "se promener au bord du précipice"', *La lettre—Actes des travaux du bureau de Rennes de l'ACF-VLB*, 9, (2006), pp. 97–102; Marie-Hélène Brousse, 'Art, the Avant-Garde and Psychoanalysis', *Lacanian Compass*, 1:11 (2007), pp. 4–13; Pierre-Gilles Guéguen, 'Manipulation of the Imaginary in a Homosexual Couple', *The Lacanian Review—Hurly-Burly*, 2 (2017), pp. 20–34. For the historical record, it is also worth pointing out that the first ever connection between Bacon's work and Lacan's contributions to psychoanalysis seems to have been made by a patient of Winnicott's, who in one of her sessions associated Bacon's desire to have his paintings being exhibited under glass with Lacan's conception of the mirror stage. See Donald W. Winnicott, 'Mirror-role of Mother and Family in Child Development', in *Playing and Reality* (London-New York NY: Routledge, 2005), pp. 149–159 and p. 157 in particular; Jacques Lacan, 'The Mirror Stage as Formative of the *I* Function as Revealed in Psychoanalytic Experience', in *Écrits*, trans. B. Fink (New York: W. W. Norton & Company, 2006), pp. 75–81.

8.  Michael Peppiatt, *Francis Bacon: Anatomy of an Enigma* (London: Constable, 2008), p. 290.

9.  See, for example, David Sylvester, *The Brutality of Fact: Interviews with Francis Bacon* (London: Thames & Hudson, 1987), p. 40; Michel Archimbaud, *Francis Bacon: In Conversation with Michel Archimbaud* (London: Phaidon Press, 1993), p. 16; Franck Maubert, *L'Odeur du sang humain ne me quitte pas des yeux. Conversations avec Francis Bacon* (Paris: Mille et une nuits, 2009), pp. 36–37.

10. Drawing on Jacques Cazotte's 1772 novel *Le Diable*

*amoureux*, Lacan posited in 'The Subversion of the Subject and the Dialectic of Desire' that the only way one can respond to the Other's desire is by saying '*Che vuoi?*', 'What do you want?', which will never generate a satisfactory answer. See Jacques Cazotte, *The Devil in Love*, trans. J. Landry (Sawtry: Dedalus, 2011); Jacques Lacan, 'The Subversion of the Subject and the Dialectic of Desire in the Freudian Unconscious', in *Écrits*, op. cit., pp. 671–702 & p. 690 in particular.

11.	Speaking to David Sylvester during the mid-1980s, Bacon disclosed that he was always trying to employ 'the most anonymous titles possible', because 'the titles lie within the images and people can read what they like into them'. More specific labels would often be added by his gallery for the purposes of identifying and cataloguing the pictures. See Sylvester, op. cit., p. 220.

12.	See Peppiatt, op. cit., p. 392.

13.	Sylvester, op. cit., pp. 21–3. Some ten years later, he told Sylvester: 'I don't think that I have that other feeling [of wanting to paint the one perfect image] any longer – perhaps because I hope to go on painting until I die and, of course, if you did the one absolutely perfect image, you would never do anything more.' See Sylvester, op. cit., p. 125.

14.	See Michael Peppiatt, *Francis Bacon in the 1950s* (New Haven & London: Yale University Press, 2008), p. 48; Peppiatt, *Francis Bacon: Anatomy of an Enigma*, p. 205; Dennis Farr, Michael Peppiatt and Sally Yard, *Francis Bacon: A Retrospective* (New York NY: Harry N. Abrams, 1999), p. 12.

15.	Sylvester, op. cit., p. 150. In his 1966 interview with Sylvester, Bacon had already underscored his fundamental 'implication' in the crucifixion paintings: '[Y]ou're working then about your own feelings and sensations, really. You might say it's almost nearer to a self-portrait.' See Sylvester, op. cit., p. 52.

16.	For 'valves of sensation', see Sylvester, op. cit., p. 161.

17.	For the difference between 'sujet de l'énoncé' and 'sujet de l'énonciation', see, for example, Jacques Lacan, 'The Subversion of the Subject and the Dialectic of Desire in the Freudian Unconscious', op. cit., p. 677.

18.	Sometime during the mid-1980s, Bacon said to Franck Maubert: 'Painting is a language in itself … No one is capable of speaking about it. And why talk about it anyway? Let's look at it.' Maubert, op. cit., pp. 79–80.

19.	See Sigmund Freud, 'On Beginning the Treatment (Further Recommendations on the Technique of Psycho-Analysis I), *The Standard Edition of the Complete Psychological Works of Sigmund Freud*, trans. J. Strachey, vol. 12 (London: The Hogarth Press and the Institute of Psycho-Analysis, 1958), pp. 121–44 & p. 123 in particular.

20.	See, for example, Sylvester, op. cit., pp. 59–60; Archimbaud, op. cit., pp. 83–4; Peppiatt, *Francis Bacon: Anatomy of an Enigma*, op. cit., p. 28.

21.	See, for example, Sylvester, op. cit., p. 25; Archimbaud, op. cit., pp. 14–21; Peppiatt, *Francis Bacon: Anatomy of an Enigma*, op. cit., pp. 91, 118.

22.	Peppiatt, *Francis Bacon: Anatomy of an Enigma*, op. cit., p. 182. Herein, I believe, also resides Bacon's definition of 'violence', which has nothing to do with representations of aggression, threat, crime or danger, but with the intensity and the immediacy of a sensation. Bacon's violence does not reflect the attribution of the meaning of 'assault' to a certain image or experience, but epitomises an unexpected, yet inescapable sensory experience, which is both immediate and intense, along the lines of what Antonin Artaud tried to achieve in his theatre of cruelty.

23.	See, for example, Archimbaud, op. cit., p. 145.

24.	Sylvester, op. cit., p. 94.

25.	Ibid., p. 136. See also Archimbaud, op. cit., pp. 73–74; Maubert, op. cit., p. 83.

26.	Sylvester, op. cit., p. 108.

27.	See, for example, ibid., pp. 31, 34, 169, 177 and 194; Archimbaud, op. cit., p. 127. Talking to Franck Maubert, Bacon said: 'Photography allows me to start off, and afterwards I'm wiping out, I subtract, I efface.' See Maubert, op. cit., p. 32.

28.	See Freud, 'Remembering, Repeating and Working-Through (Further Recommendations on the Technique of Psycho-Analysis II), *The Standard Edition of the Complete Psychological Works of Sigmund Freud*, op. cit., pp. 145–56 & pp. 155–56 in particular.

29.	Jean Laplanche & Jean-Bertrand Pontalis, *The Language of Psycho-Analysis*, trans. D. Nicholson-Smith (New York & London: W. W. Norton & Company, 1974), p. 488.

30.	Jacques Lacan, *The Seminar. Book XI: The Four Fundamental Concepts of Psychoanalysis* (1964), ed. J.-A. Miller, trans. A. Sheridan (Harmondsworth: Penguin, 1994), pp. 273–4.

31.	See Freud, 'The Dynamics of Transference', *The Standard Edition of the Complete Psychological Works of Sigmund Freud*, op. cit., pp. 98–108 & p. 99 fn. 2. The expression Δαίμων καὶ Τύχη has a long tradition in ancient Greek philosophy and culture. See, for example, Frederick E. Brenk, '"A Most Strange Doctrine": Daimon in Plutarch', *The Classical Journal*, 69:1, (1973), pp. 1–11; Dorian Gieseler Greenbaum, *The Daimon in Hellenistic Astrology: Origins and Influence* (Leiden: Brill, 2016). In *The Four Fundamental Concepts of Psychoanalysis*, Lacan revamped the opposition by substituting the Aristotelian notion of αυτοματον for Δαίμων and defining the former as the inescapable insistence of the symbolic order (the system of language, the Other). See Lacan, *The Seminar. Book XI: The Four Fundamental Concepts of Psychoanalysis*, op. cit., pp. 53–64. It should also be noted, here, that τύχη, the Greek word for chance (fortune, accident), is almost homophonic with the word πτυχή, which means 'fold' and which has entered the art world (and one of Bacon's favourite formats) in the common name for a three-part or threefold painting: triptych.

32. Josef Breuer & Sigmund Freud, 'Studies on Hysteria', *The Standard Edition of the Complete Psychological Works of Sigmund Freud*, trans. J. Strachey, vol. 2 (London: The Hogarth Press and the Institute of Psycho-Analysis, 1955), pp. 289–90.

33. See Gilles Deleuze, *Francis Bacon: The Logic of Sensation*, trans. D. W. Smith (London: Bloomsbury, 2017); Joachim Vital, *Adieu à quelques personnages* (Paris: La Différence, 2004), p. 228.

34. See, for example, Sylvester, op. cit., pp. 169, 177.

35. See ibid., p. 14.

36. Ibid., p. 60.

37. Ibid., pp. 116–19.

38. Keith Jarrett, *Keith Jarrett at The Blue Note: The Complete Recordings*, 1995, ECM Records 1575–80, Liner notes.

39. Maubert, op. cit., p. 41.

40. Ibid.

41. Ibid.

42. Sylvester, op. cit., p. 103.

43. For the notion of 'reintegration' in Lacan's work, see, for example, Jacques Lacan, *The Seminar. Book I: Freud's Papers on Technique*, ed. J.-A. Miller, trans. J. Forrester (Cambridge: Cambridge University Press, 1988), p. 193. For Lacan's critique of authenticity and other 'ideals', see Jacques Lacan, *The Seminar. Book VII: The Ethics of Psychoanalysis*, ed. J.-A. Miller, trans. D. Porter (New York & London: W. W. Norton, 1992), pp. 8–10.

44. Sylvester, op. cit., p. 23.

45. On Lacan's claim that truth is always embedded in a structure of fiction, see, for example, Jacques Lacan, 'The Seminar on "The Purloined Letter"', in *Écrits*, op. cit., pp. 6–48 & p. 11 in particular.

46. Peppiatt, *Francis Bacon: Anatomy of an Enigma*, op. cit., p. 309.

47. Perry Ogden, *7 Reece Mews: Francis Bacon's Studio*, foreword by John Edwards (London: Thames & Hudson, 2001).

48. Ibid., pp. 110–11.

49. See Ogden, op. cit., pp. 108–9; Jacques Lacan, *Écrits: A Selection*, trans. A. Sheridan (London: Tavistock, 1977). The paperback version of Lacan's book was released by Routledge in the UK and by W. W. Norton & Company in the U.S.A.

50. I am grateful to Martin Harrison, Bacon connoisseur *nonpareil*, for discussing this matter with me, and for providing me with valuable information regarding the fate of Bacon's books after his death.

51. See Lacan, *Écrits: A Selection*, op. cit., pp. 312–13.

52. Sylvester, op. cit., p. 65.

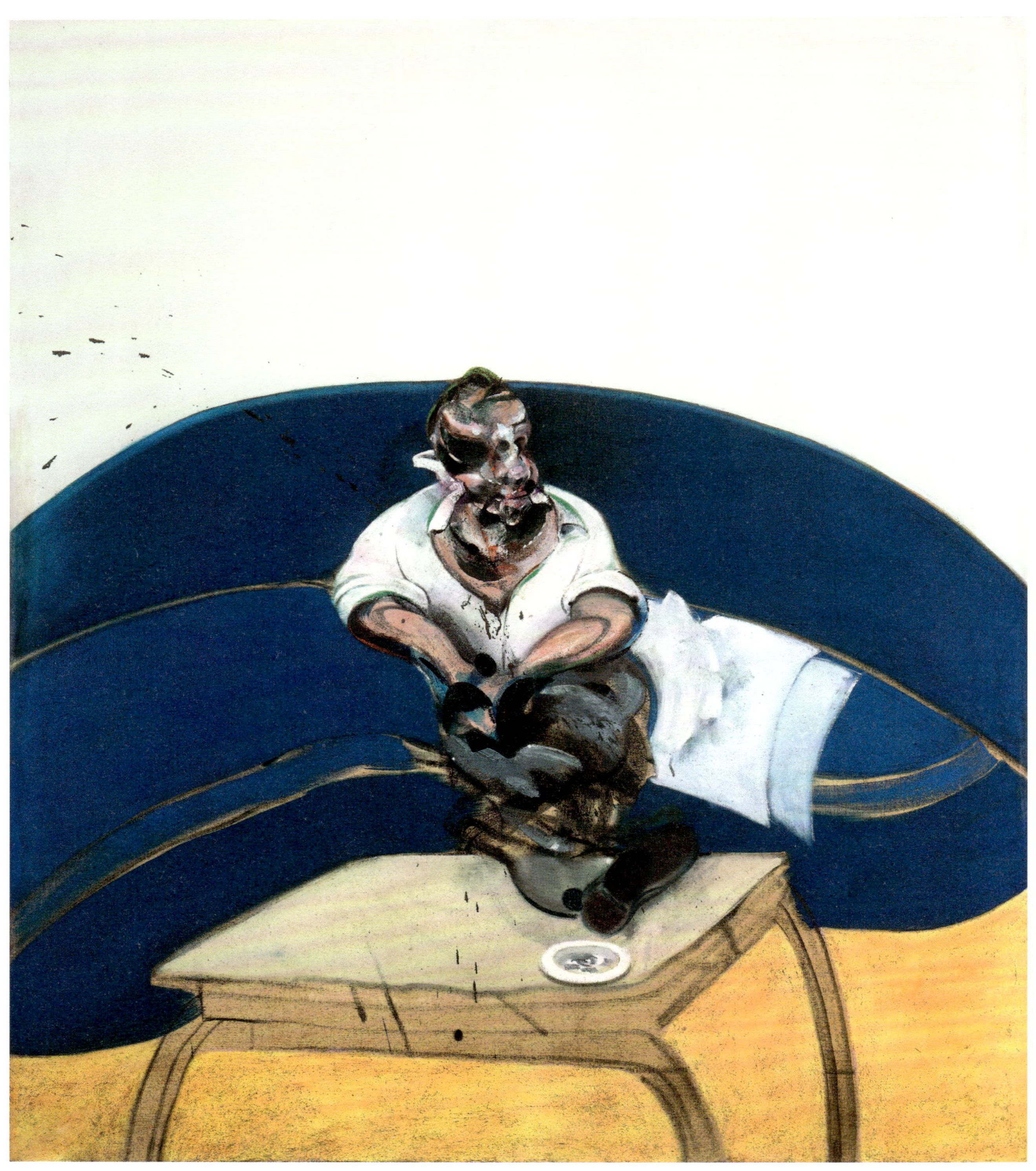

44. *Study for Self-Portrait*, 1963

# The Imposture of the Self-Portrait

Renata Salecl

How to understand a self-portrait? Moreover, how to understand a self-portrait that has no resemblance to how the artist looks? In 1970, the neurologist MacDonald Critchley wrote about self-portraits as impostors of sorts, since artists often paint images of themselves which do not resemble how they actually look.[1] As a result, Critchley concluded that self-portraits do not confirm that we know ourselves better than others. Psychoanalysts would ask whether a painter who obsessively draws himself engages in a form of self-analysis and how painting oneself differs, emotionally, from painting someone else. When a painter continuously paints himself in a form that has no resemblance to how he looks, further questions emerge: why would one name such paintings self-portraits and how do they differ from portraits of others?

Helene Deutsch linked the idea of the impostor to child's play since playing allows children temporarily to take on an adult role. The term 'imposter' has long been used to describe a person who presents himself as someone else.[2] There may be a combination of motives for doing this: financial gain, social status, the fulfilment of a fantasy about oneself, an escape from real world and/or internalised pressures; equally the steps taken by the imposter vary – while some people take the name of someone else, others fraudulently take on symbolic insignias (diplomas or military decorations) or boast of achievements they have not accomplished. Deutsch saw the reason for presenting oneself as someone else in the impostor's ego. The latter often feels devalued and guilt ridden, hence 'he needs to usurp the name of an individual who fulfils the requirements of his own magnificent ego ideal'.[3] Today, however, we have a new meaning of the impostor in the form of the 'impostor syndrome' or the 'impostor phenomenon'; this came into the public domain in the late 1970s when the psychologists Pauline R. Clance and Suzanne A. Imes wrote about high-achieving women having the feeling that they will be found out to be a fraud, or that others will somehow 'see' through them and recognise that they are far from the way they appear from the outside.[4] Certain women also suffer from the perception that their success is the result of pure luck, and that consequently they do not deserve public admiration. In both cases, we have the problem of how a person perceives herself regarding the Lacanian Big Other, the symbolic order in which she lives. If the first meaning of the term 'imposter' involves a person fraudulently taking on the symbolic role of another, or taking an identity without authorisation, the second meaning of the term involves a perception that one is not up to the symbolic role one is inhabiting – that is, one is a fraud. While the first type of impostor wants to be another, the second worries that she is someone who differs from the one socially recognised.

When Critchley observed that painters who paint self-portraits are imposters of sorts, he hinted at a third meaning of the term which has to do with the person presenting himself in an image that does not go together with his actual appearance. In this perception, self-portraiture would be a predecessor of today's selfies, which are increasingly staged or airbrushed images that have little resemblance to how a person looks in real life. While most selfies like to enhance, improve or embellish the 'real image', a whole genre (and even special technology) also exists to distort one's image. One can thus get an app that makes one's face look a different age or even preview how the face of an alcoholic changes after decades of drinking.

The question of how a person observes herself has long haunted psychoanalysts and artists alike. Lacan's theory of the mirror stage tries to give an insight into how a child goes through the process of observing herself in the mirror and then comes to the point of accepting that the reflection in the mirror pertains to her.[5] There is, however, a disjunction between the image in which the child observes herself and her bodily self-perception. The experience of the clumsy body of the little child is something the child cannot easily unite with the image of herself that she sees in the mirror. Lacan stressed the importance of the social setting, especially language, for the subject's self-recognition. For the subject to recognise herself in the mirror, it is thus essential that the primal caregiver points out that the image she is observing in the mirror is of herself.

The problem with recognition continues throughout the subject's life, but today the issues people have with their image are increasing. Social media, the perception that one has a choice over one's body, together with the proliferation of cosmetic surgery and ideals of body perfection, have contributed to the growing anxiety people experience about their image.

The subject's anxiety might be provoked not only by the prospect of having to encounter her image in the mirror, but also by the possibility of having to create her image in the form of a self-portrait or a selfie. By doing so, the subject engages with still another problem of the imposter, which involves the fabrication of one's visual identity in accordance with some imaginary concept of oneself. Before the emergence of selfies, self-portraits were used by some artists as a form in which to create a more or less likable image of themselves. While some decided to paint themselves because of the lack of funds to hire a model, others were drawn to self-portraits through narcissism, the desire to immortalise themselves, in order to explore their emotions, or even to express their political views. An example is Gustave Courbet, who in his self-portrait *The Wounded Man*, 1844–54, depicts himself as someone who has stabbed himself and then has placed his sword next to his dead body. This self-portrait has been interpreted as the artist's response to the unsuccessful revolutions that he supported – after their failure, suicide appeared the only option for the revolutionary.[6] Craig Brush, in his analysis of the difference between self-portraits and autobiographies, observes that some painters like to present themselves as younger and more handsome than they are and that, while self-portraits often depict sequences of the changes in the artist's life, they do not create an extended narration about it.[7] Henri de Toulouse-Lautrec, for example, in his *Self-Portrait before a Mirror*, 1882–83, did not reveal his disability. When he painted himself, one can see in the mirror the reflection of a young man, handsome and apparently normal in all ways that are visible.

Francis Bacon is well known for saying that he started painting himself because people had been dying around him 'like flies' and he 'had nobody else to paint' but himself.[8] One can imagine that he could have easily used photographs of other people since his self-portraits intentionally had little resemblance to how he looked in real life. Without the title 'self-portrait' one would sometimes not guess that he is trying to depict himself. Michael Peppiatt observes that it was after the death of Bacon's on-and-off lover George Dyer in 1971 that self-portraits took the principal place among the themes of his paintings. In addition to Dyer, Bacon that same year also lost his mother, Winnie. Although Bacon had suffered from painful losses before (in 1957 his friend John Minton committed suicide, and in 1962 came the death of his decade-long lover, Peter Lacy), after the losses he experienced in 1971 a change seemed to happen in his self-perception. Peppiatt suggests that the symbolic recognition that Bacon had before and the fact that he was surrounded by 'visually fascinating, eminently recordable friends'[9] did not impel him to record himself: 'The artist was enjoying his wave of success and popularity to the full, and nothing predisposed him to the guilt, melancholy, and loneliness which were later to feed his great series of paintings of himself.'[10] Peppiatt concludes that before the artist embarked on creating his series of self-portraits, too much was happening 'on the outside for Bacon to dwell on himself, and he was delighted to exercise his prowess at fracturing, then capturing, the likenesses of others.'[11]

It might very well be that the symbolic recognition at first worked as a kind of shield which allowed Bacon not to be overburdened by his traumas. Here, we are reminded of the impostors under the first meaning of the term, especially those who take on another persona as a solution for their inner turmoil. While a person might keep searching for stability in temporarily taking on a symbolic identity or in a strong identification with social status, social recognition is nothing one can rely on. As Lacan poignantly observed, the social symbolic system does not exist, but it nonetheless functions. The subject's belief in its consistency is often the necessary fantasy that holds the subject together. And should this fantasy collapse, the subject is likely to lose the ground on which he temporarily built his identity.

The tension between social recognition and the subject's self-perception is played out in both the first and the second meanings of the phenomenon of the imposter. In the first meaning, the subject searches for an identity which will give him the desired social recognition. Often, however, the impostor does not find stability in a single assumed identity but goes from one identity to another. The second meaning of the imposter, the so-called imposter syndrome, fully exposes the uncertain status of symbolic identity: it is as if the subject who suffers from this syndrome actually recognises that lack in the Big Other and can no longer rely on the fantasy of the consistency of his symbolic identity.

In the late 1950s, the psychoanalyst Phyllis Greenacre wrote a text on imposters and artists in which she observed that many young artists have the problem of feeling like an imposter since, as she says, bearing the gift of being an artist is not easy.[12] Many artists experience that they are at least two people – the personal self and the collectively recognised, creative self. Greenacre observes that these selves are sometimes nearly as separate as they are in the imposter – a division not infrequently recognised in the use of different names. An example is a writer Mary Ann Evans who took the pen name George Eliot, performance artist Stelios Arcadiou who shortened his name into Stelarc, or three Slovenian artists who officially changed their names to Janez Janša, the name of a conservative politician whose politics they opposed.

Bacon's turn to self-portraits can be read as an annihilation of the divide between the personal self and the publicly recognised self. In his self-portraits, the most intimate suddenly appear public. This intimacy, however, is nothing the viewer can easily put into words or discern in the form of a recognisable image. Observing Bacon's self-portraits, the viewer has the impression that the faces are half-rotten or the holes in them render them inhuman. The viewer often feels pulled into the holes. The fact that Bacon's self-portraits often involve circular gestures where the face appears like a vortex gives the impression that the viewer's gaze is sucked into the emptiness which is at the tip of the vortex. In the language of Lacanian psychoanalysis, this vortex would be close to the concept of the drive – the aim, the push that drives the subject and often undermines his conscious self-perception. It is what is at the place of the real, the lack that escapes the symbolic and which the imaginary cannot depict. As a result, in many of the self-portraits, Bacon presents himself as monstrous. In *Study for Self-Portrait*, 1963, [44] a person is seated on a curved, dark blue sofa. He is dressed in a white shirt and dark grey trousers. Next to the figure is something that looks like pieces of white paper. The person appears to be resting on a couch with his feet on the table, where one also observes an ashtray. The face of the person is completely distorted, and the head seems to be full of dark holes as if one is observing an alien creature. There also appears to be no division between the head and the body. As a result, the head looks like an externalised wound which protrudes out of the torso. Observing this distorted creature, one has the feeling that one's gaze is swallowed by the openings in the head. The hole at the place where one imagines the eyes in the head and where the mouth is usually positioned are joined by another hole which looks like an opening in the neck.

Why is it that Bacon so radically distorts his face? In an interview with David Sylvester, he remarks: 'I loathe my face. One of the nicest things that Cocteau said was, "Each day in the mirror I watch death at work." This is what one does to oneself.'[13] This statement seems to reflect on the fact that in one's face that one observes in the mirror, the seeds of the future decomposition are already present. However, when Bacon says that 'one does that to oneself', he also hints at the subjective inscription that is at work in one's push towards death. A person seems to observe death in the mirror, which is, however, of his own making.

One is reminded here of another of Cocteau's observations about death which he states in the conclusion of his novel *Thomas the Impostor*. In this story, the main character, the young soldier Guillaume Thomas, pretends all his life that he is someone else and this pretence does not stop even when he dies. In the final battle: 'As he heard no fire, he stopped and turned around, out of breath. Then he felt a stick strike him violently on the chest. He became deaf and blind. A bullet. I haven't a chance if I don't pretend to be dead, he said to himself. But in him make-believe and reality were one. Guillaume Thomas was dead.'[14] Is the meaning of this that even in death the imposter has the power to go on pretending – even if this time he cannot do anything but play at being what he is: dead? Or is it maybe the observer, the narrator, who looks at the dead impostor and sees double: both a dead man and one playing another of his tricks?

When artists focus incessantly on death, the first impression is that they are expressing their own anxiety over death, or mourning loved ones, or both. Depiction of death can, however, be an attempt to make death itself 'visible' in the

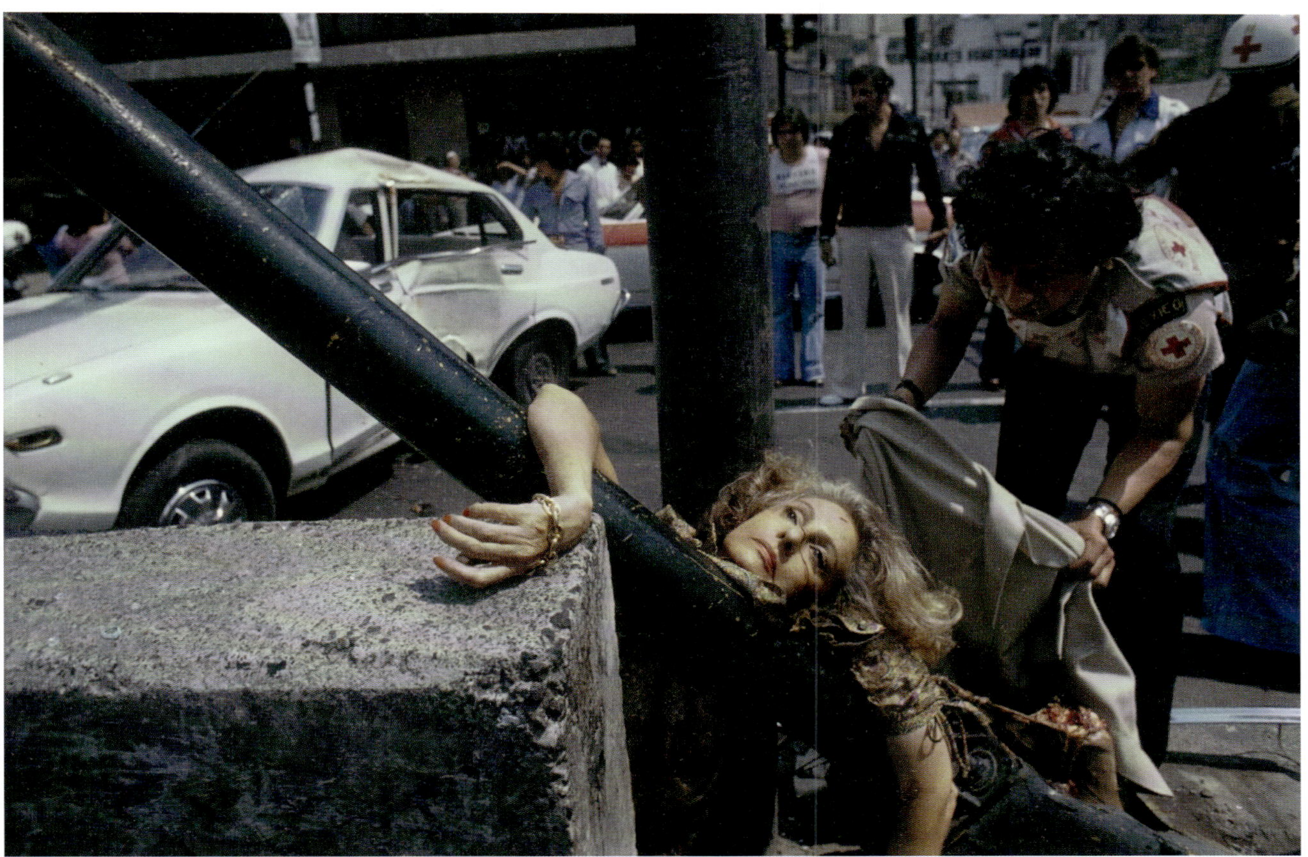

45. Enrique Metanides, *Mexico City, April 29, 1979*

endeavour to master one's anxiety over it. One example is the Mexican photographer Enrique Metinides, who became famous for capturing tragic scenes: car crashes, train derailments, street stabbings and shootings, accidental explosions, suicides and manslaughters.[15] Metinides often showed how these tragic events were reflected through the eyes of observers. In his numerous photographs of accidents, he focused on how witnesses of a traumatic scene behaved, as well as showing what dead people looked like. In his youth Metinides was very much affected by films, wanting to record how the eye of the observer functioned as a mirror in which the scene of the accident would be visible and potentially recorded in a film. When he later became a photographer his passion for depicting what death looks like was an attempt to create a distance between the event and its presentation. Metinides's photos present death as a curiosity which does not seem anxiety-provoking. In some of the images one even has the impression that dead people are still alive. [45]

With Bacon, too, death seems in a strange way appeased, tamed and sometimes almost non-dead. When one observes his *Study for Portrait II (after the Life Mask of*

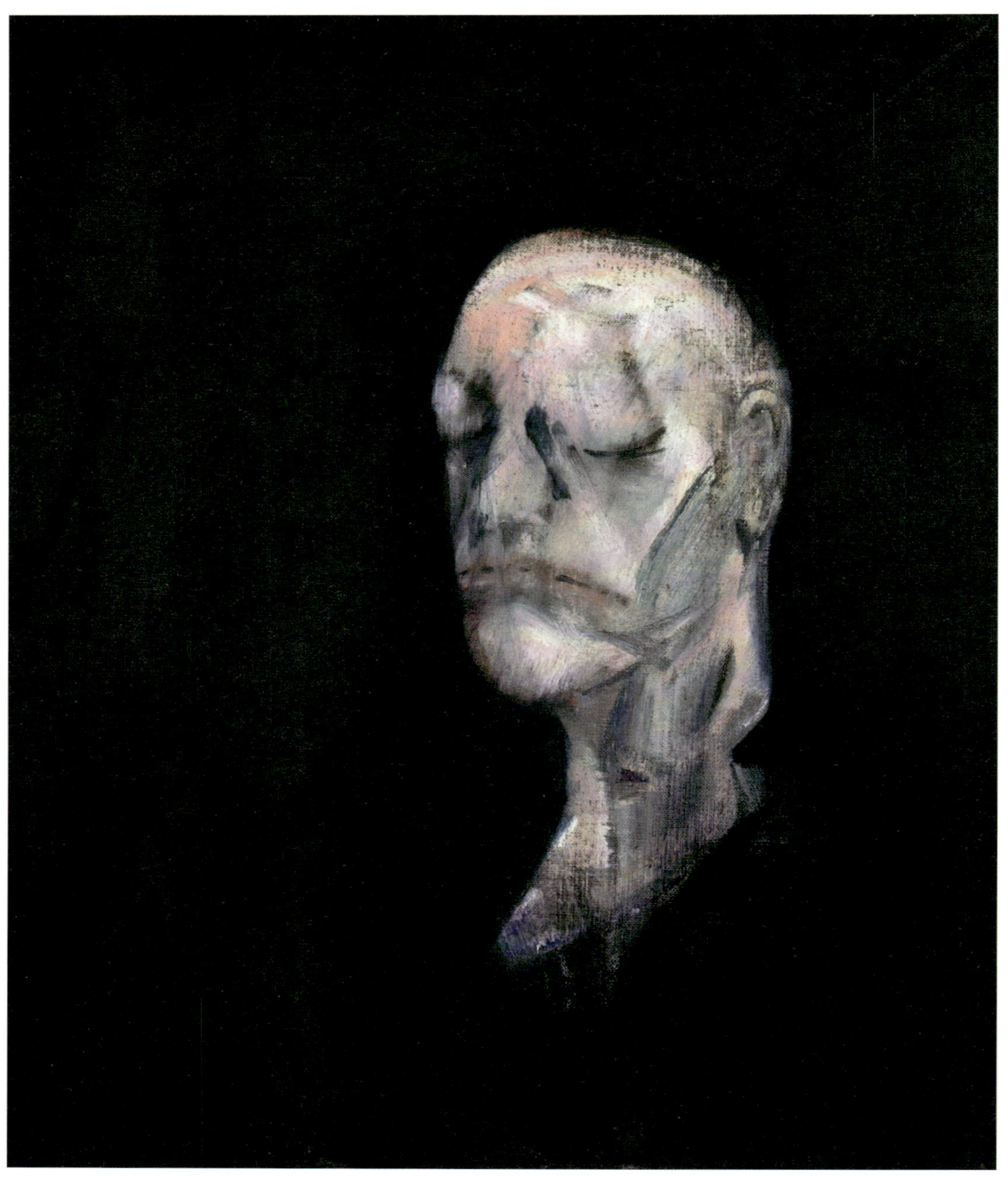

46. *Study for Portrait II (after the Life Mask of William Blake)*, 1955

*William Blake)*, 1955, [46] one has the impression that it is an image of a person asleep. There is a hint of pink colour in the face in midst of many layers of paint, which makes the portrait look alive. One does not imagine that one is looking at a mask of a dead person, but at someone who rests at the moment and who still might wake up.

During the period in which he produced this image, Bacon engaged with self-portraits for the first time. The first self-portrait was done in 1955 when he was also working on a portrait of Vincent van Gogh. Bacon found in Van Gogh's art a stimulus for developing his take on the relationship between reality and fiction. As he says in the interview with David Sylvester:

> I believe that realism has to be reinvented. It has to be continuously reinvented. In one of his letters, Van Gogh speaks of the need to make changes in reality, which become lies that are truer than the literal truth. This is the only possible way the painter can bring back the intensity of the reality which he is trying to capture. One believes that reality in art is something profoundly artificial and that it has to be re-created. Otherwise, it will be just an illustration of something – which will be very second-hand.[16]

Bacon exemplifies this by pointing out how surprised he was to visit the landscapes in Provence that Van Gogh had painted in vivid colours, creating a marvellous vision of the reality of things, while, in reality, the country was barren. It was the paint that gave it its amazing life. Bacon similarly approaches the portraits. Here, too, he challenges the reality of one's appearance. In many of his interviews, Bacon stressed that he detested it if portraits resembled a person being painted. Bacon explains his technique of painting portraits as trying to depict what emanates from the person: it is the energy within the appearance that he wants to capture. As a result, he found it most challenging to find a way to present in his portraits the pulsations of a person he was painting. Also, it was crucial for him to find subjects that absorbed him completely, since, as he says, without such subjects one might go back to decoration.[17] Bacon tried to capture the energy of the person he was painting, but also dealt with his persona and what emanated from him as a painter; he explained to Sylvester: 'I work in a kind of haze. I don't want the work to be hazy, but I work in a kind of haze of sensations and feelings and ideas that come to me and that I try to crystallize.'[18]

This haze of sensations and feelings gave life to Bacon's portraits and self-portraits which, like Van Gogh's colours, brought out something else from the person being depicted other than the reality of his appearance. When we observe portraits of Bacon's friends, we get the impression that they uncannily resemble their subjects, while they expose something in the reality of their image that goes beyond simple representation. Catching the 'likeness' of Bacon's subjects was about depicting their characteristics as well as moments when they move, change. Bacon saw his friends as in a film sequence, which is always moving and is sometimes unrecognisable from one sequence to another. In his portraits, he tried to capture these moments and the aura of a person, as well as presenting that person in such a way that he makes visible certain human characteristics which are not bound to specific circumstances. As Peppiatt notes: 'Without those drives and contradictions,

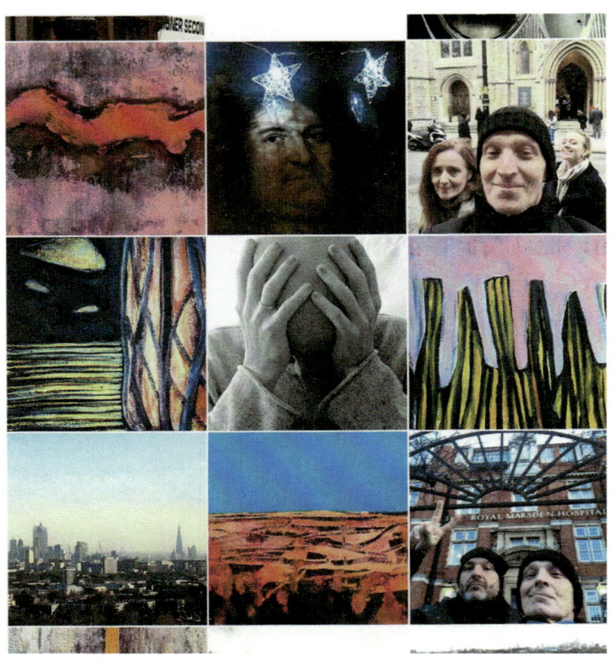

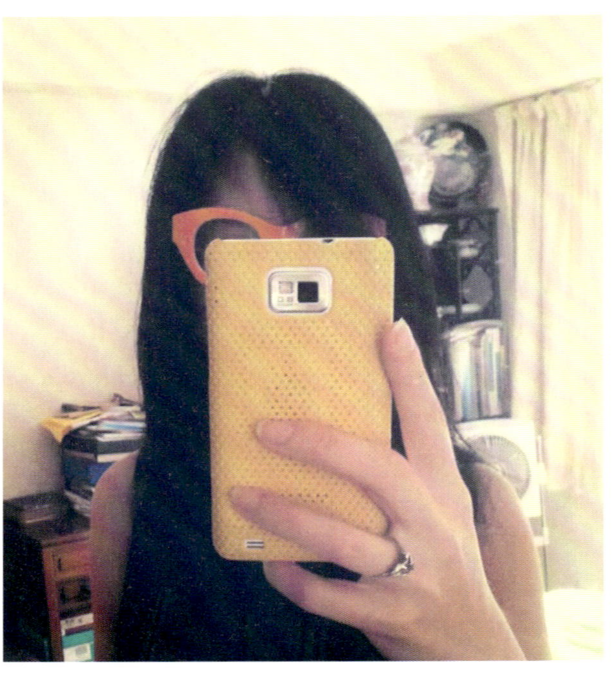

47. Ranieri Fontana Giusti, Instagram images, 2016    48. Jacqueline Tong, *The Spectacles Selfie*, 2013

which were in a sense the inner architecture of appearance, he believed, the portrait became banal, empty illustration.'[19]

One wonders how Bacon would try to convey his feelings in today's times when all kinds of new technologies allow artists and also ordinary people to share their perceptions with others easily. Numerous people are, for example, using Instagram as a platform that allows them to create a new gallery space where they curate their lives, often using a mixture of techniques (photos, paintings or computer-generated images), as well as short texts and hashtags. Some artists exhibit only in this new space, and others suddenly become artists because this new forum provides social recognition. This happened to Italian-British architect Ranieri Fontana Giusti who, after being diagnosed with pancreatic cancer, turned to art and posted daily on Instagram his paintings, artistic photos and occasional family photos, all to convey to the anonymous public his torment related to his incurable illness. Amid this collage of images, Fontana Giusti placed his self-portraits, some drawn by pencil and some in the form of photo selfies depicting his increasingly emaciated body and face. [47] The mixture of these images conveyed the feelings of wonder about life, anxiety over death, as well as optimism when the illness was not progressing. At the same time, the hashtags to the images added their interpretation. From the labels like 'endofconventionalmedicine', 'depression', 'cancerheads' and 'hangingon' one easily gets the additional impression of the feelings that incited some of the art work.

While some people turn to Instagram to express their painful feelings, many others use the platform as a place where they curate an image of themselves in which they hope to appear likable and admired. Instagram and similar social networks offer a space where a person hopes to get symbolic recognition while it also presents a new type of mirror in which one observes oneself and in which one is constantly observed by others. However, even more importantly, these new social spaces allow someone to become an impostor. On the internet, one can easily present oneself in an idealised image; one can appropriate another's identity or fabricate symbolic insignia.

In this new world of images, aggression is often very much part of how people interact among themselves as well as how they react towards themselves. Which is why, unsurprisingly, the second meaning of the term 'impostor', the impostor syndrome, is on the rise. In the space where criticism is ever present, people easily internalise these attacks and start criticising themselves. Reflecting on this uneasiness people experience in regard to their image, a whole new genre of art-selfies has appeared today, which does not show the face of the person taking the selfie realistically. Hong Kong-based art writer Jacqueline Tong only shares selfies that show her face obscured by the phone taking the image. She explains this by saying: 'I don't really like my face; it's boring – that's why I put myself behind the phone.'[20] This statement is similar to Bacon's remark about hating his face, and strangely, the phone with the help of which Tong takes her self-portrait creates a lack in her image which seems a new version of a hole Bacon was playing with in his time.

Social media today present a space where voyeurism is played out in a new way. While people are highly critical of each other, they also experience unease about their own image. Many people who observe images of others on Instagram feel terrible about their own bodies;[21] while those that post their personal images experience even more negative feelings about themselves.[22] There is a particular kind of a jouissance one can observe in this self-criticism as well as in the criticism of others. It is as if observing selfies of others and posting one's own allows the subject to find new forms of sadism and masochism. The question of how one looks in the eyes of anonymous others on the internet (which nowadays functions as the new form of the Big Other) is also reshaping the old imposter syndrome. Now, as well as the subject feeling that she will be found out as falling short of the symbolic statute, by being not good enough or exposed as lacking, she is also dealing with her image not being up to the presumed ideals.

Jouissance in voyeurism and criticism that today's new media provides is, however, not so very different from the one that Bacon engaged with in his own time. Bacon relentlessly criticised most other well-known artists, and only a few were occasionally praised. Peppiatt mentions the repetitive rhythm of Bacon's conversations, especially under the influence of alcohol, when he made unguarded remarks about himself and his experiences, and constantly denigrated other famous painters. 'It was a process of stripping away to see what – if anything – would remain after the continued verbal assault. The tone, like his approach to painting, was often provocative and aggressive, and very few were the people and themes that escaped this scrutiny unscathed.'[23]

Almost like today's internet voyeur, Bacon found particular stimulation in voyeuristic observation of the emotional distress of other people:

> After being alone in the studio, the artist loved to get out, meet his friends and observe others, particularly when they were in the grip of intense emotion or undergoing a crisis; he would often sit near a mirror so that he could

watch discreetly what he called "people carrying on". There was a detached amusement but also compassion in this obsessive interest; and if the artist knew and liked the people concerned, he would be the first to offer every kind of help, without counting the often considerable cost – in time, money or patience – to himself.[24]

What especially excited Bacon was the observation of sexual jealousy, when, for example, he had a chance to observe people fighting publicly with their partners. Bacon's portraits seem to reflect this turmoil he observed in public spaces. Some of the portraits thus look like 'scenes glimpsed through half-open doors, or happening so fast that you cannot understand what is going on'.[25]

Bacon was known for having bitter quarrels with his lovers and for his masochism, yet observing others in emotional turmoil gave him similar satisfaction. For him, as an artist, it was, however, not enough to try to depict this turmoil in his paintings. He was particularly impelled to inflict pain onto others via the paintings he produced of them. However, by doing this, he was channelling his pain through the process of painting. This was especially the case when he painted friends who died. Dead friends are brought back with the help of the painting. Bacon explains that by saying: 'If they were sitting in front of me, they would inhibit me, and I could not practise on them the injury I inflict in my work. I like to be alone with the way I remember them. Moreover, then I hope to bring them back more poignantly and violently.'[26]

Bacon liked observing people in mirrors in public spaces, while he also liked to play with mirrors in his work. However, when Bacon depicts mirrors in his painting, one often does not see the reflection of a surface in the mirror, but rather something else. In the *Portrait of George Dyer in the Mirror,* 1968, [28] we have a man sitting in front of the mirror. The painting depicts this man slightly turning into the direction of the mirror where we see his face split into two parts. The mirror does not act as a reflection of what is projected in the mirror, but rather as a frame in which a monstrous image of the face appears. In other paintings, the mirror acts as a reflective surface where the contour of the body is framed. The body as such might be deformed and its reflection too. However, the latter is framed, and therefore its deformation appears to be contained.

The mirror is also present in *Self-Portrait*, 1973. [49] Here we have a male figure seated in front of a washbasin. The face of the man is distorted, and a shadow of the face marks the white ceramics of the washbasin. On the wall appears a mirror image of the scene, which could also have been a person peeping from the outside. The ghostly figure observes the man in front of the washbasin. One wonders if the artist is observing himself from the mirror. Is that a superego gaze that looks at the artist who is vomiting into the washbasin, while the light hanging from the ceiling, which seems like an interrogation light, casts a strange shadow on the wall? Because Bacon liked to use mirrors in public spaces to observe the emotional dramas of people, one may wonder whether he is a voyeur in his portrait who enjoys observing his suffering via the intermediary of the mirror.

In psychoanalysis, the mirror is often mentioned in two ways: as a reflective surface with the aid of which the subject goes through the process of self-recognition, and as a place where the subject might experience the anxiety-provoking gaze of a

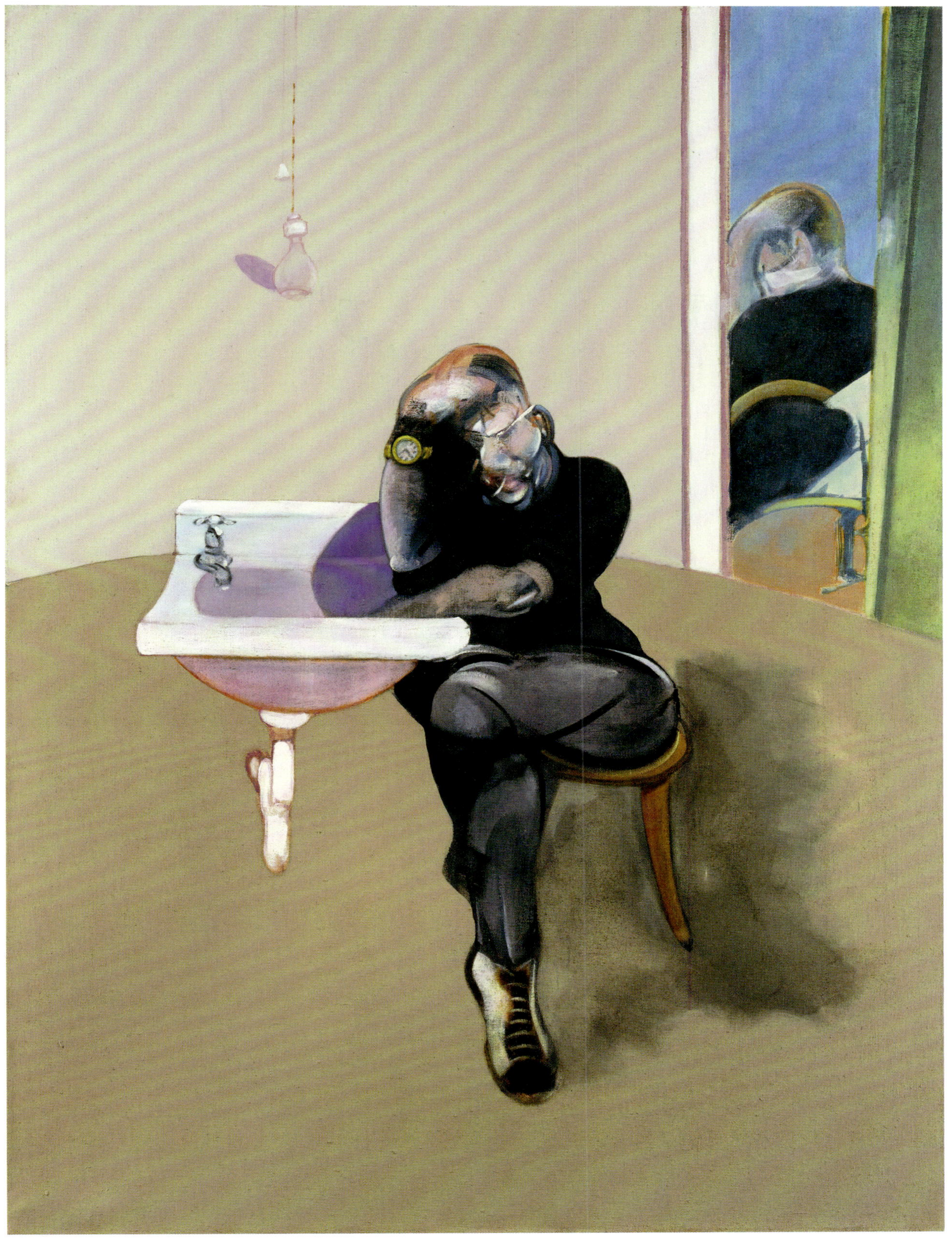

49. *Self-Portrait*, 1973

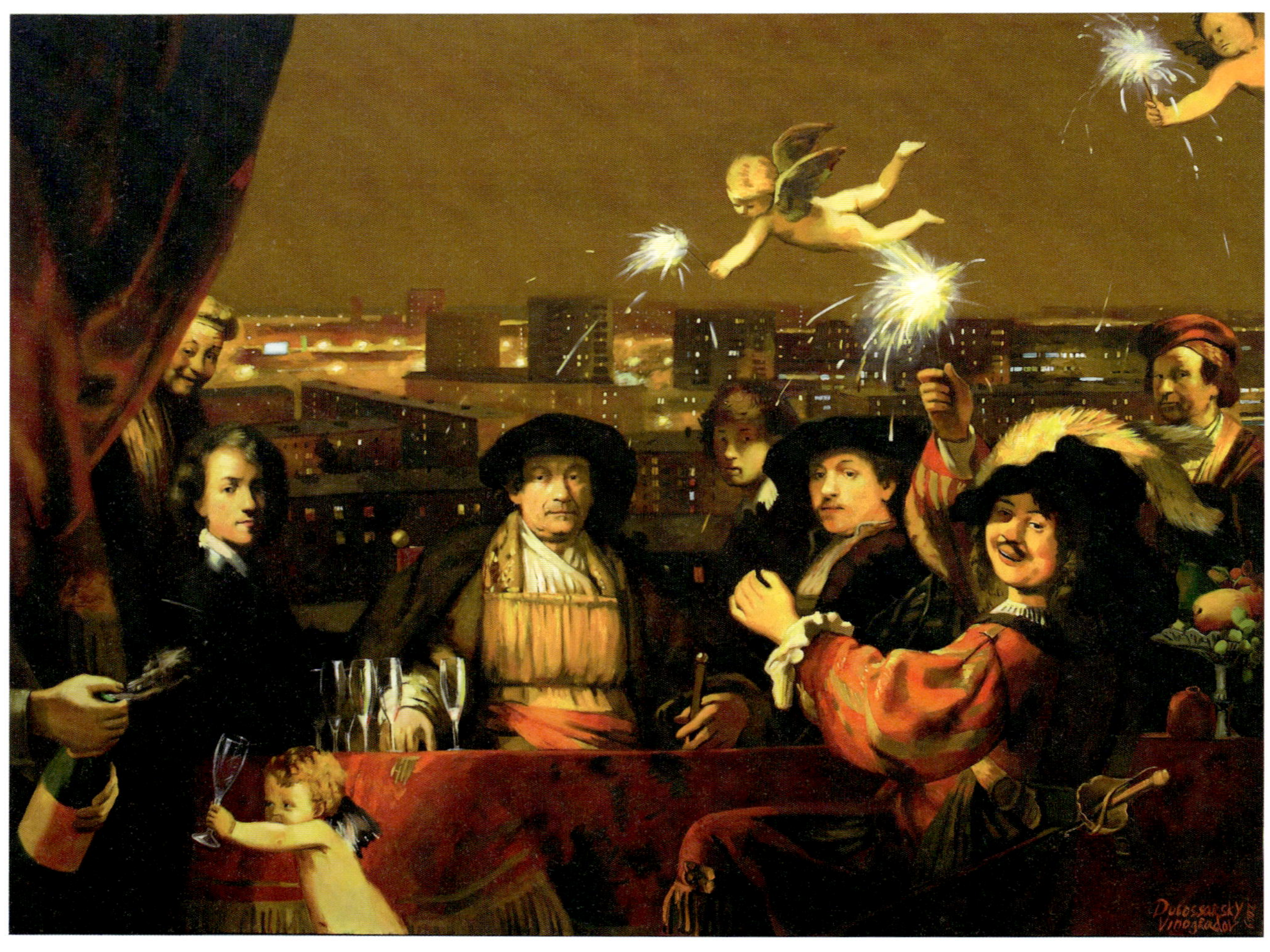

50. Vladimir Dubossarsky and Alexander Vinogradov, *Happy Birthday, Mynheer Rembrandt*, 2009

double. Lacan, on top of talking about the mirror stage, also talks about the role of the mirror in anxiety.[27] Here, the subject might have the experience of observing in the mirror her double. This could also be the moment when the image in which she is observing herself returns the gaze to her. In Bacon's portraits and self-portraits the mirror strangely plays an appeasing role. The horrifying gaze is present in the distorted faces, which are cut up and full of dark holes. The uncanny gaze in Bacon's portraits thus comes from the elements in the portraits where the portrait stops being a depiction of a person, where the portrait cracks, opens up or is marked by a hole.

A different experience with the gaze related to portraits was at work in the exhibition *'Danger! Museum!'*, by the Russian artists Vladimir Dubossarsky and Alexander Vinogradov, which was part of the Venice Biennale in 2009. The Russian duo created an exhibition full of paintings of famous people and classics of the art world, among them: Rembrandt, Joseph Beuys and Barack Obama. In some paintings the faces of contemporary figures were superimposed onto reproductions of the Old Masters. But in the case of Rembrandt, the artists combined reproductions of all of his self-portraits into one giant painting. Observing the replicas of historical portraits, the viewer was invited to guess what was altered in the old paintings or which historical figure was replaced by a contemporary one. At the end of the exhibition, the viewer entered a special room full of TV screens. Observing the screens, the viewer was able to see that she was recorded while observing the paintings. The viewer was confronted with the uncanny moment of seeing how the painting saw her. At the end of the tour through the installation, many visitors decided to return to the exhibition, chiefly with two intentions: on the one hand, they were trying to find the camera hidden in the painting; on the other hand, they were trying to pose in a more admirable way for the camera to record them.[28]

When Bacon speaks about portraits, he often evokes what is behind the image. As a result, Bacon's portraits have often been analysed in the context of the difference between face and mask. Hans Belting[29] thus sees Bacon's portraits of his friends and models as an attempt to make the mask alive. Instead of searching for the similarity between the model and the portrait, Bacon rather tries to enliven the portrait so that it gives the impression of a form of life. Gilles Deleuze, in contrast, does not see the mask as what covers the face, but as something that is the face itself. For Deleuze, Bacon was not a painter of faces, but rather heads. With his technique of painting people's portraits, Bacon challenged the very form of the portrait, since he liberated it from earlier conventions. Violence, for example, becomes in Bacon's work intrinsically connected to the very idea of the portrait. The way Bacon reformulates the portrait also extends to the area surrounding the depiction of the body or the head. Deleuze thus perceives spasms in Bacon's characters as if the body is trying to escape through one of its organs to rejoin the flat tinted area, the material structure around it. As a result, the shadow has as much presence as the body, but as Deleuze says, 'the shadow acquires this presence only because it escapes from the body'.[30] In the case of the scream, it thus looks as if the entire body escapes through the mouth. For Parveen Adams what escapes through the body in Bacon's painting is libido, lamella, the organ of the drive: 'it is lamella that is the outcome of Bacon's efforts to avoid narrative and representation and to act directly on the nervous system'.[31]

Deleuze links Bacon's work with hysteria. However, his intention is not to analyse the painter but rather to look at the special relationship between painting and hysteria. As he says: 'Painting directly attempts to release the presence beneath representation, beyond representation. The colour system itself is a system of direct action on the nervous system. This is not a hysteria of the painter, but a hysteria of painting. With painting, hysteria becomes art. Or rather, with the painter, hysteria becomes the painting.'[32] In this context, Deleuze observes Bacon's paintings of heads and his self-portraits as attempts to render visible the invisible forces:

> 'the extraordinary agitation of these heads is derived not from a movement that the series would supposedly reconstitute, but rather from the forces of pressure, dilation, contraction, flattening, and elongation that are exerted on the immobile head ... It is as if invisible forces are striking the head from many different angles. The wiped and swept parts of the face here take on a new meaning, because they mark the zone where the force is in the process of striking.'[33]

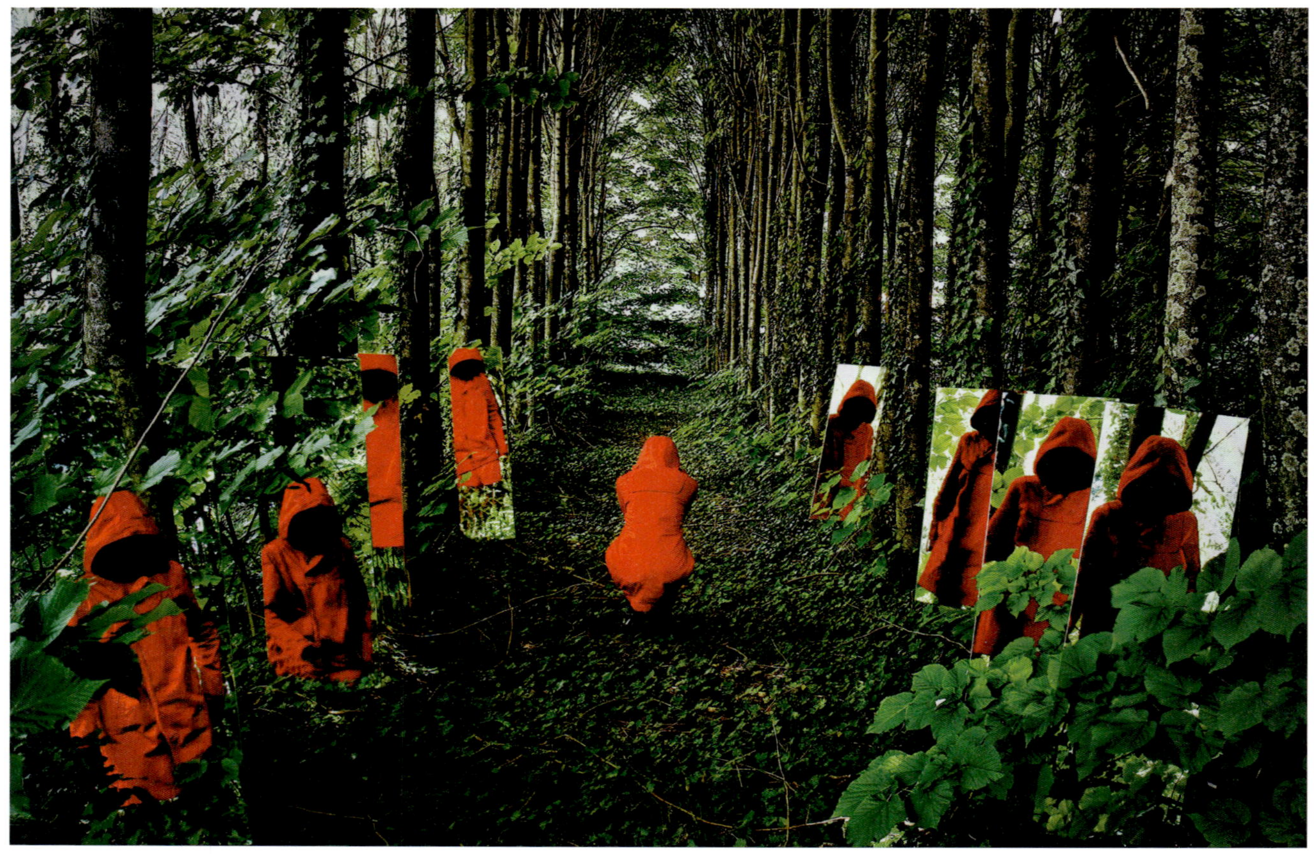

51. Manuel Colombo, *Eisoptrophobia*, 2010

These invisible forces which strike the side of the heads are, for the viewer who observes them in a gallery, often supplanted by another type of an image – the reflection of the viewer herself in the painting. Bacon insisted that his paintings were covered by a glass, which then created a reflective surface in which the viewer could easily observe herself. This was noticed by an analysand of Donald Winnicott[34] who at the time of her session described her feelings after she read in the introduction to the catalogue of Bacon's work that the artist put the glass on top of the paintings so that when the observers look at the painting, on top of the picture they also see themselves. Winnicott comments in the footnote to his patient's reflection that Bacon's preference for glazed painting is related to the painter's dependence on chance:

> 'The preference is due to the fact that glass sets paintings somewhat apart from the environment (just as his daisies and railings set his subjects apart from their pictorial environment), and that glass protects, but what counts more in this case is his belief that the fortuitous play of reflections will enhance his pictures. His dark blue pictures in particular, I heard him observe, gain by enabling the spectator to see his face in the glass.'[35]

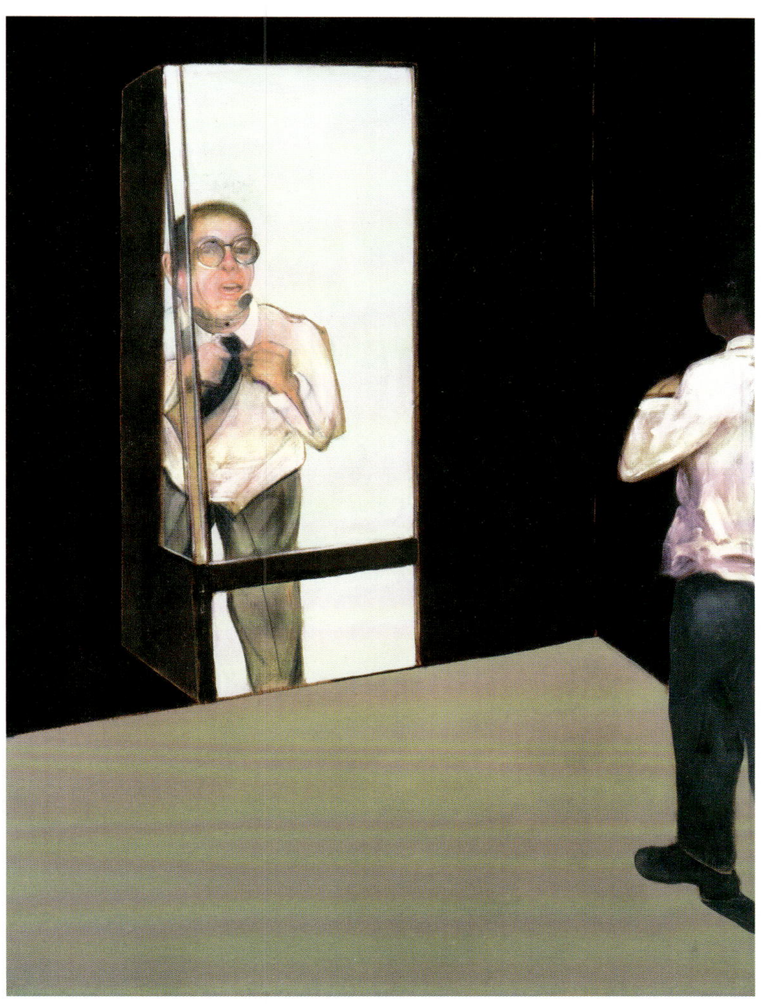

52. *Study for Portrait of Gilbert de Botton*, 1986

Observing the reflection of oneself can be anxiety-provoking. Some people even develop a phobic reaction towards their reflections. Some, who cannot stand seeing their image in the mirror, either remove or destroy all mirrors in their vicinity and try at all cost to avoid mirrors in public spaces. Their body and face appear distorted to them, and they cannot unify their self-perception with the image they observe in the mirror. This condition is often referred to as eisoptrophobia. People who suffer from it often complain that the covering up of mirrors does not help with their condition, since the person does not have a fear of the mirror, but of what she sees inside the mirror. Although the mirror might have been removed or covered, the person still fears that the horrible image will unexpectedly return. The Italian photographer Manuel Colombo tried to capture this phobia in a photograph where we see the back of a person dressed in a red hoody squatting in the woods looking at the ground and around him mirrors in which we can see red hoodies with no discernible body in them.[36] [51] Observing this image one wonders whether the squatting man tries to avoid looking at his self-reflection, but is nonetheless hunted by it in his mind.

While for some, the anxiety-provoking moment can be observing their reflection in Bacon's painting, for others the horror might be the image itself. In some portraits, the mirror that is depicted inside the paintings as the reflective surface in which the depicted head observes itself, might look like an appeasing object: something that presents a solution to putting the order together in what would otherwise be the disorderly body. This happens, for example, in the *Study for Portrait of Gilbert de Botton*, 1986, [52] with the back of a man standing in front of the mirror, and then the reflection of him in the mirror. The man is tying his tie; he looks like a businessman getting ready to go out, wearing a white shirt and ironed trousers, while large round glasses dominate his face. Surprisingly, the man's face is not distorted. The image looks quite realistic, the only perturbing thing being the half scream of the opening of the man's mouth and a dark spot on the left side of the man's chin. Although that spot is detached from the mouth, one gets the impression that it might be coming from it. As Andrew Benjamin points out, in this portrait we have a reflection that both does and does not reflect: 'The split head in the mirror mirrors and yet what comes to be viewed of that which is mirrored – the head outside the mirror – is not the same as the mirrored head. There is more involved here than the mere splitting of the self.'[37] The image in the mirror might very well be taken as an impostor of sorts; it might be that the painter sees an idealised version of his subject reflected in the mirror or that he is guessing that the man he is painting sees himself as someone he is not.

A lot has changed since the time Bacon was working on his self-portraits. Some are now even talking about the end of self-portraits. Hillel Schwartz observed the change in self-portraits already evident at the end of the twentieth century:

> our self-portraits seem neither to anchor nor extend. Why? Perhaps because our likenesses are as fragmented as our lives, and we cannot be sure of our selves from day to day. Perhaps because our false intimacies lash us on to a narcissism ever discontented with likeness. Perhaps because we carom inside a "fictive culture" whose obsession with roleplaying leads to a portraiture as clichéd as it is unstable ... Perhaps because the best we can manage in a world of simulacra is a visage unavoidably generic.[38]

In the twenty-first century, selfies are following ever more closely the ideals of generic images, which is why they are contributing to the continuous extinction of self-portraits from the past. Anxiety over how people appear in public is amplified in times where one's image appears a matter of choice, which is why the desire to look like someone else – that is, to become a 'visual' impostor – has never been greater. Bacon, in his questioning of realism, might at first appear as someone enchanted by the idea of the impostor; however, the destructions he engages in with his paintings, the cracks and lacks which dominate his portraits expose the shaky grounds that are behind the impostor's desire to hold onto a symbolic position and to create an image which will uphold it.

At the end of her study on the imposter, Helene Deutsch pessimistically concluded that the more she was researching this theme, the more she started seeing imposters everywhere: in her friends and acquaintances, and even in herself. Everyone seems to fabricate their identity in accordance with some imaginary concept of self. Deutsch questioned whether there is a difference between the 'normal' and the pathological imposter and whether the identity between ego ideal and the self is actually achieved only by saints, geniuses and psychotics: 'As one's ego ideal can never be completely gratified from *within*, we direct our demands to the external world, *pretending ... that we actually are what we would like to be.*'[39] Great art exposes the futile attempts of such pretending. While Deutsch is right to see elements of imposture in everyone, the problem is not that people pretend that they are what they would like to be, but that they are constantly guessing what they would like to be and which of their images might be socially desirable. As a result, painters in the past often experimented with different self-portraits, in the way that today people take selfie after selfie – never finding the right image.

# Endnotes


1. MacDonald Critchley, *The Divine Banquet of the Brain and Other Essays* (London: Raven Press, 1970).
2. Helene Deutsch, 'The Impostor: Contribution to Ego Psychology of a Type of Psychopath /1955/', in J. R. Meloy, ed. *The Mark of Cain: Psychoanalytic Insight and the Psychopath* (Hillsdale: The Analytic Press, 2001), pp. 115–32.
3. Ibid., p. 126.
4. Pauline Rose Clance and Suzanne Ament Imes, 'The Imposter Phenomenon in High Achieving Women: Dynamics and Therapeutic Intervention', *Psychotherapy: Theory, Research & Practice* 15:3 (1978), pp. 241–47.
5. Jacques Lacan, 'The Mirror Stage as Formative of the Function of the *I* as Revealed in Psychoanalytic Experience', in *Écrits: A Selection*, trans. A. Sheridan (New York: W. W. Norton & Company, 1977).
6. Nicholas Mirzoeff, *How to See the World: An Introduction to Images, from Self-Portraits to Selfies, Maps to Movies, and More* (New York: Basic Books, 2016), p. 42.
7. Craig Brush, *From the Perspective of the Self: Montaigne's Self-Portrait* (New York: Fordham University. Press, 1994).
8. David Sylvester, *The Brutality of Fact: Interviews with Francis Bacon by David Sylvester* (London: Thames & Hudson, 1987), p. 129.
9. Michael Peppiatt, *Francis Bacon: Anatomy of an Enigma* (London: Skyhorse, 2009), p. 164.
10. Ibid.
11. Ibid.
12. P. Greenacre, 'The Relation of the Impostor to the Artist', *The Psychoanalytic Study of the Child,* 13 (1958) pp. 521–40.
13. Sylvester, op. cit., p. 133.
14. Jean Cocteau, *Thomas the Impostor* (London ; New York: Peter Owen, 2002), p. 142.
15. Renata Salecl, *Choice* (London: Profile Books, 2010), p. 133.
16. Sylvester, op. cit., p. 172.
17. Ibid., p. 199.
18. Ibid., p. 194.
19. Peppiatt, op. cit., p. 156.
20. 'Mirrors Multiply the Selfie: The Doppelgänger Dilemma', *Hyperallergic* (8 July, 2013), https://hyperallergic.com/74877/mirrors-multiply-the-selfie-the-doppelganger-dilemma/.
21. Zoe Brown and Marika Tiggemann, 'Attractive Celebrity and Peer Images on Instagram: Effect on Women's Mood and Body Image', *Body Image,* 19 (2016), pp. 37–43.
22. Rachel Cohen, Toby Newton-John & Amy Slater, 'The Relationship between Facebook and Instagram Appearance-Focused Activities and Body Image Concerns in Young Women', *Body Image,* 23 (2017), pp. 183–87.
23. Peppiatt, op. cit., p. 164.
24. Ibid., p. 87.
25. Peter Campbell, 'Francis and Vanessa', *London Review of Books*, 15 March 1984.
26. Michael Peppiatt, *Francis Bacon in Your Blood: A Memoir* (London: Bloomsbury, 2015), p. 182.
27. Jacques Lacan, *Anxiety: The Seminar of Jacques Lacan, Book X*, ed. Jacques-Alain Miller, trans. A. R. Price (Cambridge: Polity Press, 2016).
28. When I observed the detours visitors of this show were making, I decided to join them to see how they were posing anew for the hidden camera. My voyeuristic enjoyment was, however, anxiety-provoking since I knew that I would also be recorded in my act of observing. I felt an impostor of sorts: an ad hoc anthropologist who comes to observe the strange tribe of art visitors, only to discover that she is not so much different from them.
29. Hans Belting, *Face and Mask: A Double* History (Princeton and Oxford: Princeton University Press, 2017).
30. Gilles Deleuze, *Francis Bacon: The Logic of Sensation* (London: A & C Black, 2003), p. 16.
31. Parveen Adams, *The Emptiness of the Image: Psychoanalysis and Sexual Differences* (London: Routledge, 2013), p. 120.
32. Deleuze, op. cit., pp. 51–52.
33. Ibid., pp. 58–59.
34. D. W. Winnicott, *Playing and Reality* (London: Routledge, 2005), p. 157.
35. Ibid.
36. http://www.manuelcolombo.it/phobias.html
37. Andrew Benjamin, *Art, Mimesis and the Avant-Garde: Aspects of a Philosophy of Difference* (London: Routledge, 1991), p. 32.
38. Hillel Schwartz, *The Culture of the Copy: Striking Likenesses, Unreasonable Facsimiles* (New York: Zone Books, 1998), p. 90.
39. Deutsch, op. cit., p. 131.

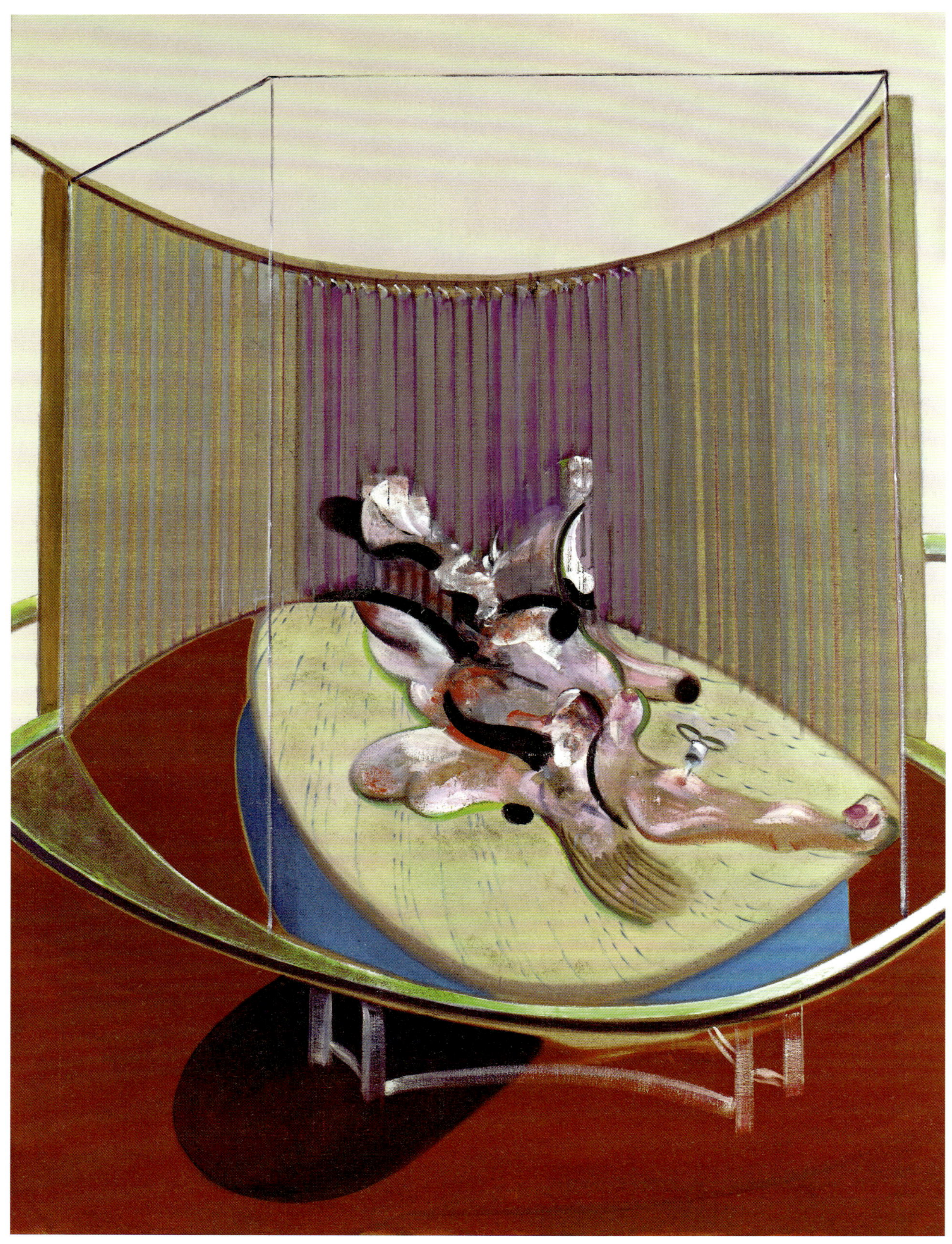

53. *Version No.2 of Lying Figure with Hypodermic Syringe*, 1968

# Looking the Negative in the Face:
# Modernist Painting after Affect

Ben Ware

## Bacon Reading Bacon

**I**

Let us begin with one kind of story about Bacon's modernism.

In a series of interviews with the art critic David Sylvester, Bacon insists that one of the key aims of his painting is to produce in the spectator a certain kind of neuroaesthetic response. The attempt, as Bacon remarks, is to bring the work 'violently' 'onto the nervous system'.[1] The success of this process depends upon the artwork breaking free from any kind of narrative structure, eliminating the 'story-telling aspect'; what has to be avoided at all costs is, the artist says, 'a long diatribe through the brain'.[2] Paraphrasing Paul Valéry, Bacon asserts that what he wants to do is to 'give the *sensation* without the boredom of its conveyance ... [T]he moment the story enters, the boredom comes upon you'.[3]

There are at least two different (but related) ideas at work here. The first, bound up with the notion of art coming 'directly onto the nervous system', is the traditional modernist category of shock. We need not spend too much time here rehearsing the classic points of reference: Baudelaire's use of the term to describe everyday urban experience in the late nineteenth century; 'war shock' as the defining psychological legacy of the great imperialist crisis, 1914–18; 'shock' as the dominant principle of artistic intent among the European post-war avant-gardes. Shock also emerges as central to the aesthetic theories of Walter Benjamin and Bertolt Brecht, where it figures as something genuinely dialectical: both a symptom of capitalist modernity *and* something which can be used against itself as part of a 'technique of awakening' [*Technik des Erwachens*].[4] Brecht's principle of alienation (*Verfremdung*) is, as has been noted, closely tied to the Russian Formalist notion of *ostranenie* – 'making strange'. In a 1917 essay, 'Art as Technique', the Formalist critic Victor Shklovsky speaks of 'the technique of defamiliarization' through which art disrupts automatised modes of perceiving and thinking, freeing the subject from a life-devouring 'habitualization' of mind:

> Art exists that one may recover the sensation of life; it exists to make one feel things, to make the stone *stony. The purpose of art is to impart the sensation of things as they are perceived and not as they are known.* The technique of art is to make objects 'unfamiliar', to make forms difficult, to increase the difficulty and length of perception because the process of perception is an aesthetic end-in-itself and must be prolonged. *Art is a way of experiencing the artfulness of an object; the object is not important.*[5]

Shklovsky's words here lead us directly back to the second key idea that we encounter in Bacon's remarks to Sylvester: namely, sensation. Philosophically speaking, sensation is an altogether more difficult notion than that of shock. In the interviews, Bacon speaks (echoing, and indeed almost paraphrasing, Shklovsky) of art 'bring[ing] [over] the sensation and feeling of life'.[6] In art 'one wants a thing to be as factual as possible and at the same time … deeply suggestive or deeply unlocking of areas of sensation' in a way that goes beyond a 'simple illustration of the object'.[7] Outlining the specific difference between an illustrational and a non-illustrational form, Bacon states: 'the difference is that an illustrational form tells you through the intelligence immediately what the form is about, whereas a non-illustrational form works first upon sensation and then slowly leaks back into the fact.'[8] Why this should be the case remains a question: '[t]his may have to do with how facts themselves are ambiguous, how appearances are ambiguous, and therefore this way of recording form is nearer to the fact by its ambiguity of recording.'[9]

There is, we might say, a kind of hidden dialectic at work here: for Bacon, the essence or truth of a subject is to be found in the distorted recording of its appearance. The artist's brutalised faces and bulging, bruised bodies are in no way 'abstract', but are, rather, a way of arriving at an irreducible truth – a 'fact', as Bacon himself calls it – about the subjects themselves. The paintings therefore *lie* (distort) in order to reveal what 'reality' itself covers over; or, to put the point another way: it is through the 'artificial' (in art) that one gets to the 'real' – a real that is, paradoxically, *more real* than reality itself. As Bacon remarks: 'What I want to do is to distort the thing far beyond the appearance, but in the distortion to bring it back to a recording of the appearance … In one of his letters Van Gogh speaks of the need to make changes in reality, which become lies that are truer than the literal truth. This is the only possible way the painter can bring back the intensity of the reality which he is trying to capture.'[10] We will return to this dialectic again shortly. For now, however, the notion of sensation requires some further unpacking.

One way of thinking about Bacon's own use of the term 'sensation' is to treat it simply as another way of speaking about 'feeling' (he frequently uses the two words together); and, in particular, the kinds of *strong feelings* he hopes his art will capture and 'give over' – as opposed, say, to the 'watered-down lyrical feelings' conveyed by abstract painting.[11] Assuming this identity between sensations and feelings, we might take the further step, suggested by a number of recent theorists, of replacing (the term) 'feelings' with (the term) 'affects' and distinguishing between 'affects' and 'emotions'.[12] Emotions, to put the matter concisely, are *cognitive states*, tied to subjects or selves, which are experienced directly and bound up with existing social and cultural regimes of meaning. Affects, by contrast, are *bodily states*, which are pre-personal, pre-subjective and pre-representational: they are 'forces' or 'intensities' which resist straightforward incorporation into language.[13] For Spinoza in the *Ethics* (who provides what is still the most elegant general definition of the concept), affects are 'affections of the body by which the body's power of acting is increased or diminished, aided or restrained'.[14] 'No one has yet determined what the body can do', Spinoza continues: 'the body itself, simply from the laws of its own nature, can do many things which its mind wonders at.'[15]

While emotions and affects follow different subjective logics, they also, as Fredric Jameson points out, pertain to different temporalities. The temporality of emotion is 'that of past and future, of time as a destiny that can be narrated'; the temporality of affect, by contrast, is 'that of a perpetual present ... a temporal perspective calculated to destroy narrative as such.'[16] Here, then, with the movement from narrative-time to non-time we arrive back with Bacon's aesthetic desire (expressed to Sylvester) to 'give the sensation without the boredom of its conveyance', but now cast in a clearer light: breaking free from narrative structure, eliminating the story-telling element, is a way of moving art beyond the traditional register of emotions and reconfiguring it as a site where one encounters affects. This, one might argue, is an ethical as well as an aesthetic move: the site of affect is also (potentially, at least) an *event site* – a location at which the spectator is jolted out of routinised modes of seeing and experiencing and, in Bacon's words, is 'return[ed] ... to life more violently'.[17] The convulsive bodily *shudder* thus becomes the Baconian aesthetico-ethical experience *par excellence*.

II

As a story about Bacon's art – and, indeed, how one ought to receive it – the preceding sketch can, I want to argue, serve only (and at best) as a partial account – *a philosophical first impression*. Reading the painting – as Bacon himself encourages us to – in terms of its action upon the 'nervous system', its dispensing with representation and narrative to unlock 'sensation', and its capturing of the 'real' through the 'artificial' is now part of a standard theoretical reading of Bacon, which, in different ways, plays out across much of the existing scholarship. At the same time, Bacon's own account of his painting is inextricably bound up with a now-familiar narrative about modernism itself – an addition to a shared set of aesthetico-ideological beliefs running through both the theory and the practice. As Todd Cronan points out: 'A central line of modernist thought turns on the effort to overcome representation in the name of something more direct, more immediate in terms of its capacity to generate bodily or affective experience.'[18] Bacon's desire to produce works that directly impact the beholder's 'nervous system' is thus part of a broader modernist structure of feeling which includes, for example, Matisse's view that '[a] certain blue enters your soul. A certain red has an effect on your blood-pressure';[19] and Kandinsky's vision of the artist as one who 'strive[s] to awaken as yet nameless feelings'.[20] If it is the case, however, that the desire for aesthetic immediacy and affective response play a significant role in the history of modernism – and continue to inform how modernism is understood – then what initial conclusions might we draw? What sorts of problems might affective modernism present? Brecht, for one, has the following to say:

> Then you paint something red and indeterminate, and some people cry at the sight of this red and indeterminate thing because it reminds them of a rose, while other people cry because it reminds them of a child covered in blood who has been torn to bits by flying bombs. Then your task is done, you have produced feelings by means of lines and colours.[21]

For Brecht, then, affective modernism is bourgeois modernism: not only does it substitute (specific) 'meaning' for (subjective) 'feeling', but the feelings which it generates are indeterminate and nameless:

> As painters and subservient spirits to those in power, you could proclaim that the most beautiful and most important feelings are produced by lines and colours ... [Y]ou would not need specific feelings, such as anger at specific injustices or desire for specific things that are being withheld, nor feelings connected with knowledge that provoke feelings which might change the world or change things in specific ways; you would only need quite general, vague, unnameable feelings which are available to everybody.[22]

Moreover, where affective modernism attempts to get the beholder simply to see things 'differently', the aim of art, on Brecht's view, is to bring one to see things 'correctly'.[23]

In what follows, I want to procced if not exactly *with* Brecht then certainly in a *Brechtian spirit*; and my argument will move through three distinct stages. First, I turn to the work of Gilles Deleuze, and specifically Deleuze's 1981 study *Francis Bacon: logique de la sensation* [*Francis Bacon: the logic of sensation* (2003)]. Here Deleuze provides what I take to be a philosophical elaboration of Bacon's own position in the interviews with Sylvester, and thus a continuation of the project of affective modernism.[24] I also take Deleuze's reading to be an important – though ultimately unsuccessful – attempt at an ethical reading of Bacon's work, and, as such, one that requires careful re-evaluation along these lines. Second, I draw the limits of what I term the Bacon/Deleuze reading of Bacon's work: a reading which, centring on the categories of shock, sensation and affect, fails, ultimately, *on its own terms*. Third, I turn to Bacon's *Self-Portrait*, 1971, exploring how the work opens up new lines of philosophical interpretation beyond the affective domain demarcated by Bacon/Deleuze. Specifically, I read the self-portrait as providing an *aesthetic response* to Hegel's remark in the Preface to *Phenomenology of Spirit* concerning beauty's lack of 'strength' and, by contrast, the power of Spirit to look 'the negative in the face'.[25]

**Deleuze and the Ethics of Affective Modernism**

I

Deleuze's book on Bacon begins with the following words:

> Francis Bacon's painting is of a very special violence. Bacon, to be sure, often traffics in the violence of a depicted scene: spectacles of horror, crucifixions, prosthesis and mutilations, monsters. But these are overly facile detours, detours that the artist himself judges severely and condemns in his work. What directly interests him is a violence that is involved only with colour and line: the violence of a sensation (and not of a representation), a static or potential violence, a violence of reaction of expression.[26]

Deleuze here thus distinguishes between sensational violence (the spectacle of mutilations, monsters and screams) and the violence of a sensation (associated with colour and line), which, for him, is the real concern of Bacon's art. Citing a line from the interviews – 'to paint the scream more than the horror' (57) – Deleuze remarks that 'Bacon has always tried to eliminate the "sensational"': he is unconcerned with what *provokes* the sensation. 'When he paints the screaming Pope, there is nothing that might cause horror, and the curtain in front of the Pope is not only a way of isolating him, of shielding him from view; it is rather the way in which the Pope himself sees nothing, and screams *before the invisible*' (27–28). Liberated from the relations of causation and effect, motivation and action, the sensation thus passes via the 'Figure' (Deleuze's term for the image-person in Bacon's work which is beyond the merely illustrative or figurative) directly onto 'the nervous system' (28). In Bacon, as Deleuze writes, '[s]ensation is what is painted. What is painted on the canvas is the body not insofar as it is represented as an object, but insofar as it is experienced as sustaining *this* sensation' (26).

In Bacon's work, then, 'there are nothing but affects', nothing but sensations (29): as Deleuze and Félix Guattari put it in *What is Philosophy?*, the work of art is a 'bloc of sensation[s]'.[27] But, for Deleuze, these accumulated sensations are always tied to movement; or, more specifically, immobility beyond movement, *movement in place*, the 'spasm': 'What fascinates Bacon is not movement [as such], but its effects on an immobile body: heads whipped by the wind or deformed by an aspiration, but also all the interior forces that climb through the flesh. To make the spasm visible' (xii). Bacon's Figures are made of flesh and his concern is thus with the 'invisible forces that model flesh or shake it'. Paul Klee's famous formula – 'Not to render the visible, but to render visible' – is particularly apt here; for, as Deleuze writes, 'Bacon's Figures seem to be one of the most marvellous responses in the history of painting to the question: How can one make invisible forces visible?' (40–1). The problem of rendering invisible forces visible – of capturing invisible forces as they impact flesh – is clearly dramatised in Bacon's series of heads and self-portraits:

> [T]he extraordinary agitation of these heads is derived not from a movement that the series would supposedly reconstitute, but rather from the forces of pressure, dilation, contraction, flattening, and elongation that are exerted on the immobile head. They are like the forces of the cosmos confronting an intergalactic traveller immobile in his capsule. It is as if invisible forces were striking the head from many different angles. (41–42)

In the heads and self-portraits, the distortions and deformations (the smudged and wiped over parts of the face) 'mark', as Deleuze puts it, 'the zone at which the force is in the process of striking' (42). But there is an important ethical dimension at work here too, which Deleuze is keen to highlight. The invisible forces 'are nothing other than forces from the future … diabolical powers of the future knocking at the door' – in a word, *death*. But by turning to face death – having life literally scream *at* death as some of Bacon's canvasses do – 'death is no longer this all-too-visible thing that makes us faint; it is the invisible force that life detects, flushes out and makes visible …. Death is judged from the point of view of life, and not the reverse, as we like to believe' (44). What we thus encounter in Bacon's work is, then, a 'declaration of faith in life' (43): the artist's Figures, through both their insistence and their presence, 'call for an even more intense life' (44).

There is another and related way in which the Deleuzean reading might also be conceived as an ethical one. The Baconian Figure is a 'body without organs' (BWO) – which is not to say an actual body deprived of organs (although Bacon's paintings are populated by collapsed bodies, reduced to mounds of pure flesh), but rather the virtual, de-stratified body that is opposed not to the organs as such 'but to the organisation of the organs called the organism'.[28] The term 'body without organs' is drawn from the late writings of Antonin Artaud (specifically his radio play *To Have Done with the Judgment of God*), where Artaud writes that 'Man is sick because he is badly constructed'; his 'true freedom' will only be 'restored' when he has been made 'a body without organs'.[29] In *A Thousand Plateaus*, Deleuze and Guattari describe the BWO as not a 'concept', strictly speaking, but rather 'a practice, a set of practices' aimed at the 'experimental' dis-organ-isation of the organic body: 'Is it really so sad and dangerous to be fed up with seeing with your eyes, breathing with your lungs, swallowing with your mouth, talking with your tongue, thinking with your brain, having an anus and larynx, head and legs? Why not walk on your head, sing through your sinuses, see through your skin, breathe through your belly?'[30] More than a mere experimental procedure, however, the BWO also names a programme of radical depersonalisation, one that is specifically opposed to psychoanalysis:

> The BWO is what remains when you take everything away' – namely, the entire domain of fantasy, interpretation, subjectification and self: where psychoanalysis says, "Stop, find your self again," we should say instead, "Let's go further still, we haven't found our BWO organs yet, we haven't sufficiently dismantled our self."[31]

Slightly different from the question of *how* one makes oneself a BWO is the question of *what* comes to pass on the BWO – what kind of a body is it exactly? To this Deleuze and Guattari provide an answer: 'A BWO is made in such a way that it can be occupied, populated *only* by intensities [affects].'[32] As Deleuze puts it in the book on Bacon, '[the BWO] is an intense and intensive body. It is traversed by a wave that traces levels or thresholds in the body according to the variations of its amplitude' (32). But the BWO is not only traversed by intensities, it also *causes* them: 'The BWO causes intensities to pass; it produces and distributes them.'[33] And here we arrive at the potentially ethical point: engaging, through Bacon's works, with the 'intensive fact of the body' can, according to Deleuze, have a transformative, enlivening effect – it can open up new desires, new combinations of affect, new possibilities of life. Indeed, engaging with Bacon's artistic dismantling of the organ*ism* ('What is a mouth at one level becomes an anus at another level' (35)), can itself be part of the process by which we make *ourselves* a BWO:

> [Painting] invests the eye through color and line. But *it does not treat the eye as a fixed organ*. It liberates lines and colors from their representative function, but at the same time it also liberates the eye from its adherence to the organism, from its character as a fixed and qualified organ: the eye becomes virtually the polyvalent indeterminate organ that sees the body without the

organs (the Figure) as a pure presence. Painting gives us eyes all over: in the ear, in the stomach, in the lungs (the painting breathes ...)' (37)

II

While Deleuze's reading significantly raises the philosophical stakes of Bacon's art, it nevertheless fits seamlessly with Bacon's own account of his work given in the interviews with Sylvester. Indeed, we might say that Deleuze's study manages to accomplish two things simultaneously: it applies the author's own ready-made philosophical system to Bacon's painting[34] *and* it provides a conceptual restatement of Bacon's own position vis-à-vis his art. The philosopher and the artist thus become bound together in an intimate and at times disorienting way. Who, we might ask, in Deleuze's book, is speaking at any given moment? Is philosophy here leading art or is art leading philosophy? Why does Deleuze (the critical philosopher) uncritically accept Bacon's reading of Bacon? Rather than attempting to answer these questions, we might instead conclude that we find ourselves with a new composite – Bacon/ Deleuze – which conceives of Bacon's work in a threefold sense: (i) as concerned with capturing *lived reality*, where reality is seen in terms of intensities, flows and forces; (ii) as engaged in a process of rethinking the human, or more specifically, thinking *beyond* the well-ordered, coherently organised human; and (iii) as bypassing representation in order to act directly upon the spectator's 'nervous system'.

While it would, of course, be entirely vacuous to claim that this Bacon/ Deleuze reading of Bacon is simply incorrect, in what follows I want to suggest that it presents us with a highly problematic account of modernist painting, one which ultimately runs up against the limits of its own logic.

### Bacon/Deleuze and the Unravelling of Affect

I

At one point in his study, Deleuze turns to Bacon's battle against the cliché. 'It would be a mistake', Deleuze remarks, 'to think that the painter works on a white and virgin surface. The entire surface is already invested virtually with all kinds of clichés' (8). The task of the artist is thus not to cover a blank canvas, but rather to 'empty it out, clear it, clean it' (61) – to sweep away the world of ready-made ideas and perceptions that is already present upon it. In Bacon's case, according to Deleuze, this fight against the cliché follows a particular logic. (i) In the first instance, there are 'figurative givens' (*données figuratives*) – representations, clichés, doxa, produced by memories, photographs, cinematic or television images, collected pieces of newspaper or magazine text – which the artist must collect and fully enter into. These form the basis of any initial image. (ii) The initial image is then subject to what Deleuze calls a *catastrophe* (71): the painter (Bacon) intervenes to disrupt 'optical coherence' with 'random' or 'chance' marks made upon the canvas; or by scrubbing, sweeping or wiping the canvas with a rag, brush or sponge; or by throwing paint, at different speeds and from different angles, onto the canvas. (iii) Finally, out of the catastrophe and chaos (and if the painting is successful), a new figuration emerges – that of the Figure. In order to evolve into the Figure, the random marks and distortions must be incorporated back into the 'visual whole' in a way that produces a 'violent' and 'precise' sensation acting directly upon the nervous system (76–77).

As a description of Bacon's artistic practice, this certainly coheres with what the artist himself has to say both in the interviews with Sylvester and elsewhere. However, one cannot help reading this account of modernist production as a sort of recipe – a recipe for a certain kind of *monotonous production*.[35] While monotony and repetition need not necessarily preclude artistic ingenuity and invention, the problem, we might say, in this specific instance, arises at the level of the *affective demand*. For Bacon/Deleuze, the artwork's ultimate success depends upon it having a certain kind of traumatic effect: each work *must* come across directly onto the beholder's nervous system, bringing about a 'violent' aesthetic shock or 'great intensity'. Returning to Brecht, however, we might ask why the ultimate purpose of an artwork should be always and everywhere *the same*: to produce in the viewer an affective response, regardless of the specific nature of this response and indeed, regardless of *who* the viewer is or *when* or *where* she is? If the focus is exclusively on affective response, then how do we account for what exactly compels our interest in a certain work (or body of work) over, say, anything else which might produce a similar response? Moreover, if affect is all that counts, then does this mean (as surely it must) that if Bacon's works fail to make an impact on the spectator's 'nerves', then they fail *tout court*, fail as works of artistic modernism? If these are questions that Bacon/Deleuze cannot answer, then this is because the problems undergirding them aren't just problems with a specific reading of Bacon's painting: they are problems with affective modernism itself – affective modernism, that is, *as a discourse about modernism*. The difficulties for Bacon/Deleuze and their account of modernism do not, however, end here.

For Bacon/Deleuze, moments of 'shock', 'sensation' and 'great intensity' in Bacon's work are tied (almost exclusively) to scenes of 'abjection' (11) – vomiting [54], screaming [55], excreting [36], intravenous drug use [53]; and thus, as Deleuze writes, '[a]bjection becomes splendour, the horror of life becomes a very pure and very intense life' (37). Not only does this connection between abjection and affect create problems for the strict separation between representation and sensation that Bacon/Deleuze wish to maintain, it also highlights a broader issue relating directly back to the problem of the cliché. Writing about the relation between art (in this case photography) and affect, Susan Sontag comments as follows:

> Photographs shock insofar as they show something novel. Unfortunately, the ante keeps getting raised – partly through the very proliferation of such images of horror. One's first encounter with the photographic inventory of ultimate horror is a kind of revelation, the prototypically modern revelation: a negative epiphany. … Once one has seen such images, one has started down the road of seeing more – and more. Images transfix. Images anesthetise. … The shock of photographed atrocities wears off with repeated viewings, just as the surprise and bemusement felt the first time one sees a pornographic movie wears off after one sees a few more.[36]

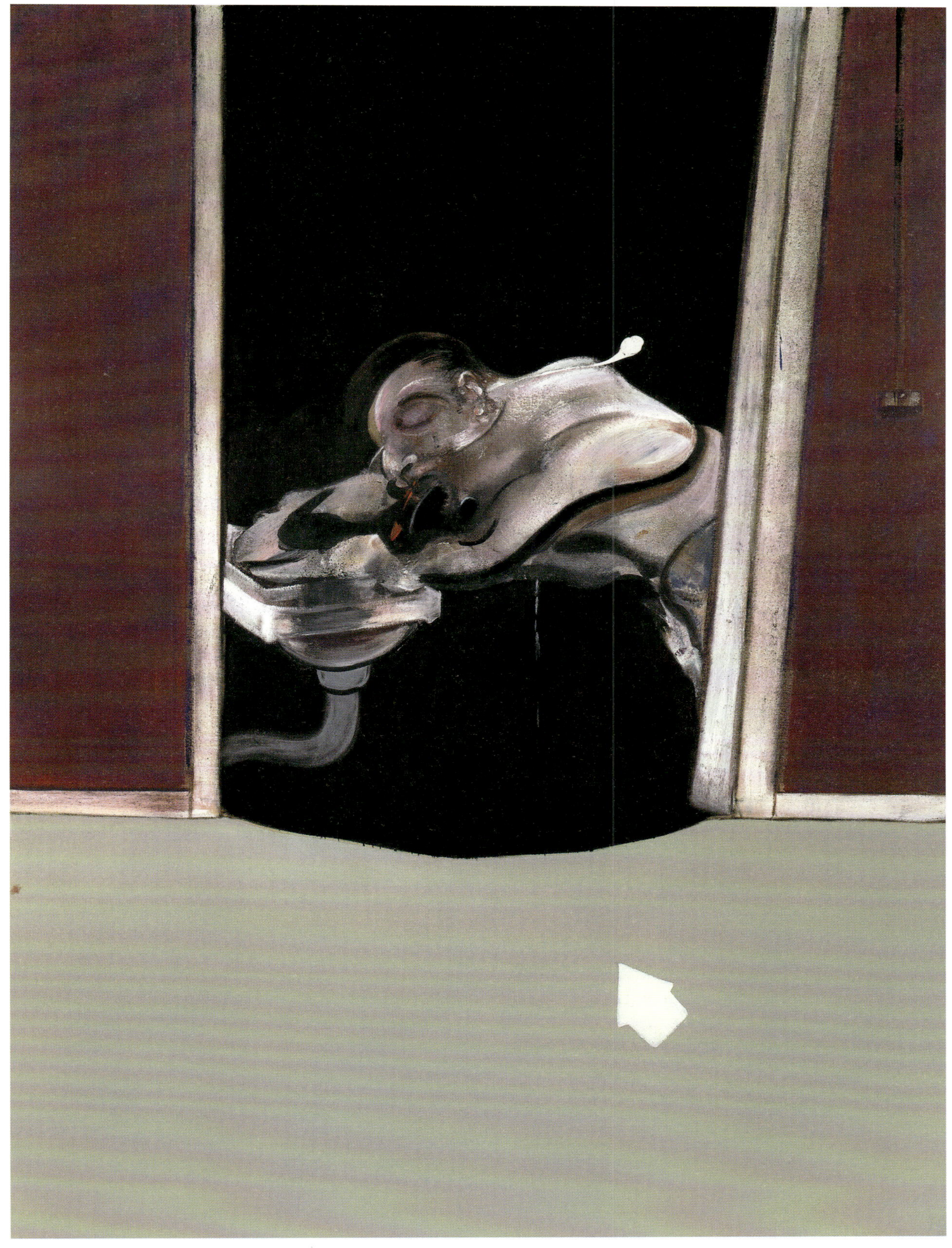

**54.** *Triptych May–June 1973* (right panel)

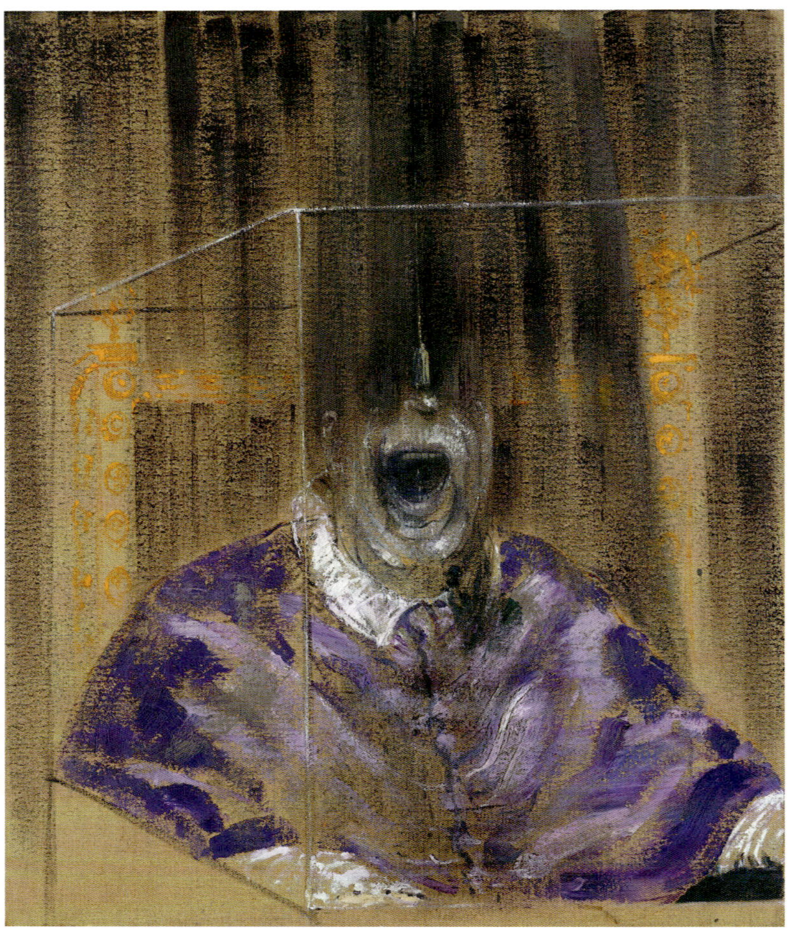

55. *Head VI*, 1949

It is not difficult to see how Sontag's remarks here might raise further conceptual questions for Bacon/Deleuze. If art operates primarily at the level of shock, sensation and affect, it forever runs the risk of not being 'enough', of the spectator always desiring 'more', and of the artist having constantly to 'raise the stakes'.[37] As Fred Botting puts it: 'A negative dialectic of shock thus emerges at the abyssal core of modern experience: the more thrills that are presented the more shocks and sensations there have to be to avoid the process of habituation and assimilation.'[38] But not only this. Rather than being the source of enlivenment, images acting violently upon the nervous system can, as Sontag suggests, have an anaesthetising effect, deadening the mind and blunting the senses: excitation gives way to boredom; moral responsiveness transforms into cynical detachment; the scream reproduces itself on the face of the spectator as a yawn. In such a context (where the desire for an affective surplus from the work of art becomes a desire for *more of the same* (the cliché); where shock-addiction and shock-absorption work together to maintain a benumbed homeostasis (the flattening of affect)), Deleuze's remark linking 'the horror of life' to the 'very pure' and 'very intense' life reads like a misplaced fantasy regarding art's redemptive power. Much more apposite here is

Walter Benjamin's observation concerning soldiers returning from the front line at the end of World War I: having experienced affective and psychic overload during battle, these individuals, Benjamin remarks, had 'grown silent – not richer, but poorer in communicable experience'.[39] If modernism is indeed 'war becoming art, an art of pure violence',[40] then it must be considered – in a way that Bacon/Deleuze simply do not – that one of the effects of this violence, as it operates directly and repetitively upon the spectator's nerves, will be a hardening to violence as such – the atrophying of a certain experiential capacity and with it a running up against *emotional indifference* and *shock-loss*.

II

Bacon/Deleuze do not stand alone: they are part of a tradition of affective modernists who place special emphasis on the potential insights derived from suffering and shock, on the transformative possibilities of the traumatic encounter – be it in art or life. Nietzsche, for example, adopting the Dionysian point of view, regards suffering as desirable. 'The discipline of suffering, of *great* suffering', he writes in *Beyond Good and Evil*, is that alone which 'has created every elevation of mankind hitherto … its strength, its terror at the sight of great destruction, its inventiveness and bravery in undergoing, enduring, interpreting, exploiting misfortune, and whatever of depth, mystery, mask, spirit, cunning and greatness'. In the face of those who wish to 'abolish suffering' and enhance 'wellbeing', Nietzsche proposes exactly the opposite: '*we* would rather increase it and make it worse than it has ever been.'[41] According to Freud, in his 1915 text 'Thoughts for the Times on War and Death', war 'sweep[s] away [our] conventional treatment of death'. With war, '[d]eath can no longer be denied; we are forced to believe in it. People really die; and no longer one by one, but many, often tens of thousands, in a single day.' And yet precisely because of this surplus of violence and suffering, precisely because of its radical proximity to life, 'life', Freud remarks, 'has … become interesting again; it has recovered its full content.'[42] Both Nietzsche and Freud here betray an intellectual debt to Schopenhauer, who, in *The World as Will and Representation*, connects 'the knowledge of death' and 'the consideration of the suffering and misery of life' with the 'impulse to philosophical reflection'.[43] However, in his essay on war and death, having noted our general tendency to exclude death from our thinking, Freud goes on to make an important observation about the relation between death and art:

> It is an inevitable result of [the general exclusion of death from life] that we should seek in the world of [art] compensation for what has been lost in life. There we still find people who know how to die – who, indeed, even manage to kill someone else. There alone too the condition can be fulfilled which makes it possible for us to reconcile ourselves with death: namely, that behind all the vicissitudes of life we should still be able to preserve a life intact. … We die with the hero with whom we have identified ourselves; yet we survive him, and are ready to die again just as safely with another hero.[44]

Freud here makes a number of points which open up a new perspective on Bacon/ Deleuze and the aesthetic ideologies underpinning affective modernism. Crucially,

Freud argues that art provides life with its missing content. Because of our tendency
to insulate ourselves against death, life becomes 'impoverished', routinised, its
interest diminished – akin, in Freud's words, to an 'American flirtation in which
it is understood from the first that nothing can happen'.[45] Art, then, provides
compensation for what has been lost in life (a point later echoed by the poet
Wallace Stevens).[46] Applying this insight to Bacon/Deleuze, we might say that the
preoccupation with 'violence', 'sensation' and new 'affective intensities' is also a way
of placing art – art, that is, of a certain kind – in the role of that which compensates
for a perceived loss of meaningful experience. As Bacon repeats in his interviews
with Sylvester, the post-war world is something 'banal', 'utterly boring', 'purposeless',
'meaningless' – people's desire for 'security' and 'social justice' has made life
'pointlessly artificial'. The artist's tone is often strikingly Nietzschean:

> I think that being nursed by the state from the cradle to the grave would bring
> such a boredom to life. … I can't think of anything more boring than that
> everything was looked after for you from your birth to your death. But people
> seem to expect that and think it is their right. I think that, if people have that
> attitude to life, it curtails … the creative instinct. … I never believe that one
> should have any security.
> [...]
> I'm not upset by the fact that people do suffer, because I think the suffering of
> people and the differences between people are what have made great art, and
> not egalitarianism.[47]

If one is to take these remarks seriously – as I think a Bacon/Deleuze-type reading
must do – then it isn't too much of a leap to read Bacon's art (at least in part) as a
response to – and indeed an attack upon – the so-called 'post-war consensus' and,
specifically, the welfare state, defined here as a social structure in which the subject
is 'nursed to oblivion'. Producing art aimed at 'unlocking sensation' and opening-up
a 'very intense life', thus becomes part of an attempt to counter a certain politically
induced creative and affective levelling; the means by which existence itself might
recover its significant depths. And yet here, precisely, is the paradox: while Bacon
repeats to Sylvester that his art captures a *deeper sense of reality* – that it gives us
the 'intensity' of things as they *really are* after various screens and veils have been
cleared away – this deeper sense of reality turns out to be, in one sense, if one
follows the logic of Bacon's own claims, nothing other than *the ideological reality of
affective modernism itself*: life is devoid of *real* meaning; the individual is a subject
of private and essentially ineffable feelings; the role of the artwork is to provoke
violent sensations which return the subject to 'life', even though life itself is 'nothing
but pure affects'.

The Bacon/Deleuze account would thus seem to arrive at a theoretical dead-
end, pointing to nothing beyond the discursive framework in which it itself is
embedded. How, then, might we begin to steer a course beyond this affective
register? How might we prise open new and hitherto unseen philosophical aspects of
Bacon's work? Turning to a specific example from the artist's oeuvre will allow us to
re-focus our investigations.

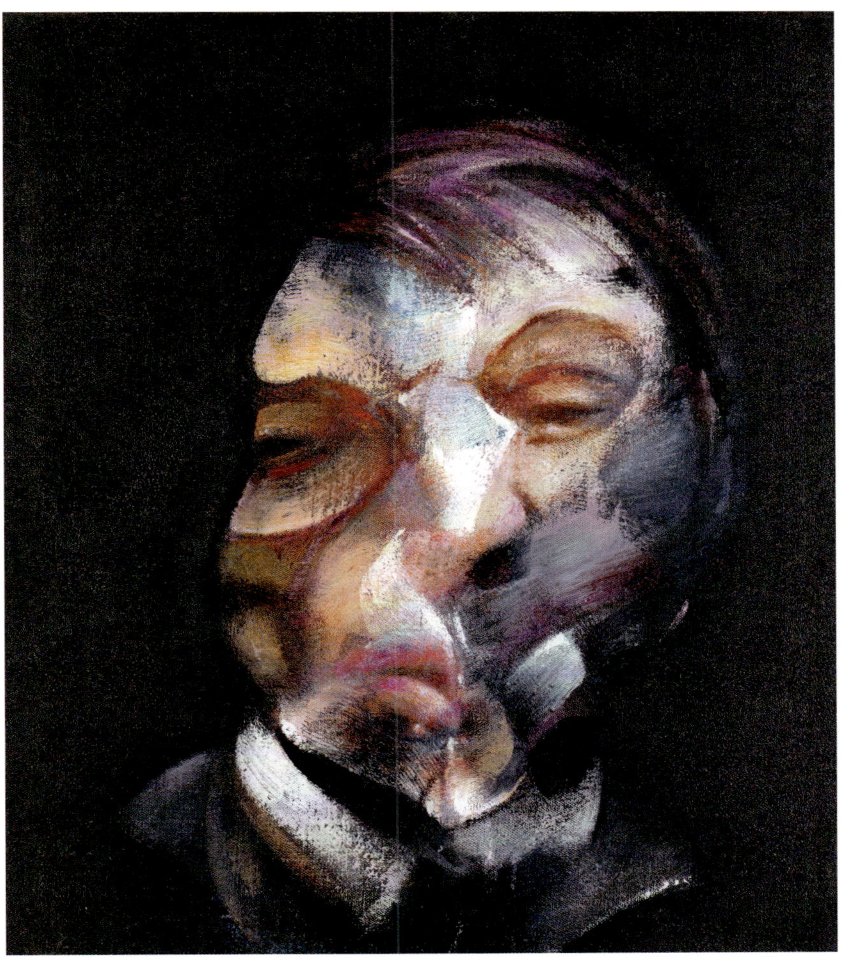

56. *Self-Portrait*, 1971

## Self-Portrait, 1971: Looking the Negative in the Face

Bacon's *Self-Portrait*, 1971, [56] is the first in a series of self-portraits which the artist painted in the 1970s, following the death of his lover George Dyer. When asked by Sylvester, at the end of the decade, why he had painted so many self-portraits, Bacon's simple reply was that there 'wasn't anyone else around to paint'.[48] At a basic level, then, the artist's gaze turns from the other (real or imagined) to the self, to the activity of self-scrutiny. But here the philosophical stakes are also raised to the next level. As T. J. Clark points out, 'the look' of self-portraiture is of a very specific kind: 'it is the look of someone looking at him– or herself looking'; or, more specifically, it is the 'look of someone looking at him– or herself looking at the look he or she has when it is a matter of looking not just at anything, at something else, but back to the place from which one is looking'.[49] But why, we might ask, is the artist necessarily best placed to judge what he (in Bacon's case) looks like when he looks at himself looking? How does the mirror or photograph come to provide access to the artist's *true* self? Isn't there always something within self-observation that remains unobserved – namely, the act of observation itself – which necessarily precludes the artist from ever *entirely* observing himself? If the artist responds that he paints simply what *he* sees (and feels), then this hardly strikes one as an adequate reply. Just as there can be (as Wittgenstein reminds us) no 'private language', so, we might say, there can be no 'private seeing': the question 'what do I see?' (or 'what am I for myself?') is always bound up with the questions 'what do *others* see?', 'what do *others* want from me?' and 'what am I for *others*?' Bacon's repetitive production of self-portraits in the 1970s (twenty-nine in total between 1971 and 1979) might thus be seen as dramatising the anxieties of a subject faced with the challenge of representing itself; representing, as Roland Barthes puts it, 'the [self] I think I am [and] the [self] I want others to think I am'.[50]

If self-portraiture poses a distinct challenge for the artist, then equally so for the viewer. While we, as spectators, might believe that we are able to look at the self-portrait from a safe and objective distance, what we quickly come to see, in fact, is that our look has already been anticipated, that our presence as spectators has already been taken into account. It is the self-portrait that gazes at us – not the other way around; and of course we can never see the self-portrait from the place at which it sees us.[51] Rather than simply standing 'outside' the self-portrait, then, we are, from the very beginning, intimately involved in it, our look, in one sense, already a part of the work's 'content'.[52] But the issue goes even further than this; for with the self-portrait not only are we involved in a relationship with the representational image of the artist, we are also brought into a relationship with the whole form of life implied by the image: an objective world of power relations, modes of production, social bonds and networks of signification. How, then, we need to ask, do specific instances of self-representation stand in relation to their own socio-historical reality? In what ways do they support or disrupt existing regimes of meaning which condition the making of 'likenesses'?

In relation to *Self-Portrait*, 1971, one of the first things that we notice is that the face isn't one face but two; or rather two faces sutured to make one (note the faint seam running from the base of the chin up to the bottom of the nose). The hair, forehead and right eye (the subject's left) appear almost realist in execution (the texture and fall of the hair, for example, with the fringe sweeping across the forehead and sitting just above the eye); what disrupts, however, is the zone of white, which covers most of this part of the face and two-thirds of the nose, giving the appearance of a mask, such as might be worn by a burns victim to conceal scar tissue. The right cheek is a smeared grey colour patch, which descends to cancel out the right side of the mouth. The left part of the mouth, by contrast, is intact (the pinkish-grey lips plump and slightly parted); while the left chin and cheek (composed of smears of brown, cream, white, black and purple) give over the appearance of someone who has been badly beaten up.[53]

This is no portrait of the artist, traditionally conceived: the artist is not 'at work' in his studio; there are no artist's tools on display; there are no clear markers of 'elevated' social status. If the subject is absorbed at all here, it is, it would appear, at least at first blush, only with his own alienation. And yet, this can't be the whole story. It is the right eye of the portrait which immediately commands our attention: the gaze, at once vulnerable and imperious, melancholic and deeply contemplative, issues down past the beholder with a kind of assured indifference. The gaze of the left eye follows the logic of the right, but the eye itself is a mere gouge, a wound, a carved subtraction from the left side of the face. Moving out to the left side of this wounded eye, we notice a thin black line running down the whole left side of the face, the purpose of which seems to be to prevent the face from collapsing, to keep the flesh securely in place. But the line also accentuates *flatness*, turning the *entire face* into a mask. Here we should avoid any obvious questions about what the mask might conceal (the artist's 'true' self? a comic mask beneath the tragic one? an infinite number of identical masks?) and instead ask: what is the meaning of *the form of the mask itself* – what sort of philosophical work is the 'appearance' doing?

The self-portrait, we might say, shares the condition of the mortuary mask: it is, by temporal necessity, always a portrait of death. The subject in the painting is caught at a particular moment in time, but that moment is forever past, and thus the subject is no longer with us (regardless of whether they are literally alive or dead). In a discussion of portrait photography (which applies equally well to self-portraiture), Barthes remarks that 'the Photograph ... represents that very subtle moment when ... I am neither subject nor object but a subject who feels he is becoming an object: I then experience a micro-version of death ... I am truly becoming a spectre.'[54] Bacon's *Self-Portrait* both confirms these observations and submits them to a neat dialectical reversal: the face-as-mask presses home the point that artistic representations of the self always involve the negation of life, a process of objectification and mortification; however, this process (becoming a spectre, in Barthes words) appears, in Bacon's case, to be the very means by which the subject is *brought back to life* – brought back to life, that is to say, *as a mask*, which looks death in the face. At this point, then, we might recall the crucial passage in the Preface of Hegel's *Phenomenology of Spirit*:

> Death, if that is what we want to call this non-actuality, is of all things the most dreadful, and to hold fast what is dead requires the greatest strength. Lacking strength, Beauty hates the Understanding for asking of her what she cannot do. But the life of Spirit is not the life that shrinks from death and keeps itself untouched by devastation, but rather the life that endures it and maintains itself in it. It wins its truth only when, in utter dismemberment, it finds itself. It is this power, not as something positive, which closes its eyes to the negative, as when we say of something that it is nothing or it is false, and then, having done with it, turn away and pass on to something else; on the contrary, Spirit is this power only by looking the negative in the face, and tarrying with it.[55]

Bacon's *Self-Portrait* might be read as an aesthetic comment upon this passage in two (related) ways. First, as suggested above, while the mask, in one sense, objectifies and effaces the subject, it is also what animates it ('converts it into being') – providing subjectivity itself with its necessary, fictional support. To the extent that the subject in the painting is looking at itself looking, it is looking right out at death, facing it head on, 'looking the negative in the face, and tarrying with it', as Hegel puts it. In the case of the *Self-Portrait*, however, this is no mere passive process: the figure is literally decomposing right in front of its (and our) own eyes, but nevertheless manages to 'endure' and 'maintain itself' in its state of utter 'devastation'. 'Every day in the mirror I watch death at work,'[56] Bacon remarks at one point to Sylvester, citing Jean Cocteau.[57]

Asked by Sylvester when the realisation of death first came upon him, Bacon replies: I realized when I was seventeen. I remember it very, very clearly. I remember looking at a dog-shit on the pavement, and suddenly I realized, there it is – this is what life is like. ... [I]t tormented me for months.[58] This humorous and apparently naïve remark conceals an astute dialectical point: the subject finds its truth – discovers the truth about 'life' – not in some positive epiphany, but rather with a little piece of 'dreadful' bodily waste – the death-like excremental element.

The second way in which the *Self-Portrait* responds to Hegel's passage is in relation to the remark regarding beauty's lack of 'strength' (a remark which, for the time being, it will be necessary to read largely apart from Hegel's account of beauty in the *Lectures on Fine Art*).[59] In the *Self-Portrait*, the subject-as-mask is not monstrous or grotesque (contra affective readings, it doesn't provoke shock or horror); rather it occupies a very specific place within the domain of aesthetics: that of the ugly. For the Hegelian Karl Rosenkranz, the category of the ugly operates primarily as beauty's dialectical foil: 'If there were no beauty, then there certainly would not be any ugliness, since the latter only exists as the negation of the former.'[60] Despite this dialectical connection, ugliness, for Rosenkranz, remains bound up with artistic imperfection and deformity. In *Aesthetic Theory*, Adorno switches the terms of this relationship: 'If one originated in the other, it is beauty that originated in the ugly and not the reverse.'[61] 'Beauty', for Adorno, 'is not the platonically pure beginning but rather something that originated in the renunciation of what was once feared, which only as a result of this renunciation – retrospectively, so to speak, according to its own telos – became the ugly.'[62] When Hegel speaks of beauty 'lacking strength' (a statement which is bound up with his general verdict on Romantic art),[63] his point is that beauty (as he sees it) is incapable of tolerating anything disruptive: it cannot countenance ambiguity and imperfection and must remain, at all costs, *pure* (a 'circle that remains self-enclosed').[64] More fundamentally, beauty cannot face 'the tremendous power of the negative':[65] it knows not (nor does it wish to know) of devastation and death. While the historical Hegel is unable to grasp the possibility of an art that is adequate to the negating/creative power of his own philosophical system,[66] he *does* suggest the possibility of a different kind of art: one involving 'the self-transcendence of art *but within its own sphere and in the form of art itself*.[67] Here, as Robert Pippin neatly suggests, Hegel can be taken to prophesise modernism.[68] Within modernism, however, it is, we might argue, the category of the ugly specifically – of which Bacon's *Self-Portrait* is a compelling expression – that does what beauty *cannot* do: it takes up for itself the radical power of the negative and looks death squarely in the face.

It would be incorrect to suggest that in our own time ugliness no longer possess aesthetic force.[69] What Bacon himself perceived (and what an artwork such as *Self-Portrait* transforms into a kind of philosophical thesis) was – and remains – true: within the context of damaged life beauty is on the side of *illusion* – failing, in its blind positivity, to register any trace of human destruction and domination; and on the side of *cruelty* – taming and idealising the 'threatening materiality of nature and the human body'.[70] In this respect, it is ugliness, and ugliness alone, that becomes the necessary means for reconnecting, via the negative (that is, via death), art, truth and the moral life.[71] But this is not an ugliness entangled in shock and sensation, an ugliness straining (and failing) to work on the spectator's 'nervous system'; but rather an ugliness which (in Hegel's words) 'invites us to intellectual consideration', which asks us to interrogate, once again, and philosophically, 'what art is'.[72] Such an ugliness is also not a 'redemptive' ugliness, one holding out the 'promise' of a new beauty to come (as if the theology of beauty had been right all along); it is instead what we might call a *negative ugliness*: one existing purely for its own sake as a kind of *death living a human life*. Can we tarry with such an idea without thought being moved from the aesthetic and the philosophical to the ethical and, finally, the political: to a world in which the bonds of mutuality and solidarity have been severed, but also one in which – as Bacon's *Self-Portrait* makes clear – the appearance of the 'natural' (dare we say, the *natural order of things*) needs to be overcome and a new kind of 'reinvented' *realism* put in its place?

# Endnotes

1.  David Sylvester, *Interviews with Francis Bacon* (London: Thames & Hudson, 2016), p. 12.

2.  Ibid., pp. 63 & 18.

3.  Ibid., p. 65.

4.  Walter Benjamin, *The Arcades Project*, trans. Howard Eiland and Kevin McLaughlin (Cambridge, MA: The Belknap Press of Harvard University Press, 1999), KI, 1.

5.  Viktor Shklovsky, 'Art as Technique', in *Russian Formalist Criticism: Four Essays*, trans. Lee T. Lemon & Marion J. Reis (Lincoln: University of Nebraska Press, 1965), p. 12 (emphasis added).

6.  Sylvester, op. cit., p. 49.

7.  Ibid., p. 65.

8.  Ibid., pp. 65–66.

9.  Ibid., p. 66.

10. Ibid., pp. 46, 194. Bacon repeats this point, which he describes as 'a very complex thing', to Michael Peppiatt. See Michael Peppiatt, *Francis Bacon in your Blood: A Memoir* (London: Bloomsbury, 2015), p. 164.

11. Sylvester, op. cit., p. 69.

12. See, for example, Fredric Jameson, *The Antinomies of Realism* (London: Verso, 2013), 29ff.; *The Ancients and the Postmoderns: On the Historicity of Forms* (London: Verso, 2015), p. 30. Jameson here follows Rei Terada's idea (derived from Kant) that affects are bodily feelings, while emotions (or passions) are conscious states. According to Jameson, 'the latter have objects, the former are bodily sensations' (*Antinomies*, p. 32). See also Rei Terada, *Feeling in Theory: Emotion after the 'Death of the Subject'* (Cambridge, MA: Harvard University Press, 2001).

13. On the emotions, see, for example, Martha Nussbaum, *Upheavals of Thought: The Intelligence of Emotions.* (Cambridge: Cambridge University Press, 2003); Amelie Rorty, *Explaining Emotions* (Berkeley: University of California Press, 1980); Robert Solomon, *The Passions: Emotion and the Meaning of Life* (Indianapolis: Hackett, 1993). On affect, see, for example, Melissa Gregg and Gregory J. Seigworth, *The Affect Theory Reader* (Durham NC: Duke University Press, 2010); Brain Massumi, *Parables of the Virtual: Movement, Affect, Sensation* (Durham NC: Duke University Press, 2002); Steven Shaviro, *Post-Cinematic Affect* (Alresford, Hants: O-Books, 2010). For an excellent critique of the contemporary 'affective turn', see Ruth Leys, *The Ascent of Affect: Genealogy and Critique* (Chicago: University of Chicago Press, 2017).

14. Benedict Spinoza, *Ethics*, trans. Edwin Curley (London: Penguin, 1996), p. 70.

15. Ibid., pp. 71–72.

16. Jameson, *The Ancients and the Postmoderns*, op. cit., p. 31.

17. Sylvester, op. cit., p. 161.

18. Todd Cronan, *Against Affective Formalism: Matisse, Bergson, Modernism* (Minneapolis: University of Minnesota Press, 2013), p. 1.

19. Henri Matisse, 'An Interview with Verdet, 1952', in *Matisse on Art*, ed. Jack D. Flam (New York: E. P. Dutton, 1978), p. 143.

20. Wassily Kandinsky, 'Concerning the Spiritual in Art', in *Art in Theory: 1900–1990*, ed. Charles Harrison & Paul Wood (London: Blackwell, 1992), p. 88.

21. Bertolt Brecht, 'On Non-Representational Painting', in *Brecht on Art and Politics*, ed. Steve Giles & Tom Kuhn, trans. Laura Bradley, Steve Giles & Tom Kuhn (London: Methuen, 2005), pp. 240–41.

22. Ibid., p. 240.

23. Ibid., p. 241.

24. Deleuze's reading has now become the hegemonic philosophical approach to Bacon, for reasons I go on to make clear. For an insightful counter to Deleuze's text, however, based on a close and detailed engagement with Bacon's work, see Martin Harrison, 'Painting, Smudging', in *Francis Bacon: New Studies – Centenary Essays*, ed. Martin Harrison (Göttingen: Steidl, 2009).

25. G. W. F. Hegel, *Phenomenology of Spirit*, trans. A. V. Miller (Oxford: Oxford University Press, 1977), p. 19.

26. Gilles Deleuze, *Francis Bacon: The Logic of Sensation*, trans. Daniel W. Smith (London: Bloomsbury, 2013), p. xii. Hereafter page numbers will be given in parentheses in the text.

27. Gilles Deleuze & Félix Guattari, *What is Philosophy?* trans. Graham Burchell & Hugh Tomlinson (London: Verso, 1994), p. 164.

28. Gilles Deleuze & Félix Guattari, *A Thousand Plateaus: Capitalism and Schizophrenia*, trans. Brian Massumi (London: The Athlone Press, 1988), p. 158.

29. Antonin Artaud, 'To Have Done with the Judgment of God', in Antonin Artaud, *Selected Writings*, ed. Susan Sontag (Berkeley: University of California Press, 1976), pp. 570–71.

30. Deleuze and Guattari, *A Thousand Plateaus*, op. cit., pp. 150-51.

31. Ibid., p. 151.

32. Ibid., p. 153 (emphasis added).

33. Ibid.

34. In the case of Deleuze's *Logic of Sensation*, all the key concepts are drawn from Deleuze's earlier writings (and are thus 'ready-mades'); with the exception of the concept of the Figure (introduced in ch. 1), which is adapted from Lyotard. See Jean-Francois Lyotard, *Discourse, Figure*, trans. Antony Hudek & Mary Lydon (Minneapolis: University of Minnesota Press, 2011).

35. We might connect this recipe for monotonous creativity to something which goes to the very heart of Deleuze's philosophy. As Alain Badiou writes: 'It is … perfectly coherent that, in starting from innumerable and seemingly disparate cases, in exposing himself to the impulsion organized by Spinoza and Sacher-Masoch, Carmelo Bene and Whitehead, Melville and Jean-Luc Godard, Francis Bacon and Nietzsche, Deleuze arrives at conceptual productions that I would unhesitatingly qualify as monotonous, composing a very particular regime of emphasis or almost infinite repetition of a limited repertoire of concepts, as well as a virtuosic variation of names, under which what is thought remains essentially identical.' Alain Badiou, *Deleuze: The Clamor of Being*, trans. Louise Burchill (Minneapolis: University of Minnesota Press, 2000), p. 14.

36. Susan Sontag, *On Photography* (London: Penguin, 1979), pp. 19–20.

37. The culmination of this logic, in recent art history, was the 1997 exhibition 'Sensation' at the Royal Academy of Art, London. The exhibition, made up of a collection of the contemporary art owned by the adman Charles Saatchi, is well described by Paul Virilio as 'the fusion/confusion of the tabloid and some sort of would-be avant-garde' culminating in a 'conformism of abjection'. See Paul Virilio, *Art and Fear*, trans. Julie Rose (London: Continuum, 2003), p. 36.

38. Fred Botting, *Limits of Horror: Technology, Bodies, Gothic* (Manchester: Manchester University Press, 2008), p. 99.

39. Walter Benjamin, 'The Storyteller: Observations on the Work of Nicolai Leskov', in *Walter Benjamin: Selected Writings Volume 3, 1935–1938*, ed. Howard Eiland & Michael Jennings (Cambridge, MA.: The Belknap Press, 2002), p. 144.

40. J. M. Bernstein, 'In Praise of Pure Violence (Matisse's War)', in *The Life and Death of Images: Ethics and Aesthetics*, ed. Diarmuid Costello & Dominic Willsdon (London: Tate, 2008), p. 42.

41. Friedrich Nietzsche, *Beyond Good and Evil*, trans. R. J. Hollingdale (London: Penguin, 1990), § 225.

42. Sigmund Freud, 'Thoughts for the Times on War and Death (1915)', in *Civilization, Society and Religion: Group Psychology, Civilization and its Discontents and Other Works*, The Penguin Freud Library, vol. 12 (London: Penguin, 1991), pp. 79–80.

43. Arthur Schopenhauer, *The World as Will and Representation*, vol. II, trans. E. F. J. Payne (New York: Dover Publications, 1966), p. 161.

44. Freud, 'Thoughts for the Times on War and Death (1915)', op. cit., p. 79.

45. Ibid., pp. 78–79.

46. Wallace Stevens, *The Necessary Angel: Essays on Reality and the Imagination* (New York: Knopf, 1951), pp. 170–71.

47. Sylvester, op. cit., p. 144.

48. Ibid., p. 163.

49. T. J. Clark, 'The Look of Self-Portraiture', *The Yale Journal of Criticism* 5:2 (1 January 1992), p. 109.

50. Roland Barthes, *Camera Lucida: Reflections on Photography*, trans. Richard Howard (London: Vintage, 2000), p. 13.

51. Here I draw on ideas regarding the gaze put forward by Lacan in his Seminar XI. Although these remarks pivot around a discussion of the anamorphic skull in Hans Holbein's *The Ambassadors*, 1533, they seem particularly pertinent to any analysis of portraiture and self-portraiture. See Jacques Lacan, *The Seminar of Jacques Lacan, Book XI: The Four Fundamental Concepts of Psychoanalysis*, ed. Jacques-Alain Miller, trans. Alan Sheridan (New York: W. W. Norton, 1981).

52. On the idea of the spectator being, from the beginning, 'in' the work, see G. W. F. Hegel, *Aesthetics: Lectures on Fine Art*, vol 2, trans. T. M. Knox (Oxford: Oxford University Press, 1975), p. 806. This idea is also taken up by Lacan in Seminar XI. For an account of the relation between Hegel's philosophy and modernist art, see Robert B. Pippin, *After the Beautiful: Hegel and the Philosophy of Pictorial Modernism* (Chicago: University of Chicago Press, 2014). For an insightful reply to Pippin's reading, see Gregg Horowitz, 'Review of *After the Beautiful*', *Platypus*, 71 (November 2014).

53. Bacon's history of sadomasochistic pursuits, including securing beatings from strangers, is by now well documented. See, for example, Michael Peppiatt, *Francis Bacon: Anatomy of an Enigma* (London: Constable, 2008).

54. Barthes, op. cit., p. 14.

55. Hegel, *Phenomenology of Spirit*, p. 19 (§ 32).

56. Sylvester, op. cit., p. 152.

57. The lines that Bacon is paraphrasing here are from Cocteau's *Orpheus* (1950): 'I'll give you the secret of secrets. Mirrors are the doors through which Death comes and goes. Look at yourself in a mirror all your life … and you'll see death at work like bees in a hive of glass.'

58. Sylvester, op. cit., p. 153.

59. G. W. F. Hegel, *Aesthetics: Lectures on Fine Art*, trans. T. M. Knox, 2 vols (Oxford: Oxford University Press, 1975).

60. Karl Rosenkranz, *Aesthetics of Ugliness*, trans. Andrei Pop & Mechtild Widrich (London: Bloomsbury, 2015), p. 33.

61. Theodor Adorno, *Aesthetic Theory*, trans. Robert Hzullot-Kentor (Minneapolis, University of Minnesota Press, 1997), p. 50.

62. Ibid., p. 47.

63. As Hegel puts it in his *Lectures on Fine Art*: 'In all these respects art, considered in its highest vocation, is and remains for us a thing of the past. Thereby it has lost for us genuine truth and life, and has rather been transferred into our *ideas* instead of maintaining its earlier necessity in reality and occupying its higher place.' Hegel, *Aesthetics: Lectures on Fine Art*, op. cit., vol. 1, p. 11. Contra certain naïve readings, this does not mean that Hegel is announcing *the end of art*. Rather, Hegel's point is that the place accorded to art in society has changed: it has ceased to matter to us in the way it once did. Which is not to say that art no longer matters at all, but, rather, that its symbolic place in our world has changed, and changed *utterly*.

64. Hegel, *Phenomenology of Spirit*, op. cit., p. 18.

65. Ibid., p. 19.

66. This inability to grasp that which is in some sense *beyond* is not, of course, specific to Hegel: his thought, like all thought, 'is *its own time comprehended in thoughts*'. G. W. F. Hegel, *Elements of the Philosophy of Right*, trans. H. B. Nisbet (Cambridge: Cambridge University Press, 1991), p. 21.

67. Hegel, *Aesthetics: Lectures on Fine Art*, op. cit., vol. 1, p. 80 (emphasis added).

68. Robert Pippin, 'What Was Abstract Art? (From the Point of View of Hegel)', in *Hegel and the Arts*, ed. Stephen Houlgate (Evanston, IL: Northwestern University Press, 2007), p. 262.

69. Such seems to be the conclusion reached by Umberto Eco's *On Ugliness*, trans. Alastair McEwen (London: Harvill Secker, 2007).

70. J. M. Bernstein, *Against Voluptuous Bodies: Late Modernism and the Meaning of Painting* (Stanford, CA: Stanford University Press, 2006), p. 283.

71. On the distinction between the ethical and the moral and how the force of the moral might be reclaimed, see Ben Ware, *Modernism, Ethics and the Political Imagination: Living Wrong Life Rightly* (London: Palgrave, 2017), ch. 1.

72. Hegel, *Aesthetics: Lectures on Fine Art*, op. cit., vol. 1, p. 11.

•   I'd like to thank Gregg Horowitz and Dany Nobus for their comments on an earlier version of this chapter.

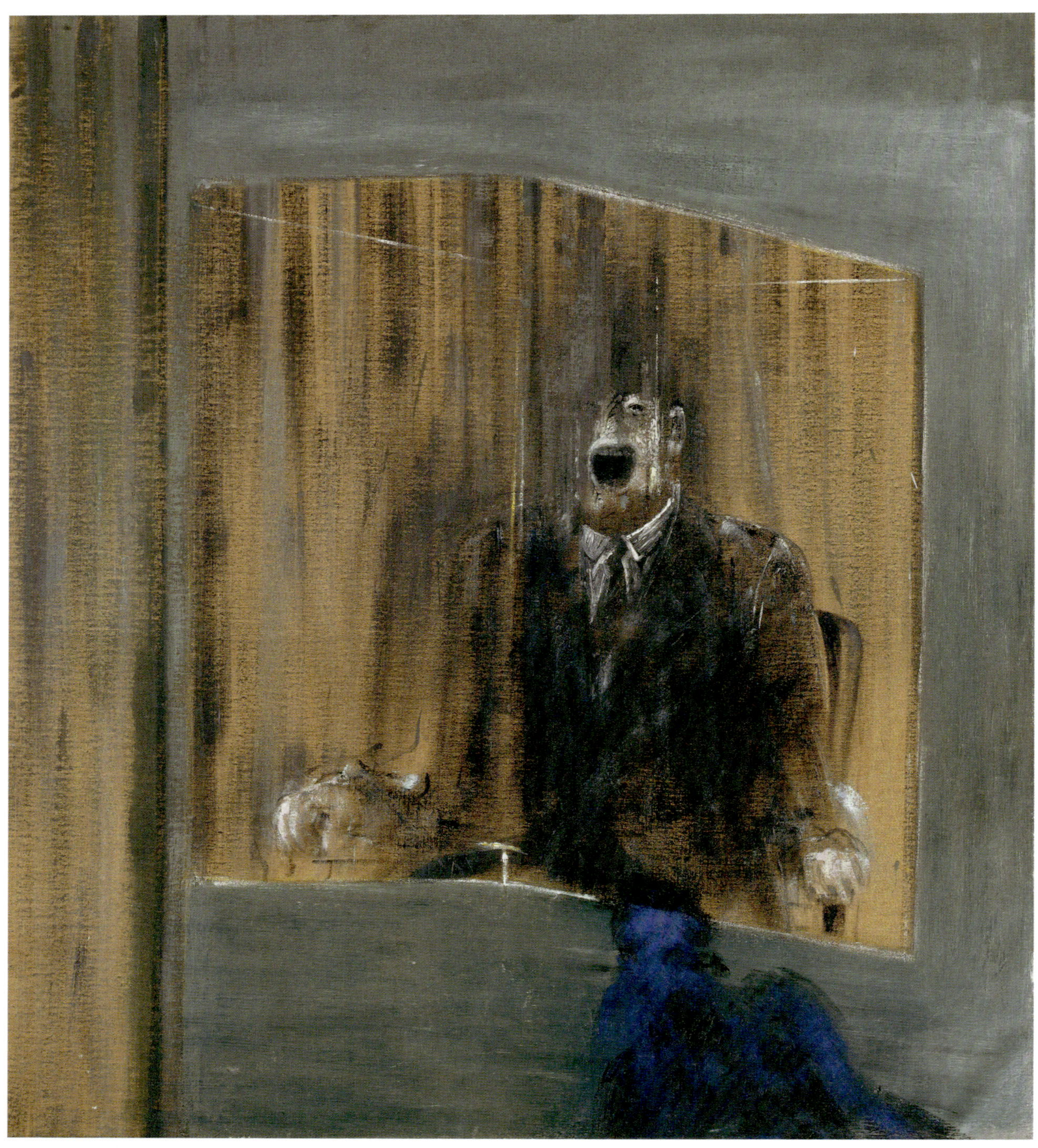

57. *Study for Portrait,* 1949

# Bacon and the Art of Objective Humour

Alenka Zupančič

In his lectures on *Aesthetics* Hegel famously concluded that art has reached its end, that it is for us 'a thing of the past'.[1] It is most interesting, and perhaps surprising, to see to what extent Hegel's account of what this actually means rhymes with Bacon's view of the situation in which modern artists find themselves: 'I think we are in a very curious position today because, when there's no tradition at all, there are two extreme ends. There is direct reporting like something that's very near to a police report. And then there's only the attempt to make great art. And what is called the in-between art really, in a time like ours, doesn't exist.'[2]

Hegel uses almost the same terms when he describes how at the end of Romantic art – which he also considers to be the culminating point of the movement in which art frees itself from all prescriptions in regard to artistic content and form, that is prescriptions springing from different 'traditions', precisely – art falls apart, it disintegrates into two extremes: 'In the course of romantic art this opposition developed up to the point at which we had to arrive at an exclusive interest, either in contingent externality or in equally contingent subjectivity.'[3]

Hegel relates the former, that is the objective extreme in art, to the 'imitation of external objectivity in all its contingent shapes', to meticulous, naturalist reproduction, 'recording and reporting' – to use Bacon's vocabulary – of what is out there. And he relates the other extreme, 'the liberation of subjectivity, in accordance to its inner contingency', to what he calls humour.[4] The latter does not refer to something like hilarious jokes, but simply to the fact that what is primarily on display in this kind of art is not this or that object, but the *wittiness* – the spirit, the cleverness, the genius – of the subject/artist herself.

In other words, humour does not stand here for a witty subject making jokes about various things, including herself. Whatever the material that is being treated in this way, this material is not its subject matter or content; it is not what is *on display* in humorist art. What is on display in it is the *humour*, the *wittiness* itself, claims Hegel. That is to say the subject. The subject does not simply joke about things, *the subject is the joke*. Hegel actually uses this ingenious expression, *der Witz des Subjektes*: 'The artist does therefore not produce a figure [*Gestalt*], but the subject makes itself seen [displays itself, *das Subjekt gibt nur sich selbst zu sehen*]... and what shows itself are the feelings/sensations, the joke of the subject.'[5]

So we have, on the one hand, a (wilful) disappearance of the subject in the attempt to do nothing else but record things as realistically as possible. And, on the other hand, we have what ultimately boils down to displaying the artistic genius itself, that is to the sole 'attempt to make great art', as Bacon puts it almost 150 years later.

It is also very interesting that in the last of his four-lecture series on aesthetics, delivered in Berlin in the winter semester 1828/29, Hegel suddenly, and very briefly, introduces a new and paradoxical notion of 'objective humour', which appears as a possible alternative to the 'end of art' thesis. The notion is paradoxical because humour constitutes for Hegel the peak of the subjective path in art, and here it suddenly becomes objective, bound to an irreducible dimension of the object as 'partial object' (the term is Hegel's). Objective humour is not reducible to either of the two extremes mentioned above, but stands for a different way of doing art, in which a new objective dimension and a new kind of necessity emerge out of intensification, or radicalisation, of the subjectivity itself. This is not the place to enter into any detailed discussion of Hegel, whose remarks about objective humour remain very scarce and inconclusive anyway – apart from the insistence that it has the capacity to *make appear something substantial out of pure contingency*. Instead, I would rather make the following suggestion: 'objective humour' is something that Hegel had only a kind of elusive anticipatory premonition about, and in fact it took Francis Bacon to show us in a concrete way what this notion could actually be all about, to invent the true art of objective humour.

We started with a strong and surprising echoing between Hegel and Bacon. Yet this echoing notwithstanding, we cannot ignore the fact that between Hegel and Bacon, *something did happen*, something that pushed, so to say, the Hegelian dissolution of art into two extremes over the edge. Bacon relates this something to the discovery of photography. In a sense photography,[6] with its capacity to record and report, closed off the 'objective' extreme of art and left only one way for art to continue, namely following its subjective path. Hence Bacon's suggestion that contemporary art is all about the 'attempt to make great art'. This way of putting it may sound like an ironic characterisation of modern artists, yet I would say that it is rather a poignant formulation of their *predicament*. For although there surely have been artists, often fashionable ones, who simply gloated in this idea of freedom to just *do* (great) *art*, it is much more plausible to say that all interesting modern artists experienced this 'freedom' as a predicament.

Bacon's dismissive views on abstract art are well known. What is perhaps less emphasised is the properly dialectical, Hegelian way in which he formulates them:

> One of the reasons why I don't like abstract painting, or why it doesn't interest me, is that I think painting is a duality, and that abstract painting is an entirely aesthetic thing. It always remains on one level. It is only interested in the beauty of its patterns or its shapes. We know that most people, especially artists, have large areas of undisciplined emotion, and I think that abstract artists believe that in these marks that they're making they are catching all these sorts of emotions. But I think that, caught in that way, they are too weak to convey anything. I think that great art is deeply ordered.[7]

What is this 'duality' that painting *is*, according to Bacon, and which accounts for the *tension* that makes it captivating, strong? It is not simply the duality or the tension between external and internal, objective and subjective, between recording the external word and displaying one's feelings and sensations. The old painters were indeed lucky in this respect: they were born into the world where they were expected to do the 'recording', the 'illustrational thing'. So, in Bacon's phrasing, they thought they were recording, and of course then they did something very much more than recording. They, at least some of them, produced artistic masterpieces. The inevitability, the necessity of recording was crucial for traditional painters; their artistic *freedom*, and what they produced on top of the recording, was inseparable from their *belief* that they had to record, illustrate things. We could also put it like this: it is quite clear in retrospect that great classical art has never been simply about illustration and recording, yet a certain misconception about it was an inherent and key element of this other thing they produced. The fact that, in a sense, painters did not know what they were doing was a pivotal factor in their doing it.

Things no longer stand this way. Mechanical means or methods of recording, starting with photography, 'have taken over the illustrational thing that painters in the past believed they had to do'.[8] Bacon further speculates on what abstract painters, realising this, have thought. Namely: 'Why not just go on in a free-fancy way, throw out all illustration and all forms of recording and just give the effects of form and colour?' It goes without saying that this particular phrasing of what abstract artists thought is above all in the service of the argument that Bacon himself is making, contrasting again this free-fancy play with a deeper necessity and tension that get lost in this move.

It is also clear for Bacon that the deeper necessity and tension (duality) cannot be regained by going back, or ignoring the historical break of modernism in all its aspects, including technological ones; it cannot be gained by saying, OK, let's continue to record things, and in this way the tension will reappear and we'll perhaps produce something more and unexpected ...

Bacon's answer – which, in his art, came long before he had the chance to formulate so elegantly the problem to which it was the answer – was to shift the focus of recording, without dismissing its imperative. This is what makes him so interesting. The imperative to record has changed. Recording is no longer about what artists are expected to do, and what they *think* they have to do (even if in fact they do something else, or more), it is about what they *really* have to do. Bacon's word for this new type of necessity is 'obsession': being stuck with something in life that you *absolutely want to record*, and have to find a way of recording it.

Abstract painting 'hasn't worked out, because it seems the obsession with something in life that you want to record gives a much greater tension and a much greater excitement then when you've simply said you'll just go on in a free-fancy way and record the shapes and the colours.'[9] The key term here is *obsession*, obsession with something you want to record, and not simply the recording itself. You get stuck in wanting to record, make appear, a singular thing that strikes you in something. This, at least, is the imperative, or rather the drive, that was there for Bacon when he painted. At the very extreme of subjectivity ('obsession' and 'stuckness' with something) there emerges a new and perhaps surprising dimension of an object, which I would suggest is a crucial feature of Bacon's objective humour.

'I want to record an image,' Bacon repeats insistently. But what *is* this image, what is the status of this image, or appearance, as he also terms it? It is not simply out there (to be properly recorded). Things, or let's say people, appear all the time. I can record how people look, or appear, to me. But how can I record how they *really appear*? This image is not a natural appearance, it can only be a *made appearance*, an 'artifice' which renders that in reality which cannot be seen in any direct way, yet which we immediately recognise as this same reality, and say: That's it, or – in the case of a portrait – that's her/him!

There is a split right there: a split between two kinds of images. There is image as resemblance ('illustration'), and there is an image that haunts me, say, in the appearance of a person, as something that I absolutely want to convey, record 'more clearly, more exactly, more violently'. It is something that I will be able to recognise immediately when I see it, but it is still waiting to *appear*, properly speaking. It's somehow like a *ghost image*. And the term 'ghost' makes some sense in this context. There is a persistent lexis in Bacon's interviews which rhymes profoundly with the famous Hamletian dictum a propos of the 'mousetrap' – the device set up to make appear what Hamlet knows only from his father's ghost: *the play's the thing wherein I'll catch the conscience of the King*. The idea of setting a *trap* that will capture the real of the situation occurs again and again in Bacon's wording. 'It's really a question in my case of being able to set a trap with which one would be able to catch the fact at its most living point.'[10]

This question of the 'trap' is directly connected to two further questions: to the question of *how* to record an image by means other than illustration or mimetic depiction, as well as to a more general interrogation of the status of appearance as such.

Again, this is all about *making* the appearance. Which has nothing to do with pretence or deceit, but with work and work process. Bacon has this ingenious formulation: 'the mystery of painting today is how can appearance *be made*. It can be illustrated, it can be photographed, but how can this thing be made so that you catch the mystery of appearance within the mystery of the making?'[11] This is about the making of appearance with means other than illustration, involving 'the whole questioning of what appearance is'.[12] This quality of pure appearance is particularly striking in paintings where Bacon produces it as a result of the lack of depth (or anything 'behind' the figure). One thinks, for example, of the extremely powerful effect of figures such as those in the *Triptych* from August 1972 (left panel). [58]

This, again, resonates strongly with the way Hegel situates what painting is all about: namely *Schein* and *Scheinen*, usually translated in English as 'pure appearance' and 'showing'. For pages and pages, he insists on how painting is all about creating a pure appearance, and not about the appearance of this or that thing: ... painting must press on to the extreme of pure appearance, that is to the point where the content does not matter and where the chief interest is the artistic creation of that appearance.[13] For Hegel, *Schein* is precisely a 'made appearance', and what he also calls an 'ensouled appearance' – a most interesting notion. Hegel explicitly states that what is at stake here is not the conformity of the painting with its object, but to show 'the correspondence of the portrayed object with itself', which is said to be 'reality ensouled for itself'.[14] Incidentally, but perhaps not accidentally, Bacon for his part likes to speak about image 'that lives on its own', has a life of its own.[15] It is very much his version of an 'ensouled appearance', and it relates directly to the art of objective humour.

The crucial point here is the idea that what is at stake is the *correspondence (or not) of the portrayed object with itself*. I believe that this idea can take us very far in understanding how Bacon does, and thinks, art. Art is not about how a painter

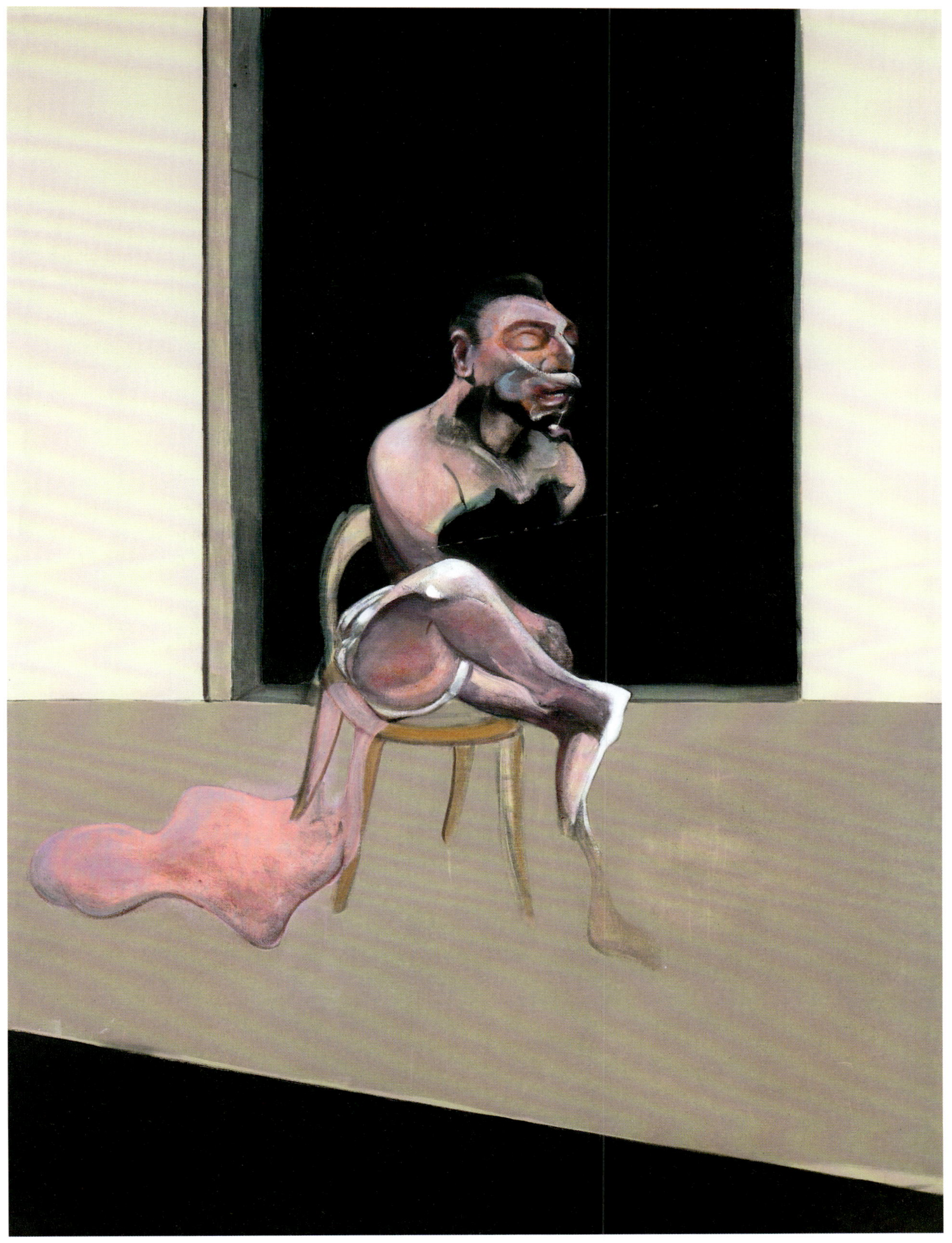

58. *Triptych August 1972* (left panel)

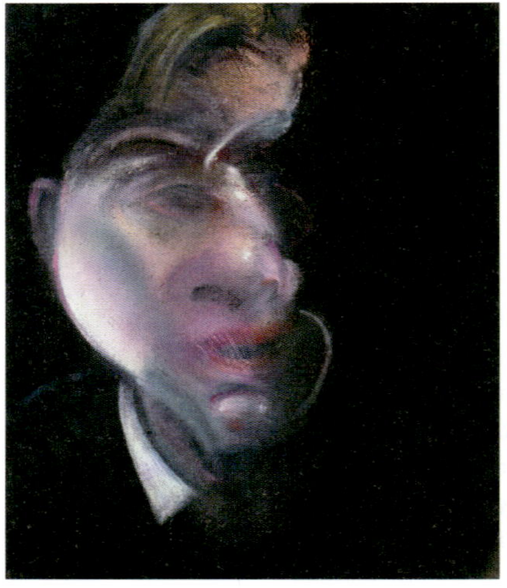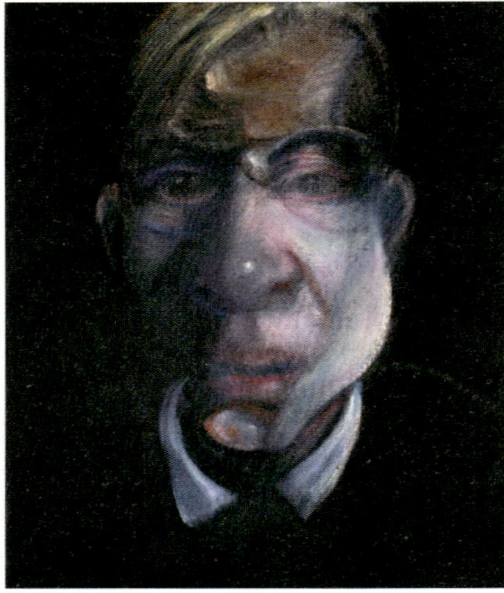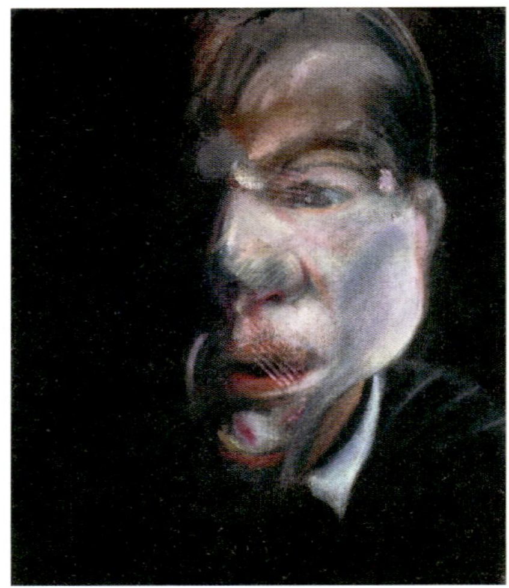

59. *Three Studies for Self-Portrait,* 1979

is affected by different objects, how she sees them ... It is also not about making an
appearance of these ('real') objects, it is about making the appearance of how these
objects relate to themselves. In this precise sense the appearance is 'ensouled', or
has a life of its own. This could also be a way of seeing and understanding Bacon's
propensity for *series.* Just think of all the paintings with titles beginning 'Three
studies ...'. Take for example *Three Studies for Portrait of Henrietta Moraes,* 1963 [17]
or, from a later period, *Three Studies for Self-Portrait,* 1979. [59] These paintings, these
appearances do not *tell a story* – Bacon very much insists on that. What does this
mean? It means that we are not dealing with a temporal sequence and with narrating
some segment of reality, but with the constellation where 'one picture reflects on the
other continuously'.[16] Figures in the series do not exactly relate to each other; they
are in a sense the same painterly object which relates *to itself* through this serial
structure, and only becomes what it is, that is *appears,* in this process. The serial or
tripartite structure is one of the ways in which painterly objects relate to themselves
and, in doing this, trap and convey the real they want to record. There is a kind of
construction going on here, with the seriality as a way for some real to return to its
place. And these considerations will also lead us to measure not only the proximity,
but also the distance between Hegel and Bacon: there is something like a historical
eventuality of which Hegel couldn't have had any idea (and it would be very non-
Hegelian to claim otherwise), and which separates them, pushing the Hegelian
edifice over its own edge.

Bacon's art, as well as his reflections on art, force us to distinguish between two
things which are often taken together or confused: i) the question of resemblance,
recognition, recalling, recording, and ii) the question of illustration, of the
illustrative and non-illustrative form.

As we have already seen, the first remains absolutely valid and imperative for
Bacon. One doesn't just go and display one's feelings on the canvas, one doesn't
present the onlooker with a soup of feelings and sensations that the latter can enter
into and be captivated by.[17] Painting is an *artifice,* a deeply ordered and disciplined
*form* that works on feelings, and not simply *with* feelings. A form that 'unlocks', as
Bacon puts it repeatedly, different layers of sensation. Abstract Expressionism is
for Bacon a running subjective commentary, an exposition of how things make us

(artists) feel, recordings of our sensations. Whereas he is in search of a form or figure that can *unlock*, simultaneously, different layers of sensation. One aims at some sort of recognition, at producing the effect of 'Yes, that's it!' But this recognition is not based on what we would call illustration as point-by-point correspondence. It can come from an image that looks very much distorted. 'What I want to do is to distort the thing far beyond the appearance, but in the distortion to bring it back to a recording of the appearance.'[18] The first thing *not* to do is to take this distortion itself as an illustration (or a metaphor), say, of the distorted world we live in. When, after the end of the war, Bacon first exhibited the *Three Studies for Figures at the Base of a Crucifixion*, 1944, [4] this was exactly what happened: their deformity was seen as 'reflecting' the horrors of the war. Bacon was completely opposed to this reading, and very rightly so. Because what he was after went much deeper than psychology. The world was shattered in its very foundation, and the question is not and cannot be 'how do we feel about it', but rather how does this affect (our) way of feeling and perception itself, at *its* own ontological core. How does this affect the way we 'recognise', record and recall things? Something has changed in the very *mode* in which the world (or the spirit/life) appears to itself, can appear to itself, or just simply *appear*. Something has changed in the world's mode of relation to itself: so the painter, as part of this process or relation, has to change her way of doing art. This is not simply about choosing more macabre objects and motives (like crucifixions, meat, screams), but about the way in which objects now relate to themselves, correspond to themselves, across a violent interruption of all immediacy in this relation.

This, for example, is at the core of Bacon's insistence that he prefers to make portraits based on photographs of his models, rather than to have these models posing directly. Because, he claims, the only thing that can bring about the *real recognition* is an artifice (that is to say an image with absolutely no immediate links with the model), and the real 'model before you, in my case, inhibits the artificiality by which this thing can be brought back'.[19] In other words, and paradoxically: when interacting with a 'live' person, this inhibits the artifice which can bring real life into the image.

Bacon's stand against illustration is so much part of the predominant way in which modern art thinks about itself that we risk missing its exceptionality, its singularity. For in Bacon this stand is absolutely bound up with the seemingly contrary imperative of recalling, of recognition, of recording (an image), of the coincidence or correspondence of the painterly object with itself. This imperative is something that he will never give up, because it is the very generator of the *tension* that makes art interesting, powerful. So we have a whole set of opposites that are made to work together. For example, and as we've already seen: the only way to unlock different layers of sensation in a most poignant way is by means of an extremely precise, ordered form.

> I think that great art is deeply ordered. Even if within the order there may be enormously instinctive and accidental things, nevertheless I think that they come out of a desire for ordering and for returning fact onto the nervous system in a more violent way.[20]

This is a very different view of sensations from the one associated with 'aesthetic painters', where sensations are to work on sensations, give rise to sensations, preferably in a most immediate way. The idea is not simply that we should 'feel' the painting, but that the latter, with the very precision of its form, unlocks areas of sensation other than a simple illustration of the object would. Only a very *clear, precise form* can have a really violent effect on sensations, going to them directly, unlocking them. 'The clearer and the more precise, the better. Of course, how to be clear and precise is a terribly difficult thing now.'[21]

Then there is the fundamental opposition between what Bacon calls a logical outcome and an illogical way of getting to it. This has to do with the difference between illustrative and non-illustrative form. Bacon wants to do a portrait of a person, but not by copying her traits. He has to do it, yet he also has to do it in a completely 'illogical' way, that is without there being any kind of direct continuity between this person (object) and the appearance.

The whole question now becomes *how*? I know what I want to do, but I don't know how to bring it about, he keeps repeating. The whole working process is about that, and the (in)famous 'chance' (like simply throwing paint at the picture), hoping for some accidental way of finding out how to do it, enters here. Sometimes, when he throws paint, an accidental mark appears that renders perfectly (or shows him how to go about it) what he wants to record, without this coming about from illustrative/descriptive activity. And when this happens, the effect must be that of *inevitability*, and not of some free-fancy freedom.[22] In other words, the ideal would be this: you are obsessed with something you want to record, you paint and throw paint, not working by means of illustration, you work in a totally illogical way, but when you succeed, the thing is 'totally real and, in the case of a portrait, totally recognizable as the person'.[23]

The only way to the logical outcome is the illogical way of going about it. Otherwise logic itself – as a relating of the object to itself – is lost in translation (illustration, copying), loses its vigour, and becomes something else, more or less anecdotic.

What exactly is going on here? *Why* this insistence on resemblance that is not brought about by an effort to create resemblance, but by means of illogical, non-voluntary, non-representational marks? What does one gain by not doing it 'logically'? There are two answers, or better, two steps in answering this question. i) The result, the image is much more powerful this way, and one can see the difference.[24] ii) One cannot do it the old way any longer: not simply because photography and other available means of technical reproduction have cut off this path of art, but because the 'illogical' proceeding marks an interruption, a gap that is essential to the new logic of appearance as such, understood as the coincidence of the object/appearance *with itself*.

It is here that the whole idea, so central for Bacon, of the accident (accidental marks) and of 'guided chance' comes in. 'I want a very ordered image but I want it to come about by chance.'[25] The ideal, says Bacon, 'would really be just to pick up a handful of paint and throw it at the canvas and hope that the portrait was there'.[26] Here we have the idea of a radical discontinuity, severance of all organic links, at the very core of an object, in its ontological constitution as appearance. Yet by saying that this would be his 'ideal' I don't think Bacon has in mind a kind of 'unattainable ideal', but rather something like his version of the end of art – this would be the painting to put an end to painting as art. Because what art as practice consists of, according to Bacon, is precisely the *work*, the dedication, the passion that makes this happen: the work that brings about the coincidence of the object with itself from within this discontinuity, or as a form of this very discontinuity. If this work were no longer necessary, there would be no room for art.

Chance, or 'accident', only becomes *chance* when you spot it and seize it. That is, when you are able to see, in the strange thing that's just happened out there, a surprising match with what you wanted to record, yet didn't know how. Now you have a way, or at least an indication of it. The work (and the art) proper only begins when something like that happens, and 'it has to do with using your critical faculty – where you suddenly see an opening'.[27]

As it should be obvious, this is not about throwing paint and seeing what happens, preserving the (aesthetically) 'interesting' results. Bacon doesn't want his images to look like thrown paint; he is quite explicit on that point. This is also not about glorifying the accident and the spontaneous, the unconscious … It is about a very disciplined selection which only works with things ('accidents') that enable one to record the image one wants to record. It is not about preserving, displaying the accident, but about using it, putting it in the service of some necessity, 'obsession' with what one wants to record. And this is what Bacon calls chance, or guided chance. It has a lot to do with luck, with something that *happens*, something that unexpectedly and quite literally enters the picture, but it has at least as much to do with the ability to recognise what happened there (and that it did happen), wanting it to happen, and being able to dismiss, discard the rest (as Bacon famously did, throwing away, destroying a lot of 'good' pictures). It is about recognising the right accident, using that accident, working in a most disciplined way to do, with its help, what you want to do. Is there a better way of understanding Hegel's suggestion that a true, objective humour makes *something substantial appear out of pure contingency*?

You throw paint, and if something happens, you *work* your way back to the appearance you want to make, the image or object you want to record. This going out and coming back is a deeply Hegelian move, yet radicalised by an element of pure discontinuity: in Hegel, it seems – at least according to predominant critical accounts of him – the spirit goes out of itself, alienates from itself and loses itself in the Other, and then comes back to itself, as if 'logically', from within that experience of loss. What is now different is that there is absolutely no necessity ('logic'), no guarantee that the spirit will find itself again. It can simply stay out of itself, wondering indefinitely in this ghostly form, in the form of a ghost image. It can only *happen* that it finds itself again: it is a question of chance, precisely. And of art, which is a 'guided chance'. And we could perhaps say: differently from Abstract Expressionism, which contents itself with recording this ecstatic forms of the spirit, its falling out of itself and erring in its ghostly form, Bacon wants to bring it back to itself, that is he wants for it to find its 'figure' – and with it the very 'itself' to which it has to return. When he speaks of the appearance, of how 'the mystery of painting today is how can appearance *be made*', he speaks precisely of the figure. There is nothing obvious, let alone easy, in making, proposing a figure today. World has no figure, and uncountable images of people, objects and landscapes that we are sunk into thanks to the 'visual media' are not really figures, they recall nothing real, or rarely. Figuration, in the classical – also painterly – sense of the term does not need to get exploded; it already has exploded. The effort is rather the opposite – it is the task to make a figure, to bring about a genuine figure. This is the 'interesting tension' that Bacon talks about, and which drives his work. Particularly in his early work it is often striking how figures literally *strive* to appear, to form themselves, out of an often very dense net of abstract patterns. Think, for example, of *Study for Portrait*, 1949, [57] *Study after Velázquez*, 1950, [60] and *Study after Velázquez's Portrait of Pope Innocent X*, 1953. [61]

So there is a fundamental discontinuity – but there remains a tension (the object does not simply fall apart), like a drive or obsession. At stake is the *inscription* of radical discontinuity, and not simply explosion of all continuity. Discontinuity is there in the very tension, and because of it. It appears all the more violently because there is a 'coming back', a 'recalling', a creation of (recognisable) appearance. Discontinuity is there because something is returning to its place, and discontinuity is 'observable' precisely at the moment something returns to its place, and not simply while wandering around. Recognition itself is a surprise, or rather, it is the surprise (what is surprising is that we recognise something at all). In the same way that Bacon will say, with humour but also quite sincerely: 'I'm always surprised when I wake up in the morning.'[28] Even at the most obvious moments there is discontinuity, a gap at work.

An exchange in the Marx Brothers' *A Night at the Opera* renders what one could rightly call the 'objective humour' of this situation. After sitting with another woman for quite a while, Groucho (Driftwood) comes to Mrs Claypool's table (she has been waiting for him all this time), and the following dialogue ensues:

> Driftwood (Groucho): That woman? Do you know why I sat with her?
> Mrs Claypool (Margaret Dumont): No.
> Driftwood: Because she reminded me of you.
> Mrs Claypool: Really?
> Driftwood: Of course! That's why I'm sitting here with you. Because you remind me of you. Your eyes, your throat, your lips, everything about you reminds me of you, except you. How do you account for that?

*Everything about you reminds me of you, except you* (that is the illustrational 'you'). In a sense, this could be taken as the gist of Bacon's art – starting with the portraits, but not limited to them – of his take on illustration, recording, discontinuity, recollection, chance and making of an appearance. Work, recognise a chance, take it somewhere, use it to bring a figure, an image, into the world. Create, in the appearance itself, the thing that this appearance resembles, recalls.

This essay may strike the reader as a rather peculiar way of writing about a painter, for it focuses on Bacon's words, more than on his paintings. And I am not acknowledging this peculiarity so as to intercept its oddness and be perhaps forgiven. I am acknowledging it in order to emphasise that it became, at some point in my thinking about Bacon – both about his paintings and about his words, interviews – a matter of explicit choice. The principal reason for this decision is the

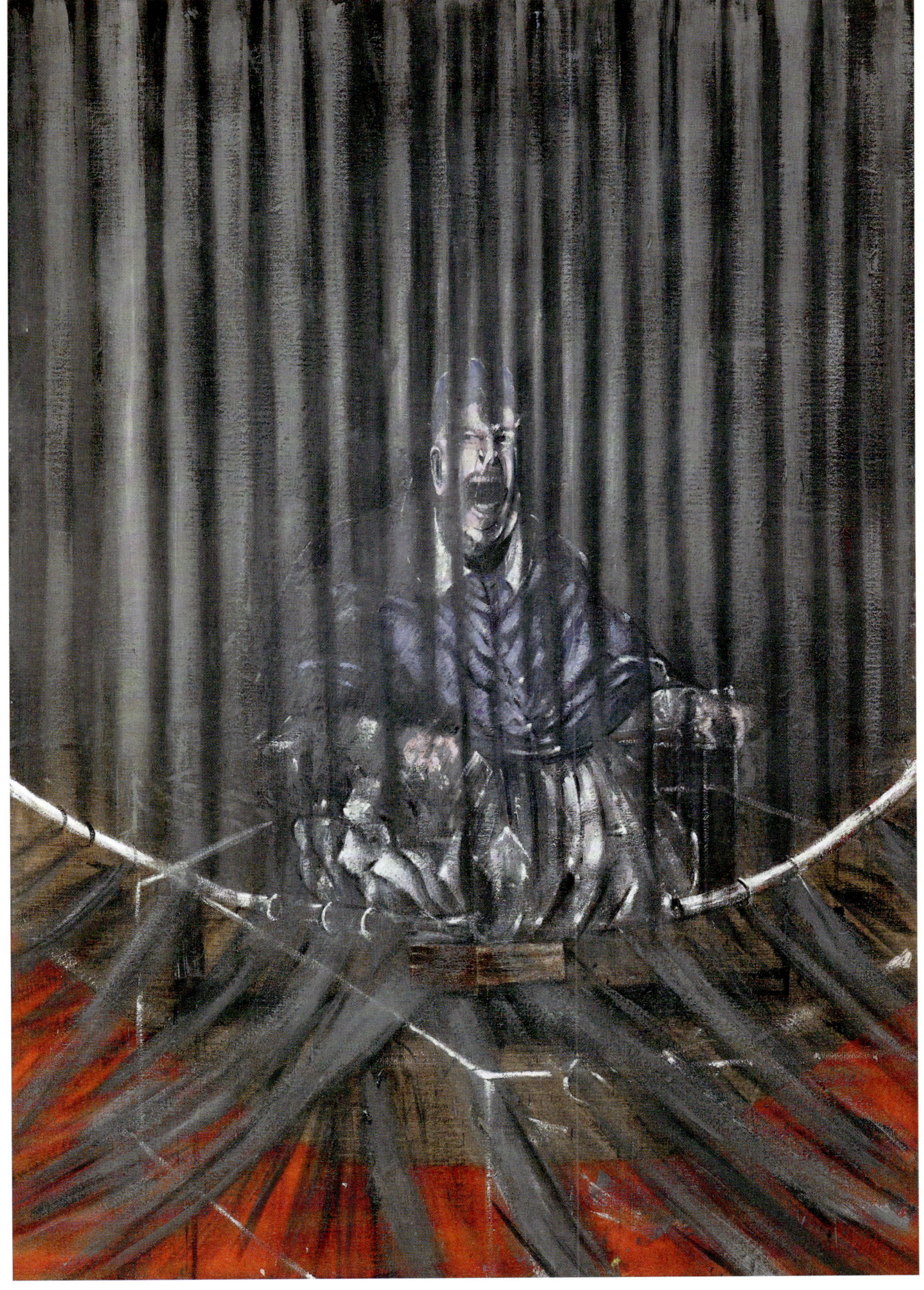

60. *Study after Velázquez*, 1950

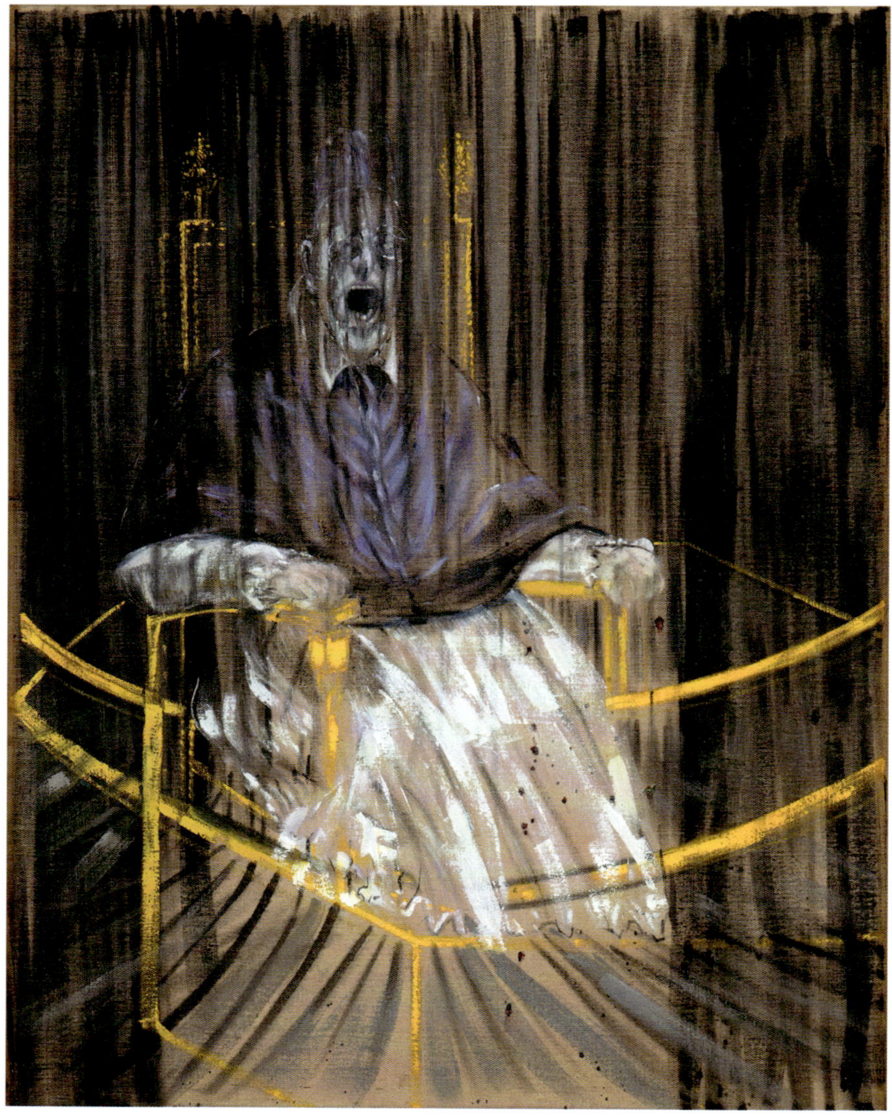

61. *Study after Velázquez's Portrait of Pope Innocent X,* 1953

following. Very much – perhaps too much? – like Bacon himself I realised I needed an 'artifice', and some chance, to perhaps get to say something real about his art. So I started throwing words, including many of his own, on the paper, pursuing *their* logic, rather than the more immediate thread of his paintings. It was a matter of choice, yes, yet at the same time not at all: I simply realised that I absolutely couldn't write about his art, his paintings, in any other way.

# Endnotes

1. G. W. F. Hegel, *Aesthetics. Lectures on Fine Art*, vol. I, trans. T. M. Knox (Oxford: Oxford University Press, 1975), p. 11.
2. David Sylvester, *Interviews with Francis Bacon* (London: Thames t Hudson, 2016), p. 75.
3. G. W. F. Hegel, *Aesthetics. Lectures on Fine Art*, vol. I, op. cit., p. 609.
4. G. W. F. Hegel, *Aesthetics. Lectures on Fine Art*, vol. II, trans. T. M. Knox (Oxford: Oxford University Press, 1975), p. 608.
5. G. W. F. Hegel, *Philosophie der Kunst. Vorlesung von 1826* (Frankfurt/M: Surkamp, 2005), p. 172.
6. It is needless to stress that photography itself cannot be reduced to this aspect of 'exact reproduction', but can have its own singular artistic dimension, which Bacon recognised very well and used it himself. But this is not the point here.
7. Sylvester, op. cit., p. 67.
8. Ibid., p. 75.
9. Ibid., p. 75.
10. Ibid., p. 62. Or: 'I think the difference from direct recording through the camera is that as an artist you have to, in a sense, set a trap by which you hope to trap this living fact alive.' Ibid., p. 66.
11. Ibid., p. 122.
12. Ibid., p. 123.
13. G. W. F. Hegel, *Aesthetics. Lectures on Fine Art*, vol. II, op. cit., p. 812.
14. Ibid., p. 834.
15. Sylvester, op. cit., p. 17.
16. Ibid., p. 21.
17. 'I think it's possible that the onlooker can enter even more into an abstract painting. But then anybody can enter more into what is called an undisciplined emotion, because, after all, who loves a disastrous love affair or illness more than the spectator? He can enter into these things and feel he is participating and doing something about it. But that of course has nothing to do with what art is about. What you're talking about now is the entry of the spectator into the performance, and I think in abstract art perhaps they can enter more, because what they are offered is something weaker which they haven't got to combat.' Ibid., p. 69.
18. Ibid., p. 46.
19. Ibid.
20. Ibid., p. 67.
21. Ibid., p. 13.
22. 'I want the paintings to come about so that they look as though the marks had a sort of inevitability about them. I hate the kind of sloppy sort of Central European painting. It's one of the reasons I don't really like abstract expressionism. Quite apart from its being abstract, I just don't like the sloppiness of it.' Ibid., p. 108.
23. 'It's an illogical method of making, an illogical way of attempting to make what one hopes will be a logical outcome – in the sense that one hopes one will be able to suddenly make the thing there in a totally illogical way but that it will be totally real and, in the case of a portrait, recognizable as the person.' Ibid., pp. 122–23.
24. Can one see the difference between resemblance acquired by illustration and resemblance achieved by a guided chance? Yes, one sees it in the marks, and in how they *form* a picture. The eye, for example, is not done in what would be the logical way of drawing an eye. Involuntary marks on the canvas 'may suggest much deeper ways by which you can trap the fact you are obsessed by'. Ibid., p. 60.
25. Ibid., p. 62.
26. Ibid., p. 123.
27. Ibid., p. 218.
28. Ibid., p. 91.

# Picture Credits

**(Unless otherwise stated, all images of Bacon's artwork
are © The Estate of Francis Bacon).**

1. Perry Ogden, Francis Bacon's studio, 7 Reece Mews,
London, 1998

© The Estate of Francis Bacon. All rights reserved.

4. Francis Bacon,
*Three Studies for Figures at the Base of a Crucifixion*, 1944

Image © Tate, London

5. Titian, *The Death of Actaeon.*

© The National Gallery, London. Bought with a special grant and
contributions from The Art Fund, The Pilgrim Trust and through
public appeal, 1972.

8. Francis Bacon, *Elephant Fording a River*, 1952

PHOTO: © Sotheby's, NY

13. Chaim Soutine, *Carcass of Beef*, 1925

Minneapolis Institute of Art, Gift of Mr. and Mrs. Donald
Winston and an anonymous donor, 57.12

PHOTO: © Minneapolis Institute of Art

15. Lucian Freud, *Lying by the Rags*, 1989–90

Private Collection. © The Lucian Freud Archive/Bridgeman Images

16. Francis Bacon, *Portrait of Henrietta Moraes*, 1963

PHOTO: © Christie's Images / Bridgeman Images.

17. *Three Studies for Portrait of Henrietta Moraes*, 1963

PHOTO © The Museum of Modern Art, NY.

32. Francis Bacon, *Study for Portrait of P.L. No. 1*, 1957

PHOTO: © Sotheby's

45. Enrique Metinides, *Mexico City, April 29, 1979*
(Adela Legarreta Rivas is struck by a white Datsun on Avenida
Chapultepec, 29 April 1979)

CREDIT: Enrique Metenides

47. Ranieri Fontana Giusti, Instagram images, 2016

CREDIT: Ranieri Fontana Giusti

48. Jacqueline Tong, *The Spectacles Selfie*, 2013

CREDIT: Jackie/Jacqueline Tong / 唐文曦

50. Vladimir Dubossarsky and Alexander Vinogradov,
*Happy Birthday, Mynheer Rembrandt*, 2009

CREDIT: Vladimir Dubossarsky and Alexander Vinogradov

51. Manuel Colombo, *Eisoptrophobia*, 2010
Courtesy Saatchi Art

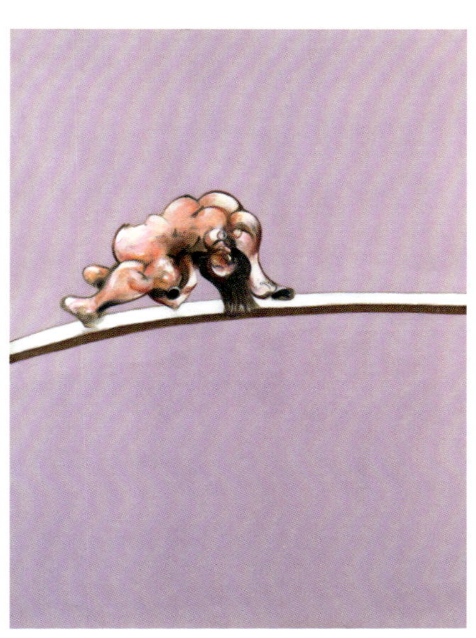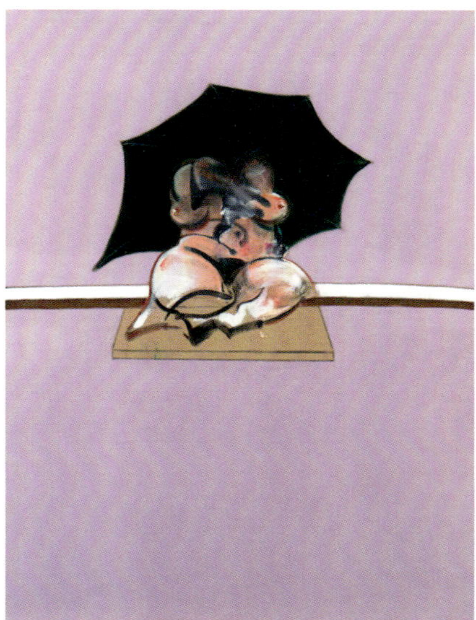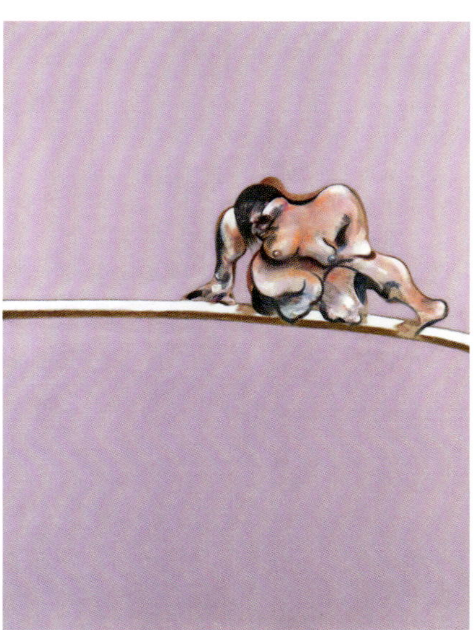

62. *Triptych – Studies of the Human Body*, 1970

First published in the United Kingdom in 2019 by
EFB Publishing and Thames & Hudson Ltd, 181A High Holborn,
London WC1V 7QX

www.francis-bacon.com

www.thamesandhudson.com

First published in the United States of America in 2019 by
EFB Publishing and Thames & Hudson Inc., 500 Fifth Avenue,
New York, New York 10110

www.thamesandhudsonusa.com

Reprinted in 2021



British Library Cataloguing-in-Publication Data
A catalogue record for this book is available from the
British Library

Library of Congress Control Number 2019940654

ISBN 978-0-500-97098-0

Printed by Fuller Davies Ltd., Ipswich
Bound by Diamond Print Services Ltd., London
Design and production: Brett Harrison
Picture researcher: Francesca Pipe
Copy editor: Liane Jones
Proofreading: First Edition Translations Ltd, Cambridge, UK.